What America Can Learn from School Choice in Other Countries

What America Can Learn from School Choice in Other Countries

in Other Countries

Edited by David Salisbury and James Tooley

CATO
INSTITUTE
Washington, D.C.

Library of Congress Cataloging-in-Publication Data

  What America can learn from school choice in other countries /
    edited by David Salisbury and James Tooley.
    p. cm.
  "The book is, in part, the product of the May 2004 Cato Institute
conference, 'Looking Worldwide: What America Can Learn from
School Choice in Other Countries'"—Introd.
  Includes bibliographical references and index.
  ISBN 1-930865-75-9 (cloth)
    1. School choice—Cross-cultural studies.   2. School choice—
United States.   I. Salisbury, David F., 1951–   II. Tooley, James.
III. Cato Institute.   IV. Title.

LB1027.9.W52 2005
379.1'11—dc22
                                                                2005045783

Cover design by Jon Meyers.
Printed in the United States of America.

CATO INSTITUTE
1000 Massachusetts Ave., N.W.
Washington, D.C. 20001

Contents

Acknowledgments

The Cato Institute expresses its appreciation to the Achelis and Bodman Foundations, the Ernest and Mildred Martha Mario Foundation, the Gleason Foundation, and the Milton and Rose D. Friedman Foundation for their support of the May 2004 conference that led to the production of this book. We also thank Ron Rankin and the Kern Family Foundation for its support of the Center for Educational Freedom.

Introduction

There are a number of sound reasons to believe that an education system based on consumer choice and free markets would produce better results than one based on bureaucratic structures and government operation. All over the world, markets and consumer choice have proven superior to government control and distribution. Schooling, like medical research, computer software production, or law, is essentially an information-sharing activity; and the free market, not government provision, is demonstrably better suited to efficient production and distribution of those services. There is no reason that the education industry should be an exception.

Education reformers and policymakers are starting to recognize that, and more states and localities are implementing market-based reforms. In the United States, at least 10 states have enacted school choice programs, and Congress recently funded a voucher program for children living in Washington, D.C. Other states have allowed charter schools and choice among public schools.

In some other countries, school choice is commonplace. Americans might be surprised to learn that in countries such as Australia, Sweden, and the Netherlands parents can choose private, even religious, schools without incurring any financial penalty. Today, in many ex-communist countries, parents have more educational freedom than American parents. In those countries, parents can choose private schools and also work with others to create new independent schools.

As we move toward more school choice in America, we ought to be aware of the lessons offered by the experiences of other countries. What school choice policies are most effective? How well do private schools serve the poor? Does school choice lead to social divisions along religious, economic, or ethnic lines? What policies are necessary to promote the widest selection of education opportunities for the largest number of children? Also, what controls and regulations are most harmful to the development of a competitive education

1

industry? Has school choice in other countries led to a freer education market, or has it, at least in some cases, led instead to increased regulations, regimentation, and uniformity among private and public schools?

This book seeks to answer those questions. The book is, in part, the product of the May 2004 Cato Institute conference, "Looking Worldwide: What America Can Learn from School Choice in Other Countries," at which international scholars shared their research and conclusions about school choice policies around the world. The conclusions, in many cases, were eye opening and provide some important lessons for America.

Although a number of nations have embraced school choice, recent experience in those countries shows that politicians and entrenched interests can easily stifle the potential positive effects of increased choice and competition in education. In many of the countries with school choice policies, regulatory barriers and politically motivated controls have prevented school choice from developing into a mature competitive education market. School choice in New Zealand, for example, includes only public schools. All schools of choice must have registered teachers and follow the national curriculum. Pay and benefits for teachers are set centrally. So that country's education program cannot be described as a legitimate example of a competitive market in education. Sweden is another country where school choice has become the predominant policy. In Sweden, children and parents are free to choose among public or private schools, and enrollment in private schools has grown by almost 600 percent over 10 years (from about 15,000 in 1993 to more than 100,000 in 2004). Nevertheless, private schools in that country must seek approval from the National Agency for Education to become established and must operate in accordance with the national curriculum. Also, price controls exist; private schools are not allowed to charge more than public schools.

Whether such programs will lead to fully competitive education markets remains to be seen, but the improbability of that is arguably one of the genuine lessons of the parental choice programs in other countries. Perhaps the main lesson to be learned from the school choice experiences of other countries is that a reform is inadequate if it leaves in control the people who benefit from the status quo. If it does, then those in power can use their positions to stifle competition and specialization by imposing government control on private schools.

Findings

Claudia Hepburn of Canada's Fraser Institute describes the school choice programs in several Canadian provinces. The programs in the provinces differ substantially in terms of the freedom they allow parents and the regulation they impose on private schools. Because of that, Hepburn is able to assess the effect of those policies on the quality and diversity of education in both private and public schools. Her assessment shows that, although public funding of private education tends to make private schools more like public schools, it also makes public schools more diverse, autonomous, and successful. The province of Alberta, for example, has offered some school choice for decades and since 1994 has increased the diversity of schools and offerings within the public system. Since that time, fewer children have migrated from public to private schools, probably because of the regulatory burdens on private schools that make it difficult for them to distinguish themselves from public schools. Decreasing regulations on private schools would undoubtedly increase the positive effects of the program.

Next, Mikael Sandström describes the Swedish education reforms that introduced school choice nationwide in both primary and secondary schools. Before the reforms, regulations dictated what both public and private schools should do and specifically how they should do it. Those regulations have now been replaced by national academic achievement "targets" in various subjects; so in practice, both public and private schools are less regulated today than before the reforms. For-profit private schools are allowed to participate, and school companies have come to play an important role in Swedish independent schools. Sandström discusses the conflicts that exist between the people who want to go back to centralized "command-and-control" schools and those who wish to continue the current system based on choice.

Chile has had a voucher program in place since 1982, and its effects have been the subject of numerous studies and evaluations, many of which have been contradictory in their conclusions. Claudio Sapelli examines both the policies and the results of the Chilean voucher system and discusses the other reported evaluations of the system. His chapter is more technical in nature than the other selections in this volume, but his conclusions are straightforward: students who attend private schools experience significant academic gains. Perhaps even more important, Sapelli points out the design features of the Chilean system that detract from its potential effectiveness: private schools are highly regulated, and the funding they receive is much less per student than public schools receive. Also, public schools do not face the incentives of competition, since they work with special budget subsidies. No Chilean public school has closed since the voucher system was instituted. Instead, those that fail often receive further subsidies. Rather than motivate public schools to improve, such budgeting policies are a perverse incentive for public school teachers to teach smaller classes.

Critics in the United States who attempt to discredit school choice by suggesting that it would harm hard-to-educate students should read Lewis Andrews's chapter in which he looks at the effect of school choice on handicapped students and students with learning disabilities. He finds that school choice has been successful in helping disabled students in foreign countries. As they do in the United States, parents of disabled children in other countries tend to take advantage of school choice programs at a higher rate than other parents. The enthusiasm of parents of special needs children for school choice should not surprise us, since those parents are often the most dissatisfied with the public school system. In a school choice environment, the parents of a special needs child are free to place their child in a school with a pedagogical, philosophical, or academic emphasis compatible with the child. Under those conditions, a special needs child can not only learn but thrive.

Boston University professor Charles Glenn focuses on the lessons that America can and should learn from the experiences of other countries. One important lesson is to allow schools (both private and public) to differ from each other in significant ways. Schools that differ in ways that are meaningful to families not only are more satisfactory to those families but also are more likely to be educationally effective. That's because the staff agrees about what the school is trying to accomplish and shares values and beliefs about the central mission of the school. Specialized schools can respond to the needs of the particular group of students and parents to whom it is committed rather than to the politically bargained preferences of society as a whole. Using evidence from the Netherlands, Glenn points out that allowing schools to specialize and to be distinctive has not led to weird or extremist schools or to segregation and social division.

James Tooley's research on private education in developing countries shows that private education is not for just the rich or the academically bright. As part of his ongoing examination of the role of private schools serving low-income families, Tooley and his team of researchers have walked the streets of shanty towns, slums, and villages throughout the developing world. What they discovered may be a surprise. In those neighborhoods, either a majority or a substantial minority of children are served by private, rather than government, schools. In general, the private schools are run as businesses, dependent more or less entirely on student fees for their income, set up by local entrepreneurs who want both to make a living and to serve their own communities. Most significant, although fees are very low and affordable to the poor, the private schools are generally better in terms of student-teacher ratio, facilities, and teaching commitment than their public counterparts and have higher academic achievement, even after controlling for family background.

The New Zealand education system is often held up—by both proponents and opponents of school choice—as a large-scale example of market competition and choice. Indeed, the reforms that took place in the late 1980s and early 1990s abolished school zoning laws and introduced considerable school choice for students. However, since that time, there have been significant changes in the regulatory and funding policies that have affected the degree of choice available to parents in New Zealand. As Norman LaRocque puts it, "School choice policies [in New Zealand] have had more ups and downs than Disneyland's Thunder Mountain rollercoaster." LaRocque's chapter sheds light on New Zealand's education reforms, pointing out how the reforms created a more competitive environment for schools (at least within the public sector), eliminated an entire level of education bureaucracy, and increased choice for students, particularly students from low-income families. Nevertheless, we should be careful about drawing too many lessons from the New Zealand experience with school choice, since the reforms are very limited. School choice in New Zealand is effectively limited to public schools because private schools receive a much lower per student funding amount than state schools, thus limiting access to independent schools, especially for students from lower-income families. The main lesson from New Zealand is this: half measures cannot be expected to yield the full demand- and supply-side response needed to generate the benefits that could be derived from more universal choice.

Ludger Woessmann's extensive research on school choice and school governance structures in 61 countries provides some additional lessons for America. Using data from several prominent international achievement tests, Woessmann shows that students perform better in countries where more schools are privately managed and where a larger share of enrollment is in such schools. Performance is further enhanced if those countries use external exit exams as a measure of quality. The ideal recipe for an effective education system is a high level of school autonomy combined with external measures of school quality. In countries that have both, external exams provide something like "price information" for consumers. That gives consumers a way to judge the value of individual schooling choices. Although Woessmann advocates external exams, he notes that they do not necessarily need to be provided by government. As long as they are external to the individual school and provide a comparable yardstick for all schools, they can be provided by the private sector.

Many critics of market-based education policies argue that the nongovernment education sector could never serve more than a small fraction of students. Andrew Coulson's international examination of marketlike education systems reveals that nongovernment schools can and already do serve the greater part of primary and secondary education students in several nations. As a result of Chile's nationwide voucher program, nongovernment schools now enroll nearly half of that country's school-age children, an increase of nearly 50 percent since the program began in 1982. In the Netherlands, the nongovernment school sector enrolls 76 percent of all primary and secondary students. In some of the poorest countries, private schools, not government schools, serve the bulk of school-age children. In India, nearly 80 percent of children in some cities attend private schools. In Lahore, Pakistan, even the poorest parents are as likely to enroll their children in private fee-charging schools as in government schools. Coulson's examination of the nongovernment education sector in those and other countries leads to his conclusion that universal choice plans provide the greatest and most meaningful array of educational options for children at all income levels.

In the final chapter, economist John Merrifield examines the degree to which existing school choice programs (both in the United States and abroad) constitute what could be described as a competitive education industry. Merrifield lists five essential ingredients for a competitive education industry and then evaluates existing school choice programs on the basis of the presence or absence of those necessary ingredients. The five ingredients are freedom to specialize, nondiscrimination against private schools, low formal entry barriers, avoidance of price controls, and little private school regulation. No current school choice program includes many, let alone all, of those necessary economic features. In the United States, all of the operating school choice programs include some form of price control, and participation is limited to low-income children, children in failing public schools, or children living in particular cities, such as Milwaukee. Those restrictions dilute the potential positive effects that might be derived from the universal choice of a fully competitive education market. If those programs are to become a catalyst for larger educational change, they will need to be expanded beyond their current size and scope. Otherwise, they cannot be a starting point for a true marketplace in education.

Lessons for America

Taken as a whole, the chapters of this book provide a valuable look at school choice around the globe and draw out critical lessons for the expansion of school choice in America and elsewhere. The following nine points summarize the basic lessons that can be derived from the research and experiences reported here.

1. Prohibitions on pricing, for-profit schools, and student participation dampen the potential benefits that could be derived from a school choice program.
2. Barriers to entry that prevent new school operators from entering the education market deprive students of new and potentially beneficial teaching methods and shield existing school operators from new competitors.
3. Schools of choice should be allowed to differ from each other in significant ways. Schools that specialize have many advantages over general purpose schools.

4. Distinctive, specialized schools do not necessarily exacerbate ethnic, income, or religious divisions. Indeed, the evidence points in the opposite direction.
5. Private schools can adequately serve the needs of hard-to-educate students, including students with disabilities.
6. Private schools can meet the educational needs of students from families with very low incomes. Private schools typically do a better job of educating poor students than do government schools.
7. Students seem to perform better in countries where more schools are privately managed and where a larger share of the enrollment is in such schools.
8. External exams and other third-party information provide a yardstick that can be used to measure the qualities of different schools. Those measures help consumers judge the value of individual schooling choices.
9. Funding and regulatory policies have profound effects on the success of school choice programs. Programs that operate with significant regulatory barriers and restrictions should not be viewed as legitimate "tests" of free-market education.

People who read this book and remain unconvinced that markets can serve the educational needs of children better than government may at least agree that America should continue to test the effects of market-based reforms in education. But to test them properly, we need school choice programs that are structured to harness the full economic power of the marketplace. Limited school choice programs, with restrictions on enrollment and pricing and that discriminate against new private school operators, will not provide such a test. If we want the positive results that a market-based education system can provide, we will need to seek more universal, less restricted school choice programs.

David Salisbury
James Tooley

1. Public Funding of School Choice in Canada: A Case Study

Claudia R. Hepburn

Education policy in Canada offers insights into the effects of public funding on school choice. Several of the larger Canadian provinces have had publicly funded choice of private education for many years. British Columbia, Alberta, Manitoba, and Quebec all offer about a third of total public school spending per pupil (up to 50 percent of operating costs) to students attending private schools. The other six provinces (Ontario, Saskatchewan, Nova Scotia, New Brunswick, Prince Edward Island, and Newfoundland) offer no funding for private education. One province, Alberta, also provides public funding to parents who choose to educate their children at home.

Many proponents of school choice promote public funding of private educational choices in the form either of direct subsidies to independent schools or of tax credits to parents or third-party payers of a child's school tuition. They argue that allowing families of all income levels to access private schools will improve education, not only for families choosing private schools, but also for children remaining in the public system faced with greater incentives to improve. Other proponents of school choice see public funding as a false hope. They argue that government funding is always eventually followed by government regulation so that its long-term effect is to destroy the freedom of the private sector and the distinct choices it offers by making private schools like public schools in unintended but undesirable ways.

Does public funding increase educational choice or hinder it? This chapter outlines Canadian education policies regarding choice of private education and considers the effect those policies have had in four areas: the ease with which parents can choose private education, the numbers of families choosing private education, the autonomy of private education providers, and the effect of private choice

9

on the quality and diversity of education in the public sector. The findings shed light on the question of whether public funding is a boon to real school choice or inevitably damages the very choices it was intended to support.

In Canada, primary and secondary education is the responsibility of the provinces, not the federal government. The provinces have complete freedom to pursue their own education policies and, partly as a result of their different histories, founding populations, and cultures, have very different policies regarding private education. Some provinces regulate private education heavily while others give private schools considerable freedom. Some provide partial funding for students who choose private schools, and others do not. Three provinces (Alberta, Ontario, and Saskatchewan) provide complete public funding to Catholic or Protestant schools, or both, that are run by "Separate" public school boards. Those religious school boards and schools are not private but another version of public education that, for historical reasons, caters to a minority religious group.

Differences between Voucher Restrictions in Canada and the United States

Public regulations and restrictions on funding for private schools are based on different criteria in Canada than they are in the United States, where educational voucher programs were developed more recently. Different treatment of religion is the most striking example of that.

In Canada, there is no equivalent of the U.S. First Amendment prohibition of publicly funded religious schools. Indeed, in many provinces, public education was initially established through religious school boards, Protestant and Catholic. Though religiously based public schools have been transformed in many instances to nondenominational public schools,[1] Separate Catholic school boards still serve more than 20 percent of the population in three provinces (Alberta, Ontario, and Saskatchewan), and a few small Protestant school boards exist in two provinces (Alberta and Saskatchewan). In addition, Canadians in all provinces who choose to send their children to private schools are eligible for a federal income tax credit for any portion of tuition that applies to religious instruction.

In the United States, voucher programs are often restricted not only by First Amendment issues but also by the desire to help only certain disadvantaged populations.[2] For instance, the publicly funded voucher programs in Cleveland and Milwaukee are only for students from low-income families, Florida's McKay Scholarships Program is for students with special education needs, and Florida's A + program is for students attending chronically failing schools. That may reflect an American motivation to support vouchers in order to remove children most at risk from harmful environments— as certain public schools or school districts have proven themselves to be. In contrast, Canadian policy reflects a desire to allow public funding for only those private schools that fit the government-endorsed view of education. In many Canadian provinces, public funding of private schools is restricted, not to disadvantaged children who would otherwise be unable to access a good education, but to private schools that are willing to submit to state regulations. In other words, Canadian provinces generally discriminate, not on the basis of who uses a voucher, but by the practices of private schools.[3]

Those tendencies can be seen more clearly by looking at the specific policies of the provinces that offer public funding of private education. The history of publicly funded school choice in those provinces also offers insights into how changing governments and times affect school choice years after public funding for private education was established. Alberta is the most striking example.

Alberta

Public Funding and Regulation of Private Schools

Alberta is the province that provides the most public funding for private education. Qualifying private schools receive subsidies worth approximately 60 percent (about C$2,500) of the basic per student grant available to public schools, or approximately 35 percent of the total cost of educating a public school student. They receive no grant for capital costs. Special needs students who attend private schools receive the same funding as they would if they were attending public schools, as long as the parents follow strict guidelines in order to qualify. Public funding also extends to students whose families choose to educate them at home. Accredited independent schools receive public funding for supervising those

11

students' education, and parents of home-schooled children may receive public funding equal to approximately 16 percent of what is spent to educate a child in the public system.

Both private schools and home schooling are more heavily regulated in Alberta than they are in many other provinces. Funded private schools are obliged to teach the government-approved curriculum; they must hire certified teachers as instructors or supervisors of instructors; the schools may not operate for profit and must operate for at least a year on totally private funds before they are eligible to receive government funding.

Public Funding and Regulation of Home Schooling

Though Alberta is the only province that provides direct funding to home-schooling families, that funding, like the province's funding of private schools, comes at the cost of some government interference. Before parents may start to home school their children, they must ask permission from the government. Home-schooling parents must also report and prove their children's educational progress to the government on a regular basis in order to retain the right to teach their children themselves. In comparison, three provinces (British Columbia, Ontario, and Quebec) provide homeschoolers with no funding and no regulation; three provinces provide no funding but have either permission or reporting requirements; and three provinces provide no funding but, like Alberta, have both permission and reporting requirements.

Figure 1.1 shows those differences and ranks Alberta in a four-way tie for the most free province in which to home school. The Canadian Centre for Home Education disagrees with that ranking. Its executive director, Dallas Miller, claims that home-schooling families in the three provinces without regulation are better off than home-schooling families in Alberta, where the government interferes with their children's education, even though it helps to pay for it. He believes that government funding is not worth the cost of government interference.[4] The interference is made worse by the fact that home-schooling parents may not choose to opt out of the regulatory requirements, as private schools may, even if they do not accept public funding.

Figure 1.1
FREEDOM FOR HOME SCHOOLING IN CANADA BY PROVINCE

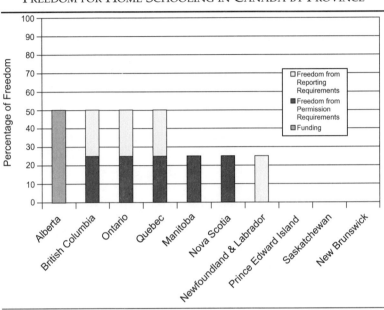

SOURCE: Adapted from Claudia R. Hepburn and Robert Van Belle, *The Canadian Education Freedom Index*, Studies in Education Policy (Vancouver, BC: Fraser Institute, 2003).

History of Public Funding of Private Education

Alberta has supported private education through public funding since the 1960s, but it increased that funding 10 years ago when it enacted changes to enable public schools to compete more effectively with private schools. The changes encouraged the public system to be "goal-oriented, service-oriented, and responsive to market forces."[5] Alberta did that by implementing provincial standardized testing and grade 12 diploma examinations, introducing charter school legislation, and promoting site-based management of public schools. The changes made public school boards more accountable for their students' academic results but encouraged diversity in how they achieved those results. In short, the reforms gave public schools more of the freedoms and responsibilities of private schools.

13

The Effect of Private School Funding on Public Schools

A common argument both for and against public funding of private education is the effect of such funding on public education. Many people who oppose public support for private schools claim that that support will result in an exodus of the best students and teachers from the public system, leaving them drained of talent, resources, and hope and creating a vicious cycle that exacerbates inequity and creates ever-increasing demand for private schools. Those who favor public funding of private schools argue that public schools will respond to increased competition from private schools by improving the quality and diversity of their programs and by focusing more attention on parental satisfaction and academic results, which parents tend to care about. The result will be improved equity and quality for all: a better education, not only for the minority of children whose parents choose the subsidized private schools, but also for the majority that continue to be educated in public schools.

Alberta's example seems to support the theory of proponents of school choice. During the past 10 years, funding for private schools has increased and public schools have been given more flexibility and autonomy. Over that time period, the province has consistently scored at the top of national and international tests of academic performance.[6] It has achieved those impressive results while spending less per student than any other of Canada's wealthy provinces (Figure 1.2).

Funding for private schools has resulted neither in the deterioration of academic achievement in the public system (as measured by academic achievement on national and international tests) nor in the flight to private schools predicted by opponents. In fact, the percentage of students enrolled in private elementary and secondary schools in Alberta is 25 percent below the national average (Figures 1.3 and 1.4). According to the most recent figures available from Statistics Canada, in 1998–99, 4.5 percent of students attended private schools, up from 3.1 percent in 1987–88 and 4.1 percent in 1994–95. That compares with a Canadian average of 5.6 percent in 1998–99, up from 4.6 percent in 1987–88.

Alberta's fully funded, Separate public system of Catholic schools may be part of the cause of the province's surprisingly low private school enrollment. Children of the 22 percent of the province's population that are Catholic may attend Separate schools free of charge.

14

Figure 1.2
CANADIAN SPENDING PER FULL-TIME-EQUIVALENT STUDENT, 1999

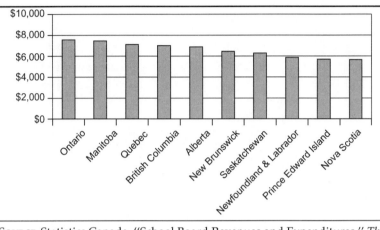

SOURCE: Statistics Canada, "School Board Revenues and Expenditures," *The Daily*, July 23, 2002.

Figure 1.3
ENROLLMENT IN PRIVATE SCHOOLS: CANADA COMPARED
TO ALBERTA

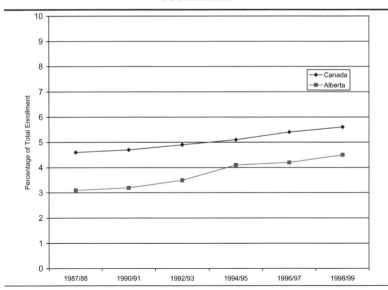

Figure 1.4
PERCENTAGE OF ELEMENTARY AND SECONDARY STUDENTS
ENROLLED IN PRIVATE SCHOOLS BY PROVINCE

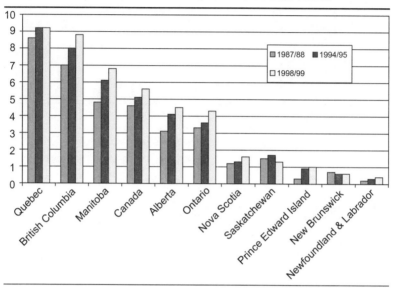

SOURCE: Statistics Canada, *Trends in the Use of Private Education*, 2001.

Only Ontario and Saskatchewan have similar Separate systems for their Catholic students. However, enrollment in Ontario's unfunded private schools is almost identical to that in Alberta's, though Ontario's Catholic population—28 percent of the total, who may also attend Separate schools free of charge—is significantly higher than Alberta's. That suggests that the Separate school factor cannot be the only reason that Alberta's private school enrollment is below the national average.

Because Separate Catholic schools have existed in Alberta for as long as public schools have, Separate schools cannot account for the fact that enrollment in private schools did not increase dramatically when their public funding was increased in 1994. Rather, since 1994 parents seem to have been given new reasons to choose Alberta's public schools that have mitigated the effect of subsidization of private schools. Those reasons include increased public school choice, both within the jurisdiction of public school boards and outside it, in the form of charter schools.

Alberta enacted charter school legislation at the same time it increased funding for private schools. The legislation is weak in comparison with many charter laws in the United States,[7] and after a decade there are only 13 charter schools in Alberta for parents to choose. The paucity of charter schools may also be the result of a far-sighted superintendent in Edmonton, one of the province's two large cities. Emery Dosdall responded to the demand of parents and educators for new programs by encouraging them to open as new schools under his board rather than as charter schools. The board even persuaded two formerly private Christian schools to become public, while retaining their Christian character. The result is that, today, Edmonton is home to more than 30 different educational programs, available at more than 140 locations. Included are advanced placement; international baccalaureate; bilingual and immersion programs in many languages; Christian schools; all-girls schools; and arts, music, and sports schools. The board has rid itself of "catchment areas" and offers a bus service for elementary students so that all students have access to the public school of their choice.[8]

The result of that policy has been an incredible amount of student movement within the public school system. In research Robert Van Belle and I conducted in 2001, we found that only 51 percent of public school students attended their local public school—49 percent attended another Edmonton public school.[9]

Calgary, the province's other major city, was initially slower to offer choice within its municipal school district. Though through the 1990s the school board denied all charter proposals on the principle that "neighborhood schools ought to be able to accommodate the learning needs of all children,"[10] Calgary became home to six charter schools, all granted charter status by the provincial minister of education against the wishes of the school board.[11] Since then, the Calgary District School Board has changed its attitude toward choice and is now embracing it warmly. In 2000 a new school board "approved a vision to redefine public education . . . based not just on choice, but on equitable access to all programs including programs of choice."[12] All of the school board's decisions are now based on "equity, access, excellence and choice."[13] Since 2001 the board has opened 26 new programs or program locations. It currently offers six international language programs, an all-girls school, two Montessori programs, an aboriginal culture school, four arts schools, 17 programs for high-risk students, and dedicated online programs and support for home-educated students.[14] Though Calgary's educational choices are still fewer than those available in Edmonton, they are generous in comparison with those in much of the rest of Canada.[15]

That aggressive approach to offering school choice within the public system may have made it harder for private schools to attract students and may be a large part of the reason why attendance at private schools has not risen more since 1994. The government's persistent regulatory burden on private schools adds to the challenge for private schools to distinguish themselves from public schools.

The province's Conservative government, which implemented the changes in 1994, is still in power 10 years later. Though this government is the most market friendly in the country and has enjoyed a strong hold on power for over a decade, it has chosen not to loosen its regulatory grip on either private or home schools. The continuity of governance has not given us an opportunity to see how an opposition party might treat these policies.

British Columbia, where the policies have weathered several changes in provincial government, provides us with an example of how successive governments have treated private school funding. It is the first of the four other Canadian provinces that fund education at private schools.

British Columbia

British Columbia has offered public funding to students attending private schools since 1977, when it passed the Independent Schools Support Act. Since then, the province has allowed public funding to support operating costs at private schools that comply with certain regulations. No grants are available for capital costs. Operating grants are tiered so that schools may comply with more or fewer regulations and receive more or less public funding.

Group one schools must follow the provincial curriculum, employ certified teachers, have been operating for at least one year, not operate for profit, and have operating costs that are *not more* than the per student operating costs of the local public school district. They receive grants equal to 50 percent of the operating costs of local public schools (about a third of the total per student cost). Group two schools are subject to the same restrictions as group one schools but may have operating costs greater than the per student operating costs of the local public school district. They receive grants equal to 35 percent of the operating costs of local public schools. In general, schools that do not follow the provincial curriculum or that operate for profit (groups three and four) are not eligible for funding.[16]

Those policies have weathered many changes in political leadership since 1977, including a decade of government by the socialist New Democratic Party in the 1990s. Perhaps surprisingly, that socialist government did not acquiesce to demands from the teachers' unions to abolish the policies. Rather, that government abolished the category of grant that permitted a smaller amount of funding to schools not employing certified teachers, and it reduced the other grants for private school students.[17] British Columbia has the second-highest private school enrollment in the country[18] (Figure 1.4).

Manitoba

Manitoba allows approximately 50 percent of net operating costs per student at public schools to follow students to private schools, as long as those schools teach the provincial curriculum, employ certified teachers, and have been operating for at least three years. Manitoba is one of only two provinces that allow funding for schools that operate for profit (Quebec is the other). Furthermore, Manitoba allows students with special needs to take 100 percent of their funding to the private school of their choice. In 2003–04 that amounted to C\$8,780 for a Level II special needs student and C\$19,530 for a Level III special needs student.[19] Like all the other provinces, Manitoba refuses funding for capital costs of private schools.

Quebec

Quebec has allowed public funding for students attending the majority of private schools since 1968. The grant, worth about 55 percent of the basic per student grant in the public system (about 60 percent for secondary students), is indexed to costs in the public system. The grant is worth about 35 percent of the total costs per student in the public system. Private schools in that province are eligible for funding as soon as they start up but are heavily regulated. They must teach the approved provincial curriculum and hire only certified teachers. Private schools that do not wish to comply with the regulations receive no funding.

Ontario

Ontario briefly offered parents a refundable tax credit for private school tuition. It was the first province to use that approach, which has been praised for keeping parents as the purchasers of their children's education. Unfortunately, that exciting policy experiment was short-lived.

The Equity in Education Tax Credit was introduced by a Progressive Conservative government in 2002. The refundable credit was initially worth 10 percent of tuition up to an annual maximum of $700 per child, and it was scheduled to grow over five years so that it would eventually be worth 50 percent of tuition up to a maximum of $7,500 per child per year. The province has long had a laissez-faire policy toward private schools, and the government did not use the tax credit as an opportunity to impose any new regulations. Private schools in Ontario do not have to hire certified teachers, teach a government-approved curriculum, or submit to government testing of their students. They are free to teach what they want to whom they want and charge what they like, as long as they do not violate any basic human rights.

In October 2003, the Progressive Conservative government was defeated in a provincial election, and the Liberals, who had made the cancellation of the private school tax credit part of their election platform, won a strong majority. The new government quickly fulfilled its promise; with a minimum of public consultation, it canceled the credit retroactively to the beginning of 2003.

Other Provinces

None of the other Canadian provinces—Saskatchewan,[20] New Brunswick, Nova Scotia, Prince Edward Island, and Newfoundland—allows public education funding to leave the regular public system. Enrollment in private schools in all those provinces is considerably below the national average.

Conclusion

The Canadian experience with government funding of private education suggests that that funding may make private schools more like public schools, but it also seems to make public schools more like private schools. Alberta, compared with other Canadian provinces, shows us a private education system that is generously funded but heavily regulated. Its public system, however, nurtures considerable school autonomy and diversity and high academic standards. The two largest public school districts have developed the broadest range of school programs available in the country. The system also tolerates charter schools. Although charter schools have not proliferated, they may have contributed to public school choice in other ways.

As for the question of private school independence, all of the Canadian provinces that fund private schools allow the schools to opt out of funding if they do not wish to comply with the regulatory requirements attached to it. In four Canadian provinces, private school funding has survived for a generation or more, testifying to its compatibility with a variety of different political philosophies and its long-term acceptability to voters. The Canadian experience suggests the potential for private school funding to benefit not only the children who attend private schools but also those who continue to attend public schools, if coupled with legislation to encourage school autonomy and academic accountability. Alberta's success gives us hope that other provinces will one day follow suit, not only with public funding of private schools, but also with the high school exit exams and school autonomy that have combined to make Alberta's students some of the world's highest academic achievers.

Notes

1. This is particularly true of Protestant school boards, which have gradually become secular in most provinces.

2. Robert C. Enlow, *Grading Vouchers: Ranking America's School Choice Programs*, School Choice Issues in Depth 2, no. 1 (Indianapolis, IN: Milton and Rose D. Friedman Foundation, 2004).

3. The exception to this rule is funding for students with special needs. Several provinces provide better funding for students with special needs being educated in private schools than they do for other students.

4. Dallas K. Miller, "A Report on the Canadian Study on Home Education 2003," Question and Answer Session, Fraser Institute Policy Briefing, Toronto, March 11, 2004.

5. L. Bosetti, R. O'Reilly, and D. Gereluk, "Public Choice and Public Education: The Impact of Alberta Charter Schools," Paper presented at the Annual Meeting of the American Educational Research Association, San Diego, CA, 1998, p. 2.

6. Council of Ministers of Education, Canada, *Measuring Up: The Performance of Canada's Youth in Reading, Mathematics and Science*. 2004, www.cmec.ca/pisa/2000/highlights.en.pdf. See also Claudia R. Hepburn and Robert Van Belle, *The Canadian Education Freedom Index*, Studies in Education Policy (Vancouver, BC: Fraser Institute, 2003), p. 17.

7. By the standards set out by the Center for Education Reform in *Charter School Laws across the States: Ranking and Scorecard,* 8th ed., 2004.

8. Most school boards in Canada divide their districts into catchment areas, or neighborhoods assigned to a particular public school. Children must attend the school assigned to their residence's catchment area unless they receive special dispensation from the board to attend another public school.

9. Claudia Hepburn and Robert Van Belle, *Ten Case Studies of Urban School Choice in Canada,* available from the author.

10. Lynn Bosetti, "The Alberta Charter School Experience." In *Can the Market Save Our Schools?* ed. Claudia R. Hepburn (Vancouver, BC: Fraser Institute, 2001), p. 106.

11. Charter applicants in Alberta must apply for status first to their school board. If the school board denies them a charter, they may appeal to the minister of education.

12. Kally Krylly, system coordinator, program renewal, Office of the Chief Superintendent, Calgary Board of Education, letter to the author, March 8, 2004.

13. Ibid.

14. After publishing an article on school choice in Alberta earlier this year, in which I contrasted the attitude toward school choice of the Calgary Board of Education with that of the board in Edmonton, I was contacted by Brendan Croskery, chief superintendent of schools, Calgary Board of Education, and his office has sent me considerable amounts of information since then in an effort to convince me of how earnestly the board is attempting to create a broad choice of programs in its district schools.

15. When doing research in 2002 on programs of choice in 10 large urban school districts across Canada, Robert Van Belle and I had difficulty finding any information on choice programs in 8 of the cities we surveyed. Vancouver, with its 11 school districts, and Edmonton's single school district were the exceptions.

16. Schools that employed uncertified teachers used to be eligible for a smaller per student grant, but that category of funding was abolished in the 1990s.

17. William Robson and Claudia R. Hepburn, *Learning from Success: What Americans Can Learn from School Choice in Canada,* School Choice Issues in Depth 1, no. 2 (Indianapolis, IN, and Vancouver, BC: Milton and Rose D. Friedman Foundation and Fraser Institute, 2002), p. 13.

18. Statistics Canada, "Trends in the Use of Private Education," *The Daily,* July 4, 2001, www.statcan.ca/Daily/English/010704/d010704.pdf. See also Federation of Independent Schools in Canada, *Enrolment Trend,* 2004, www.independent-schools.ca/trend.htm.

19. Manitoba Education, Citizenship and Youth, "Special Needs Funding Support: Guidelines for Level II and III Support," 2003, http://www.edu.gov.mb.ca/ks4/specedu/funding/level2-3.html.

20. Saskatchewan does provide some financial support to eight "historical" secondary schools, four "associate" schools, and three alternative schools. Other private schools are ineligible.

2. School Choice in Sweden: Is There Danger of a Counterrevolution?

F. Mikael Sandström

It is now more than a decade since Sweden introduced school choice reforms. Two laws, the Government Bill on Freedom of Choice and Independent Schools[1] and the Government Bill on School Choice,[2] established the right of any nongovernment school that fulfills certain basic requirements to receive public funding on terms equal to those of public schools. Because of those two bills, it is probably easier to establish an independent school in Sweden than in any other country.[3]

All kinds of schools, including religious schools and schools run by for-profit companies, are eligible to receive vouchers. Under the new laws, the National Agency for Education (NAE), the government body responsible for overseeing the school system, must approve any school that fulfills the requirements for receiving vouchers. Local government municipalities, which in Sweden are responsible for financing schools, are obliged to give independent schools per capita funding equal to the amount given for students in government schools. Parents are free to place their children in the public or independent school of their choice.

There are some provisions for approval of an independent school. The schools must meet certain quality requirements and must show that they are working toward the academic achievement targets set for the compulsory educational system. They must also be open to all children. Thus, they may not base admission on ability or on religious or ethnic origin. Finally, they are not allowed to charge tuition. The municipalities are allowed to give an opinion on whether they consider the establishment of an independent school to be harmful to existing schools, and their views are taken into account by the NAE. However, the municipalities have no veto and are bound by law to finance an independent school once it has been approved. On several occasions, the NAE has approved schools against the will of the municipalities.

The school choice reforms were a dramatic shift from past practice in Sweden. Before the reforms, independent schools played a marginal role. A few private schools existed, but they either catered to specific groups (such as Sweden's small Jewish community or the Estonian minority) or applied some distinct pedagogical concept, such as that of Steiner/Waldorf or Montessori schools. Also, before the reforms, the number of independent schools had been declining. Up until at least the 1960s, quite a few independent schools existed, especially at the upper secondary level. However, they were gradually taken over by the municipalities. Independent schools received financial support from the state only by government decision on a case-by-case basis. Generally, such support was granted only if a school was judged to make a "valuable contribution" above what was offered by the public school system.

Since the school choice reforms, the number of independent schools has increased fivefold. Today, about every third upper secondary school and 1 in 10 primary and lower secondary schools is an independent school. The number of students attending independent schools increased from approximately 15,000 in 1992–93 to close to 100,000 in 2004. That is still a small fraction of a total student population of around 1.4 million, but, compared with that of many OECD countries, the Swedish rate of increase has been impressive.

The reforms were controversial when they were enacted, but the basic principles of school choice have won widespread acceptance. Although the reforms were enacted in 1991 against the opposition of the Social Democrats, that party did not reverse the reforms when it came back into power in 1994. Of the seven parties represented in the Swedish parliament today, only the former communist party (now known as the Left Party) is outright opposed to school choice, and it represents less than 10 percent of the popular vote.

School choice is popular with parents and is seen as beneficial. In a survey undertaken by the NAE, more than 90 percent of respondents agreed with the statement that "parents and children should have a right to decide for themselves which school the children should attend." About 60 percent agreed that it is good when schools compete with each other. Only one-fourth said they disagreed. Almost 40 percent thought that having more independent schools would be good, and only about a quarter said that it would not be good.[4]

Although the basic principle of school choice is relatively well accepted by both the main political parties and the population at large, there are sharp disagreements over the effects of the school choice reforms on the public schools: Is competition beneficial, or does it lead to a depletion of resources in the public schools? A related issue is whether costs increase for the municipalities when they have to pay for students in independent schools. Another hotly debated issue is whether school choice increases or decreases racial and economic segregation. There has also been disagreement on the need to impose stricter regulation on the independent schools. That debate has focused partly on the general need to secure the quality of education, but the main issue has been the treatment of religious schools. Thus far, however, very few new regulations have been imposed.

In the following sections I describe the development of the Swedish school system since the school choice reforms were instituted; comment on the effects those reforms have had on school quality, costs, and segregation; discuss the risk the school choice reforms pose for independent schools in terms of additional government regulations; and draw some tentative conclusions about the lessons to be learned from the Swedish example.

A Decade of Freedom of Choice

Sweden is not outstanding among European countries when it comes to the share of students attending independent schools. For historical reasons, a large number (around 65 percent) of students in the Netherlands go to independent schools.[5] Sweden's southern neighbor, Denmark, also has a larger number of students in independent schools (about 13 percent). Thus, from an international perspective, Sweden's 6 percent of children of compulsory school age and 10 percent of upper secondary school children who attend independent schools are a small share of the total student population.[6]

However, the relatively few restrictions that Sweden places on independent schools' eligibility for vouchers sets Sweden apart. For example, in Denmark, private schools have received public funding for a long time, but only parent-controlled, nonprofit schools receive funding. Further, the Swedish system applies to children of all income levels. That sets the reform apart from most voucher experiments in the United States, such as the so-called Milwaukee experiment that provides vouchers only to children from low-income families.[7]

The treatment of religious schools in Sweden deserves special attention since the picture is somewhat complicated. There are no restrictions on religious (officially called "confessional") schools' eligibility for vouchers. However, according to national regulations, teaching in all schools that receive public funding has to be "nonconfessional." It is not entirely clear how that should be interpreted. Although it appears that the schools cannot teach creationism as the sole truth in a biology class, there is no ban on religious teaching per se. In practice, the requirement that teaching be nonconfessional does not seem to be a serious limitation on the 66 confessional schools that were in operation during the 2002–03 school year. It is clear that religious schools are treated far more generously under the Swedish voucher system than they are under voucher systems in the United States.

The Swedish school reforms stand out as radical in most international comparisons. Before the reforms, teachers were employees of the national government, and the municipal schools were strictly regulated by the powerful National Board of Education. There were national regulations on the maximum number of students in each class, on teaching methods, on classroom size, and so on. Under the reforms, that system of regulation was replaced by national academic targets and a general curricular framework, within which municipalities and schools were given wider autonomy. Teachers became employees of the municipalities, and specific grants to schools were replaced by general grants to the municipalities. The National Board of Education was replaced by the much less powerful National Agency for Education. Thus, in a few years time, Sweden moved from a highly centralized system with strict government regulation of education to a decentralized system with freedom for parents to choose among private or public schools and freedom to establish independent schools that have a large degree of autonomy.

As pointed out above, the rate of increase in the number of independent schools has been impressive (Figure 2.1). However, there is considerable variation between municipalities. In the Stockholm and Gothenburg regions, for example, 20 to 40 percent of upper

Figure 2.1
THE DEVELOPMENT OF INDEPENDENT SCHOOLS

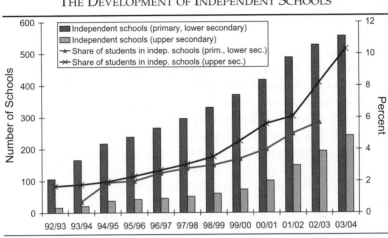

SOURCE: National Agency of Education (*Skolverket*).

secondary school students attend independent schools. In about 50 of Sweden's 290 municipalities, the share is below 2 percent. At the compulsory school level, the independent school share of student enrollment is above one-tenth in about 30 municipalities and below 1.5 percent in more than half of the country's municipalities.

More students attend independent schools in the main urban areas, but it would be wrong to conclude that independent schools are mainly an urban phenomenon. Some of Sweden's most sparsely populated municipalities are in the northern county of Norrbotten. Yet those municipalities are among the municipalities with the largest share of students in independent schools (above 10 percent). Thus, Sweden provides clear evidence that independent schools can work well in rural areas.

Moreover, independent schools have expanded rapidly in some less-privileged areas. The third-largest share of students in independent compulsory schools is found in Älvkarleby, which is a mainly rural, working-class community, heavily dependent on a paper mill. Several municipalities with a large immigrant population are also among those with a comparatively high proportion of independent schools. Botkyrka has the highest proportion of foreign nationals in the Stockholm region and is characterized by a high unemployment rate and serious social problems. Yet it has the 11th-highest proportion of students in independent schools in the country. Thirteen percent of Botkyrka compulsory-age students attend independent schools.[8]

In addition to the spectacular rate of growth, there are two other interesting points about the development of independent schools in Sweden. First, a large and growing share of the independent schools is owned by limited liability companies. Only two years ago, that share was around 30 percent. Today, more than half of the independent schools are owned by limited liability companies. Several companies run a number of schools. An example is Internationalla Engelska Skolan, the International English School, which was started in Stockholm in 1993 and has now expanded to six schools in different parts of the country. Kunskapsskolan, the Knowledge School, began with four schools in 2000 and has now expanded to more than 20 schools. Two other limited liability companies are Pysslingen and Vittra, which operate 12 and 25 schools, respectively. Although most schools, including the ones just mentioned, were started partly to realize the founders' educational visions, there is also a clear profit motive driving the expansion.

Second, religious schools constitute a small minority of independent schools in Sweden. That contrasts sharply with the Netherlands where more than 90 percent of the independent schools are run by religious institutions.[9] In Sweden religious ("confessional") schools constitute only 12 percent of the total number of independent schools at the compulsory school level.[10] The share of the student population is even smaller—less than 10 percent of all students who attend independent schools (Figure 2.2).

The declining share of religious schools is perhaps not so hard to explain. Before the school choice reforms were implemented, parents who wanted to send their children to a particular school were forced to pay twice for education. They paid taxes for the municipal education system as well as fees to the private schools their children were attending. Under those circumstances, only parents who strongly preferred a private school would choose the private alternative. It is not surprising then that it was mainly parents with strong religious beliefs who chose private schools. Furthermore, religious organizations often subsidized the tuition fees for students in religious private schools, which made those schools more affordable than the more expensive nonreligious private schools.

Figure 2.2
DEVELOPMENT OF INDEPENDENT SCHOOLS ACCORDING
TO SPECIALIZATION

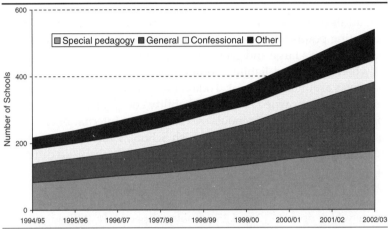

SOURCE: National Agency of Education (*Skolverket*).

A school voucher system transforms schooling from a government enterprise into a more normal market where schools compete on the basis of the quality of their educational programs or focus on special subjects or children with special needs. Confessional schools certainly continue to exist, but, at least in Sweden, the market that they appeal to appears to be limited.

The Impact of Choice

It is thus clear that the Swedish school choice reforms have had a dramatic effect on the number of independent schools as well as on the share of students attending such schools.[11] However, an important subject of debate has been how the reforms are affecting the public school system. Opponents of the reform have raised concerns that the independent schools "drain" resources from the public schools, with a detrimental effect on quality. Proponents, on the other hand, cite the increased competition as a way to improve results.

The evidence thus far clearly indicates that competition improves student results. Students in independent schools generally seem to have better results than students in public schools, even after

29

controlling for socioeconomic differences.[12] A recent study by Sandström and Bergström indicates that both grades and test results in
mathematics for public school students improve when the degree
of competition from independent schools increases.[13] Another conclusion from the study is that the share of students in independent
schools is likely to be larger if the academic achievement of public
school students was low, ceteris paribus, before the reform was
enacted. Thus, it seems that independent schools are, at least partly,
a response to inadequacies in the public schools.

A study by Åsa Ahlin found a significant positive effect on public
schools from competition in mathematics, but not in English and
Swedish.[14] Ahlin also found that immigrant children tend to gain
more from increased school competition. The same is true for students in need of special education. Ahlin does, however, find that
competition has an adverse effect on the results in English and
Swedish for students from low-education families.

Björklund et al. also studied the effects of competition on student
grades and test results.[15] Their results are largely consistent with
those of Sandström and Bergström and Ahlin. However, Björklund
et al. also found a positive and significant effect from competition
on results in English and Swedish. In contrast with Ahlin, they found
evidence that students from a low socioeconomic background benefit
less from competition.

Closely related to the issue of the effects of competition on public
schools is the question of how school choice affects the overall cost of
schooling. If students leave the municipal school for an independent
school, the municipality has to pay money to the independent school.
At the same time, it may be hard to reduce costs in the municipal
schools, at least in the short run. On the other hand, if competition
increases school productivity, the resulting efficiency gains may
work to reduce costs.

Two studies have addressed that issue. Björklund et al.[16] find no
evidence that costs either increase or decrease as a result of competition from independent schools.[17] Waldo uses data on 851 upper
secondary schools (out of 1,064) in 1994–95 to estimate the schools'
efficiency. He finds that the schools could, on average, use 9 to 19
percent less money and still produce the same results. More interesting from our point of view, he finds that competition from independent schools improves efficiency.[18]

A final issue that has been debated in Sweden is what effect school choice has had on segregation, both among immigrants and native-born Swedes and among people with different socioeconomic backgrounds. Historically, Sweden has been more ethnically homogeneous than most European countries and certainly more homogeneous than the United States. However, immigration during the last two or three decades has created what can be described as a minority problem in Sweden. The immigrants have been partly foreign labor and partly refugees and have originated from a large number of countries both in and outside Europe. Some immigrant groups have not been integrated into Swedish society. There are housing areas, especially around the country's major cities, with a large share of immigrants and also high rates of drug addiction and high unemployment and other social problems. Some observers have been concerned that school choice would cause inhabitants of areas with a large number of immigrants to become even more isolated from the rest of the population and that school choice would lead to segregation by parents' educational background and economic situation.

Unfortunately, no systematic study of that issue has been undertaken. Instead, anecdotal support for different points of view has been presented in the public debate. Those who claim that segregation is increasing refer to statistics, mainly for the Stockholm region, showing that the difference between schools in regard to the share of pupils with immigrant background, parents with low education, or parents with low incomes has increased. The data usually referred to include only public upper secondary schools and not the independent schools. Thus, that part of the debate has to do with the right to choose different public schools rather than with vouchers to independent schools. Those who claim that segregation is decreasing refer to the fact that the share of pupils from suburbs with many immigrant inhabitants and with considerable social problems has increased in the popular schools in the center of the city.[19]

A related concern is that the independent schools may exclude students with special needs such as those with physical disabilities or limited proficiency in Swedish. There is, however, no evidence that that is the case. A government committee, appointed by the Social Democratic government to evaluate some aspects of the school reforms, made the following statement:

> The view that independent schools are segregated and do
> not have students with special needs is sometimes heard in
> the debate. None of the committee's findings indicates that
> independent schools have fewer students with special needs
> than municipal schools. To the contrary, many independent
> schools have many students from this category. Parents who
> do not think that their children get the support they require
> in the municipal school often take their children from the
> municipal school to independent schools.[20]

The committee also noted that a number of independent schools
are explicitly focused on students with special needs.

In conclusion, the Swedish school choice reforms have led to an
impressive expansion of independent schools. That has certainly
increased the diversity of schools in the Swedish school system.
Today, there are schools specializing in music, Russian, mathematics,
English, French, German, Arabic, and information technology. Some
schools apply the Steiner/Waldorf pedagogy and some practice the
theories of Maria Montessori. There are Christian, Muslim, and Jewish schools. Naturally, the largest number of choices is available in
the larger cities, but students in a large number of rural communities
also have a choice between the public schools and one or several
independent schools. The available evidence indicates that freedom
of choice has had a beneficial effect on student achievement, and
the fact that municipalities have to pay for students in independent
schools has not caused costs to rise. To the contrary, one study
indicates that competition increases efficiency and thus may reduce
costs. Further, there is no evidence that freedom of choice has
increased segregation along racial or economic lines, although that
is certainly an issue that deserves further attention. Overall, it is fair
to claim that the school choice reforms have been a tremendous
success.

A Dawning Counterrevolution?

There is general agreement in Sweden that school choice and
independent schools have, on the whole, been beneficial to the school
system. Nevertheless, voices have been calling for closer regulation
of independent schools. In a few cases, new regulations have in fact
been imposed.

Before going into that issue, it is necessary to point out that independent and public schools alike are less strictly regulated today than they were before the 1990s. The previous system included regulations not only on what the schools should do but also on how they should do it. That has now been replaced by national academic achievement targets for the school system and a large degree of autonomy for municipalities, municipal schools, and independent schools in meeting the targets.

However, the targets have not been met. About a tenth of compulsory school children do not meet the requirements for entry to upper secondary school, and a quarter fail in at least one of the compulsory subjects. Generalizing slightly, one may say that two opposing views on how to remedy the problem have emerged. One proposed remedy is to demand tighter regulation of schools, both public and independent.

Demands for tighter regulations have led to, among other things, government funds directed to municipalities for the purpose of increasing the number of "adults" in schools, thus removing some of the municipalities' and schools' autonomy in deciding how best to staff their schools and spend resources.[21] In addition, there is some evidence that independent schools have been unfairly treated in the distribution of money from the grants, thus violating the principle of equal treatment of all schools. Also, the NAE has been transformed from what it was originally supposed to be—a small, knowledge-intensive organization to oversee how the schools and municipalities implemented government policy—into an administrator of government grants. Thus, the NAE has a much more intrusive role in the school sector than was originally envisaged.[22]

An alternative proposal to remedy the problem of unmet targets is to impose stricter quality control over schools, both independent and public. Basically, the line of argument is that more frequent and thorough inspections of schools and more frequent centralized tests should remove much of the need to regulate the operation of schools. As long as schools meet the targets set by the government and fulfill the requirements to be eligible to receive vouchers, the organization of teaching and other decisions may be left to the schools.

Admittedly, there have been severe deficiencies in the NAE's supervision of schools and municipalities. In 2001 the Swedish National Audit Office drew the conclusion that the NAE focused mainly on catching formal errors of the schools, such as unsatisfactory administrative routines, and other peripheral issues.[23] The quality of education was rarely an issue. As a result, there has been some movement toward better evaluation of school results. The NAE has recently been split into two agencies—the NAE and the Swedish National Agency for School Improvement—leaving the former to focus somewhat more on evaluation. The NAE has since improved the assembly of data on student results and has increased the number of school inspections. However, thus far, few discernible improvements in supervision have resulted.

What can be seen from this discussion is that the lack of adequate supervision of schools easily gives rise to demands for new regulation. That does not have to do so much with the voucher system as with the dramatic change in the Swedish government's approach to regulating schools—from command and control to management by objectives. A lack of inspections, evaluation, and sanctions against schools or municipalities that do not meet the objectives has sparked a movement back toward command and control. Generally, however, the independent schools seem to be less affected by increased government interference than the municipal schools, partly because the specially directed grants have been directed to municipalities rather than to the independent schools.

The concern for quality has been specifically focused on independent schools. Under present regulations, municipal schools have to hire formally qualified teachers, if available, while independent schools have greater freedom to determine which personnel they should hire. There have been proposals to reduce that freedom, but thus far, such proposals have not resulted in any legislation.

One issue that has a more direct bearing on independent schools is the treatment of religious schools. Many of the complaints to the NAE and also from NAE's inspectors have been directed at religious schools. However, a large share of the complaints has had to do, not with the fact that the schools are religious, but rather with their failure to meet the general teaching standards and lack, in some cases, of competent teachers.

In addition, a few Christian as well as Muslim schools have been accused of violating the provision that education should be nonconfessional. As pointed out above, it is somewhat hard to judge what that provision really entails, since religious schools are eligible for vouchers. A recent press statement by an NAE official indicates how unclear the policy is: "While independent schools may be confessional, they must at the same time follow the national guidelines which state that the *teaching* should be non-confessional" (emphasis added). In practice, the NAE has stipulated some practices that schools need to follow in order to meet the "nonconfessional" requirement. Generally, it has not been hard for the religious schools to follow the directions of the NAE. In one case, the school chose to introduce a new subject, Bible studies, and keep confessional teaching out of the other subjects. That was deemed adequate by the NAE. In a few cases, Christian and Muslim schools have had their approval removed, not because the teaching was religious, but because it was of too low quality.

Concern over the Muslim schools is a bit more complex. One complication is that, while most students in Christian schools are of Swedish origin, the students in Muslim schools are usually immigrants. Often, the Muslim immigrants are not well integrated into Swedish society. Thus, segregation arguments are more relevant in that context. Also, because of problems with integration of this group of immigrants, many parents of children in Muslim schools may distrust Swedish authorities. In addition, Muslim schools are more susceptible to the suspicion that teaching may be based on values that are alien to a modern democratic society (for example, teachings about the position of women in society and general attitudes toward democratic institutions). A recent television program showing the headmasters of some Muslim schools admitting to physical abuse of students brought forth calls for increased inspection of those schools. However, the resulting NAE inspections were not considered adequate, even by the minister of education. Thus, although the inspections led the NAE to demand that some of the Muslim schools improve on a number of points, and to the dismissal of at least one headmaster, many politicians and others remained unconvinced that those Muslim schools really meet the standards.

As a result, demands have been raised that confessional schools not be eligible to receive vouchers. Naturally, it would be impossible to bar Muslim schools while allowing Christian or Jewish schools; thus the demand is to exclude all religious schools from the voucher system. The lack of appropriate supervision and the unclear regulations covering what is permissible under the "nonconfessional" statutes have given rise to demands to restrict the freedom of independent schools.

Another point that has caused the NAE to act and has also led to stricter regulation of independent schools is grading practices. In Sweden, students in public schools do not receive grades until eighth grade. For reasons that are hard to explain to non-Swedes, it is considered harmful to receive grades earlier than that. However, until two years ago, there was no law banning independent schools from giving grades to younger students. When some independent schools did so, however, the law was quickly changed. The reason given by the then–minister for schools was that allowing independent schools to give grades earlier would give them an unfair competitive advantage over the public schools. Also, the NAE has forced some independent upper secondary schools to change their grading practices to conform to the national standards.

Yet another frequently voiced opinion is that it is not right that voucher-financed schools be allowed to make a profit. However, no such limitation has been imposed thus far. The adverse attitude toward profits is not uniquely Swedish. In Norway, which is introducing a school choice reform partly modeled on the Swedish reform, for-profit companies will not be allowed to receive vouchers. That will mean that the kind of for-profit companies that provide many Swedish independent schools will not appear in Norway.

In conclusion, the demands for stricter regulation of independent schools have not resulted in such regulations being introduced. It should be kept in mind, though, that the initial regulations on independent schools placed some rather severe restrictions on the operation of those schools, in particular the restrictions on how students are admitted and the ban on tuition fees to "top-up" the vouchers.

The ban on tuition fees has likely been important in gaining popular acceptance of the independent schools. The allegation that independent schools are for only the well-off simply does not stick, since independent schools cost the same as public schools. Also, independent schools are allowed to charge fees for extracurricular activities, which may include music classes or extra language training. Thus, this is perhaps not a severe restriction on the operation of the independent schools, even though it may have negative effects on efficiency. The restrictive rules on how students are admitted may be more serious, since they preclude ability testing. Basically, only a "first come, first served" admission policy is acceptable.

Lessons from the Swedish Experience

The main lesson from the Swedish school choice reform is simple enough: Vouchers work! Even with the caveats discussed in the previous section, it should be clear that the Swedish voucher reforms have had a tremendously positive impact on independent schools, simply by allowing them to exist. If school choice had not been introduced, the number of independent schools would have continued to decline. Instead, Sweden has set an example for successful reform. Students have a choice. Independent schools with innovative educational ideas or ideological or religious outlooks that differ from the majority view can prosper in Sweden. Although the Swedish education system suffers from many deficiencies, it seems clear that competition from independent schools has improved quality.

The Swedish experience also offers at least two lessons on how to avoid demands for tighter regulation of independent schools. First, the original school choice legislation must be clear about any requirements that schools must meet to be eligible to participate in the voucher system. Second, when tax money is used to finance schools run by private entities, there will be requirements for some government supervision. Politicians will not be content to rely on parents or private accrediting bodies as the sole overseers of private schools. In view of that, it is important to keep requirements to a minimum and not burden private schools with onerous regulations. If politicians and the public do not feel confident that money distributed through the voucher system is used responsibly, that may give rise to demands for tighter regulation of the independent schools or even undermine the whole voucher system. Thus, paradoxically, limited but strictly enforced regulations and adequate supervision are important to guarantee that the autonomy of the independent schools is preserved in the long run.

Swedish regulation of religious, or "confessional," schools is an example of regulation that has not worked very well. It is difficult to draw the line between what should be tolerated in the name of freedom of religion and what should be deemed unacceptable and in violation of basic principles of a free and democratic country. Obviously, Muslim schools should be allowed to teach the Koran. But what if they refuse to talk about Israel in geography class and instead call it "the Zionist Entity," or call the United States "the Great Satan," teach that the Holocaust never took place, or treat the

Protocol of the Elders of Zion as a historic document? That view of the world is widely shared in many parts of the Arab world, so the idea that a school may teach such views is not far-fetched.[24] It could reasonably be asked whether such schools should be subsidized by the taxpayers. Also, if knowledge of biology is a national requirement, then schools that teach only creationism could not claim to be meeting the requirements.

The point, however, is not that certain practices should be allowed and that others should not. The point is that the conditions required for schools to participate in the voucher program must be clearly specified. If they are not, then the credibility of the whole system may be undermined. Most religious schools in Sweden seem to work very well, teach according to the national guidelines, keep scientific facts and religion apart, and foster respect of other religions and the fundamental principles of a democratic society. However, a few bad apples may spoil the whole barrel. In fact, the failings of some religious schools have been used as arguments against the entire school choice reform.

In conclusion, Sweden proves that vouchers can be an important tool for improving education and foster pluralism in the school system. Sweden has made the transition from an almost completely centralized education system to a system based on decentralization and choice. As a result, the number of students in independent schools has more than quadrupled, and the number of independent schools has increased more than fivefold.

The Swedish experience also provides some lessons in accountability and regulation. Primarily, those lessons are that clarity and minimal regulations are the best way to foster respect for the system and, at the same time, allow for innovative approaches by schools. Changing from a command-and-control system of education to an environment of choice has not been easy in Sweden, but the problems that we have experienced do not suggest that choice will lead to strong demands for tighter regulations.

Instead of giving rise to a "counterrevolution," school choice has become universally accepted and greatly popular among parents, teachers, and the public in general. The popularity of choice has made the political demand for restrictions on independent schools relatively weak. Although there certainly are politicians who want to limit the freedom of choice, opposing school choice simply is not a vote winner.

Notes

1. "Proposition om valfrihet och fristående skolor" (Prop. 1991/92:95). This bill established freedom of choice for grades 1–9 of compulsory schools.

2. "Valfrihet i skolan" (Prop. 1992/93:230). This bill established freedom of choice in upper secondary schools, roughly equivalent to high school.

3. To avoid terminological confusion, I use the term "independent" school to denote a school that is owned and run by an agent other than a local or national government, regardless of whether the school receives public funds. An independent school may cover all, parts, or none of its operating costs with public funds. Thus, charter schools, schools financed by vouchers, and tuition-based private schools would all fall under my definition of independent schools. I use the term "public school" to refer to a school run by local or national government bodies. Thus, using my terminology, a school is either an independent school or a public school, depending on who runs it, regardless of who finances it.

4. Skolverket (National Agency of Education), "Valfriheten och dess effekter inom skolområdet" (Freedom of choice and its effects in the school sector), Stockholm, 2003.

5. For descriptions of the Dutch school system, see F. J. de Vijlder, "Choice and Financing of Schools in the Netherlands," in *Nachfrageorientierte Bildungsfinanzierung. Neue Trends für Kindertagestätte, Schule und Hochschule*, ed. D. Dohmen and C. Cleuvers, Scriften zur Bildungs- und Sozialökonomie (Bielefeld, Germany: Bertelsmann, 2002); and J. M. M Ritzen, J. Van Dommelen, and F. J. de Vijlder, "School Finance and School Choice in the Netherlands," *Economics of Education Review* 16, no. 3 (1997): 329–35.

6. Compulsory school in Sweden comprises primary and lower secondary school, grades 1–9. Upper secondary school (roughly equivalent to high school) is usually three years.

7. C. E. Rouse, "Private School Vouchers and Student Achievement: An Evaluation of the Milwaukee Parental Choice Program," *Quarterly Journal of Economics* 113, no. 2 (1998): 553–602; and J. P. Greene, P. E. Peterson, and J. Du, "Effectiveness of School Choice," *Education and Urban Society* 31, no. 2 (1999): 190–213.

8. For upper secondary schools, Botkyrka ranks 21st, with more than 18 percent of students attending independent schools.

9. de Vijlder, "Choice and Financing of Schools in the Netherlands." Only 16 percent of U.S. private school students are enrolled in nonreligious private schools. See National Council on Educational Statistics, *Private School Universe Survey: 1999–2000* (Washington: National Council on Education Statistics, 2001).

10. Only three upper secondary schools are religious.

11. For a more detailed account of the Swedish reforms and the discussion they have provoked, see F. Bergström and F. M. Sandström *School Choice Works! The Case of Sweden*, School Choice Issues in Thought 1, no. 1 (Indianapolis: Milton & Rose D. Friedman Foundation, 2002).

12. Åsa Ahlin, "Does School Competition Matter? Effects of a Large-Scale School Choice Reform on Student Performance," Working Paper Series, no 2003:2, Department of Economics, Uppsala University, 2003; and A. Björklund et al., *Den svenska skolan—effektiv och jämlik?* (The Swedish school system—Efficient and equal?) (Stockholm: SNS Förlag, 2003).

13. F. M. Sandström and F. Bergström, "School Vouchers in Practice: Competition Won't Hurt You!" *Journal of Public Economics* 89, nos. 2–3 (2005): 351–80.

14. Ahlin.

15. See Björklund et al. They use repeated cross-sectional data for the years 1998–2001. Test results are available for a selection of 30 municipalities per year, and grades are available for the full cohorts. Thus, they can control for unobserved heterogeneity between municipalities, even though they cannot use the value-added approach. The empirical strategy used by Björklund et al. is to estimate the effect of changes in test results on changes in the share of students attending independent schools.

16. Ibid.

17. I have used various statistical models to assess the effect of competition on cost. The preliminary results indicate that competition decreases costs. However, the results are highly unstable and not robust to specification; thus, these results support the conclusion of Björklund et al. that there is no reason to believe that costs are affected either way.

18. S. Waldo, "Efficiency in Public Education," Working Paper 2002:10, Department of Economics, Lund University, 2002. Waldo uses so-called data envelopment analysis.

19. Unlike that of many American cities, the central part of Stockholm is considered an attractive and socially privileged area. The social problems are instead more pronounced in some of the city's suburbs.

20. SOU 1999:98 "Likvärdiga villkor" (On equal terms), Final report from the government committee on the distribution of resources to independent schools, Stockholm: Department of Education, p. 48 (author's translation).

21. There is no requirement to hire teachers, so personnel other than teachers count; hence the phrase "more 'adults' " in schools.

22. Riksdagens Revisorer (Parliamentary Auditors), "Statens styrning av skolan- från målstyrning till uppsökande bidragsförmedling," report 2001/02:13.

23. Under the Swedish constitution, the government "cabinet" is responsible to parliament. Government agencies have, from an international perspective, a large degree of autonomy. Ministers are barred by the constitution from interferring in the operation of government agencies. Instead, the government issues formal instructions to the agencies, which they then have to follow. The Swedish National Audit Office (SNAO) served the government with audits of government agencies to ensure that government guidelines were followed and that tax money was used efficiently. The "old" SNAO has now been merged with the Parliamentary Auditors into a new agency serving directly under parliament, which has kept the Swedish National Audit Office as an English translation of its name.

24. For an interesting insight into militant Islamist schools, see Andrew Coulson, "Education and Indoctrination in the Muslim World: Is There a Problem? What Can We Do about It?" Cato Institute Policy Analysis no. 511, March 11, 2004.

3. The Chilean Education Voucher System

Claudio Sapelli

Chile's education voucher system, introduced in 1982, is the only nationwide education voucher system with evaluative data stretching over such a long period. Therefore, the program is of great interest in assessing the effects and proper design of a national voucher system.

The most recent studies find significant differences in test scores between students educated at private voucher schools and those educated at municipal voucher schools. The key problem here is how to disentangle the effect of the school from the effects stemming from differences in family background. To do that, data on individual student and family background are required; those data have only recently been made available.[1]

In this chapter, I discuss the improvement in test scores associated with attending a private voucher school as opposed to a public school. My research takes into account the fact that in the Chilean voucher system different types of schools work with different budgets.[2] The funding differences between municipal and private voucher schools will be described below, but the key point is that many municipal schools receive substantial funding in addition to the per student voucher, whereas private voucher schools do not. In a previous study conducted by Sapelli and Vial, we found that, when public and private voucher schools receive similar per capita subsidies (i.e., when private voucher schools work with up to 25 percent less funds than public schools), test scores for students who attend private voucher schools, all else being equal, are higher and that this number is both statistically significant and large.[3]

Some analysts fear that that result is the consequence of sorting (the selection of the best students by private schools) or the peer effect (the fall in the achievement of the worst students due to the

41

extraction of the best students from a class), or both, and not the consequence of the effectiveness of private voucher schools.

Sapelli and Vial analyzed the importance of peer effects and found that, all else being equal, the result that private voucher schools are better is unaffected by controlling for peer group characteristics.[4] In other words, even when we control for peer group characteristics, we find a positive effect of private voucher schools in geographic areas where public and private voucher schools receive similar per capita subsidies.

Those results are important because the discussion surrounding voucher systems in general and the evaluation of the Chilean system in particular have centered on whether private schools are better than public schools and on the importance of sorting and the peer effect. The debate has often assumed that private voucher schools are not significantly more effective than public schools in Chile.[5]

The fact that we find significant positive effects is all the more important if we take into account the many limitations that prevent the Chilean voucher system from fulfilling its potential. For the system to improve, those limitations must be removed. One of the key lessons of the Chilean experience is that the design of a voucher system is of central importance.

I begin by considering the characteristics of the Chilean voucher system, then discuss the other reported evaluations of the system and the methodology employed in those evaluations. I conclude with a discussion of the flaws in the design of the system.

The Chilean Education System

Education in Chile is provided by three types of schools: municipal (MUN), private subsidized (PS), and private nonsubsidized (PP or private paid) schools. PP schools are 100 percent financed from tuition payments, while PS and MUN schools are usually free and are fully funded from the fiscal budget. The money is distributed, in part, according to a per capita subsidy (the voucher). The purpose of the subsidy is to promote competition to attract students to and retain them in schools financed from the fiscal budget, since the amount of money they receive depends on enrollment. However, there are several exceptions that soften schools' dependence on enrollment as a determinant of funding; those exceptions complicate empirical work. They are discussed below.

Table 3.1
PER CAPITA SUBSIDY

| | Multiple of the USE | |
Type of Education	Without Longer School Day	With Longer School Day
Preprimary	1.4495	
Primary (1st to 6th)	1.4528	
Primary (7th to 8th)	1.5781	
Primary (1st to 8th)		1.9906
Special education (3rd to 8th)	4.8216	6.0516
Secondary (humanities)	1.7631	2.3824
Secondary (technical, agriculture)	2.6209	3.2345
Secondary (technical, industry)	2.0410	2.5183
Secondary (technical, commerce)	1.8290	2.3824

NOTE: USE (1998) = US$22, approximately.

Overall, MUN schools have about half of total enrollment, PS schools have a third, and PP schools have about one-tenth. Those percentages vary in Santiago, where PS and PP schools have a larger share.

In 1988 a standardized test was established to generate information on the quality of education in different schools.[6] It consists of tests in language, mathematics, social sciences, and science. Students in all schools are tested in the fourth and eighth grades of primary school and in the second grade of high school. The raw scores show that PP schools have the highest test scores, while MUN schools have the lowest.

Although the evolution of test results through time may appear to be of interest—and many analysts make much of its trajectory—it is in fact meaningless, since the test is not designed to be comparable across years. The test was not "equated" until 1997. It was administered by the Universidad Católica until 1992 and was then transferred to the Ministry of Education.

MUN and PS schools receive a per capita subsidy. The subsidy is expressed as a multiple of a unit called *Unidad de Subvención Educacional* (USE). The multiple varies according to different characteristics of the school (Table 3.1). That subsidy is the voucher.

The subsidy paid to the school every month is based on average attendance over the previous three months. Generally, in MUN schools the subsidy is not enough to cover the entire budget, and so the majority of MUN schools receive additional subsidies from the municipalities. Since 1993 PS schools have been eligible to receive additional financing from two sources: the system of shared financing (*financiamiento compartido*) and tax-deductible educational donations.

The *financiamiento compartido* system allows parents to make direct payments to the school, without the school losing 100 percent of the subsidy, as was the case before 1993. Currently, once a school chooses to participate in the system, it can charge up to four USEs (approximately US$88), and the per capita subsidy is reduced according to the average fee paid by parents. The discount corresponds to (a) 10 percent off the voucher if the parents pay between one-half and one USE, (b) 20 percent off the voucher if the parents pay between one and two USEs, and (c) 35 percent off the voucher if the parents pay between two and four USEs. As Vial has shown, that system unambiguously increases total financing for education, reducing the distortions created by the either/or choice between fully parent-financed and voucher schools.[7] The system of *financiamiento compartido* has proved a huge success: about 40 percent of PS schools (about 65 percent of total PS enrollment) had switched to the system by 1996.

Assessment: Are Private Subsidized Schools More Effective?

Some analysts have asserted that test scores do not differ between municipal and private subsidized schools if one considers differences in pupils' backgrounds and concluded that there has been no improvement in educational outcomes attributable to the introduction of the voucher system.[8] Over the last 15 years those beliefs have pushed educational policy toward increasing the Ministry of Education's influence over the operation of the system and generating multiple additional incentives running in parallel with the voucher system.

Since municipal schools work within a very different incentive framework than that faced by PS schools, the result that municipal and private voucher schools do not differ in the quality of their "product" would imply that incentive frameworks cannot contribute to solving the problems of the education sector.

However, over the last few years better data have been made available, and evaluations have been conducted using previously unavailable individual-level data. Research using those data has produced results different from those of the previous "generation" of studies (which used school averages instead of individual data). The most recent studies provide evidence that PS schools are better than MUN schools.[9]

The most recent literature tries to solve some or all of the following problems faced by the earlier researchers: the use of inappropriate variables as controls, not testing for the direction of causality, lack of control for selection bias, and lack of adequate structure on the supply side. I shall consider each problem in turn.

Use of Inappropriate Controls

In addition to using school average data, the methodology of the earlier generation of studies was often unsatisfactory. Those studies confused the literature of policy evaluation with that of production functions: in the production function literature all possible inputs are included to ascertain which are of use in obtaining better results. The policy evaluation literature aims to identify the effects of a new policy and does not concern itself (at least at the first level of analysis) with how those effects are obtained. Some researchers, in trying to evaluate the effect of the voucher system, used variables controlled by the school as explanatory variables (thus controlling for them). But since one of the voucher system's advantages is that it allows schools to experiment with different combinations of inputs—and hence variation in this respect is a choice variable for the school— those researchers were removing from consideration one of the main channels by which the voucher system affects test results and hence biasing the results toward finding no effect.

On occasion, the literature has appeared to argue that controlling for "enough" variables causes the difference in test scores between school types to disappear. However, some researchers wanted to exclude from the controls all those variables that may be affected by the voucher system because they are the channels by which voucher schools are able to improve their results. Hence the estimation strategy followed by those researchers is incorrect and biases results toward finding that being educated at private voucher schools has no effect.

Not Testing for the Direction of Causality

Even when it is accepted that significant differences in test scores exist, some analysts argue that they are not the result of the greater effectiveness of private voucher schools but rather stem from the "cream skimming" of the best students by private schools and the deterioration in test scores that results from this cream skimming in municipal schools via the peer effect. The literature argues that, if sorting and the peer effect are important, one has to evaluate the educational system as a whole; one cannot just evaluate whether the private schools are better than the public schools. However, having made this point, the key issue is whether either or both sorting and the peer effect are empirically important in the case of Chile. Regrettably, the literature contributes little to answering that question.[10]

The key problem in assessing the importance of sorting and the peer effect is the methodological issue of causality. If we find that municipalities with higher enrollment in private schools also have lower test scores in the public school system, we cannot necessarily infer that there is a causal link that goes from a larger private voucher school system to cream skimming and the deterioration of test scores in the public school system through the peer effect, as some papers claim.[11] Without explicitly testing for causality, we cannot know whether what is occurring is instead that municipalities with particularly bad municipal schools attract private voucher schools. The methodology must take into account that the entry of private voucher schools to a district is endogenous and that it naturally occurs first in districts where the population is most underserved by municipal schools.

For example, even though Hsieh and Urquiola provide evidence in their paper that poor tests in public schools cause entry of private schools, the authors do not perform a test that explicitly controls for endogeneity. Gallego finds that the issue is crucial: results with and without controlling for endogeneity differ significantly.[12] Gallego's results, when controlling for endogenous entry, show that competition from private subsidized schools actually increases the test scores of municipal schools. Those results are the opposite of the results reported by Hsieh and Urquiola and show how important it is to adequately control for endogenous entry.[13] I discuss the peer effect further below.

Selection Bias

Virtually all of the empirical studies of Chile's voucher system conducted prior to 2000 failed to take into account the existence of selection bias, as data to correct for it were unavailable until then. Selection bias is relevant, for example, when attempting to interpret the difference in raw test data from different types of schools. Two effects can be confused: that of a better-quality entering student due to more family or home production of human capital and that of an improved student-school match brought about by parents with higher human capital, which allows them to better select the appropriate school for their child. Econometric methods must be used to separate the value added by the school from that due to the better quality of the input (the student).

Until 2000, analysts used regression analysis to determine the influence of family characteristics and type of school on test scores. If the differences in raw scores could be fully explained by different family characteristics, then the authors generally concluded that schools did not differ in the quality of education provided. However, since the decision about which type of school a child is sent to is endogenous—that is, it depends on the parents—not controlling for that endogeneity may result in mistaken inferences. Also, family characteristics influence test scores through two channels: first, through the choice of the type of school the child attends and, second, through the child's ability to learn. If all the influence of parental education is channeled through the choice of school, then what makes the difference is the school. Only if most of the influence were through the learning abilities of the child would the conclusions in the Chilean empirical literature be correct.

In the Chilean literature, Contreras[14] and Tokman[15] control for selection bias and find significant differences in scores between MUN and PS schools; those differences favor PS schools.

How Much Structure Should We Give to the Supply Side?

Most of the studies in the literature implicitly assume that MUN and PS schools are a homogeneous pool, facing similar incentives and working with similar budgets. That is mistaken. There are several differences that should be controlled for, or at least taken into account when interpreting the data. Those include the different budgets of MUN schools (partially determined by the municipality in which they are located), the inclusion of schools in Ministry of Education programs, the extra subsidy received by rural schools, and the increased funding of schools in the *financiamiento compartido* system.

Discussion of Results

Comparing Private Subsidized and Municipal Schools

Sapelli and Vial[16] ran separate regressions for private subsidized and municipal schools, controlling by income group, parental education, a dummy indicating that the child comes from an indigenous family, and three dummy variables indicating the maximum education level that the respondent believes the student will attain.[17] In the selection equation they include the variables that determine test score results and dummy variables for province of residence.[18] Regional variables are included to capture the effect of school availability on the choice of school.

The regression results show that the family background variables are important in determining test results at both PS and MUN schools. The most important result, however, is that incorporating self-selection is central to proper estimation: Sapelli and Vial obtain positive and significant selection coefficients in both sectors. People with a higher comparative advantage for a particular type of school select that type of school. The underlying hypothesis is that people are characterized by several qualities and that those traits are exploited differently by different schools, resulting in different outcomes for the same person depending on which of the different schools he attends. People choose the school that makes the best use of their mix of unobserved traits (in addition to cost considerations).

When Sapelli and Vial correct for self-selection, they obtain a small "average treatment effect," or ATE (i.e., the benefit that a student selected at random would gain by moving from a municipal school to a PS school), but a much larger "treatment on the treated" effect, or TT (i.e., the effect of moving from a municipal school to a PS school for those who moved). The size of the TT effect (20 and 23 points on average in language and math, respectively) corresponds to 0.41 and 0.48 standard deviation, a magnitude considered large in the literature (effects of 0.1 standard deviation are considered slight, 0.2 to 0.3 moderate, and 0.5 large).[19]

It is also of interest to note that estimates of the TT are almost constant across income groups. That implies that the traits that make

Table 3.2
ATE AND TT ON 1998 LANGUAGE TEST SCORES BY
TRANSFER QUINTILE
(treatment is attending PS school)

	ATE	TT
Average test score	248.7	248.7
Test score standard deviation (TSSD)	47.6	47.6
1st quintile (closest to pure voucher system)	5.7	23.7
Standard deviation*	(3.0)	(7.4)
Percentage of the TSSD	12%	50%
2nd quintile	6.1	14.0
Standard deviation*	(1.4)	(3.0)
Percentage of the TSSD	13%	29%
3rd quintile	7.4	16.0
Standard deviation*	(1.5)	(4.2)
Percentage of the TSSD	16%	34%
4th quintile	−3.6	−2.0
Standard deviation*	(1.7)	(2.9)
Percentage of the TSSD	−7%	−4%
5th quintile (MUN schools receive substantially more funding)	−75.2	−97.6
Standard deviation*	(2.9)	(3.1)
Percentage of the TSSD	−158%	−205%

* Standard errors are estimated using parametric bootstrapping.

students perform better in PS schools are present in all income categories. Moreover, it implies that students choosing PS schools—whatever their income level—will see their test scores increase by a similar amount.

The case discussed so far is the comparison that most approximates a "pure" voucher system, that is, where MUN and PS schools work with similar budgets. Sapelli and Vial separate students into five equal groups (quintiles) ordered according to the additional subsidies MUN schools receive over and above the voucher (Table 3.2). The first quintile consists of schools whose budgets are most similar (in each quintile the comparison is made with PS schools in the same geographic area). In the second and third quintiles (where MUN budgets are larger than PS budgets) we still find a TT effect that is considered moderate in the literature. In short, despite receiving less money per pupil than MUN schools, PS schools in these funding categories perform moderately better.

When Sapelli and Vial replicated their estimations using 1999 data (for the fourth grade of elementary school), they obtained a similar pattern of results. Indeed, they found an even larger TT for the first quintile: 42.2 (almost one standard deviation).

In Short, Which Schools Are Better?

Sapelli and Vial estimate a TT that is substantially positive and significant and an ATE that is small and sometimes zero when controlling only for student characteristics. When we consider funding differences between schools and group schools by the size of the transfer they receive in addition to the voucher, then the TT for the lowest quintile of transfers to municipal schools (closest to a pure voucher system) shows a large positive effect, while negative TT effects are found in municipal schools that work with budgets substantially larger than those of PS schools (in the fifth quintile they work with budgets on average almost three times as large). In summary, when MUN and PS schools work with similar budgets, PS schools produce much better results.

Empirical Evaluation of the Importance of Peer Effects

The preceding section presented evidence showing that in areas where public and private voucher schools receive similar subsidies, the same voucher student attains higher test scores if he attends a private voucher school instead of a public one. Some analysts fear that this result is the consequence of the sorting process and its associated peer effects and does not stem from superior performance by private voucher schools. In this section I discuss empirical work that tests and rejects this hypothesis.

Sapelli and Vial[20] directly test this assertion by estimating the treatment parameters when controlling for the mean and standard deviation of the mothers' education of all the students in every school.[21] The education of the mother of the student is used as a proxy for the human capital the student brings from his home to the school and hence for the potential effect he can have on his peers. This test involves theoretically moving a student with all his

Table 3.3
ATE AND TT ON 1998 LANGUAGE TEST SCORES BY TRANSFER QUINTILE, CONTROLLING FOR PEERS
(treatment is attending a PS school)

	ATE	TT
Average test score	248.7	248.7
Test score standard deviation (TSSD)	47.6	47.6
1st quintile (closest to a pure voucher system)	1.5	18.7
Standard deviation*	(2.5)	(7.7)
Percentage of the TSSD	3%	39%
2nd quintile	2.1	6.1
Standard deviation*	(1.3)	(3.1)
Percentage of the TSSD	4%	13%
3rd quintile	3.7	5.9
Standard deviation*	(2.1)	(4.7)
Percentage of the TSSD	8%	12%
4th quintile	−8.3	−11.6
Standard deviation*	(1.9)	(3.2)
Percentage of the TSSD	−17%	−24%
5th quintile (MUN schools receive substantially more funding)	−43.1	−54.5
Standard deviation*	(4.5)	(5.6)
Percentage of the TSSD	−90%	−114%

* Standard errors are estimated using parametric bootstrapping.

or her classmates (hence eliminating all possible peer effects) from a private to a public voucher school. Results change only slightly. If the treatment parameter estimated in the first section were exclusively the result of the sorting process and the peer effect, the new treatment parameter should be zero. The data used by Sapelli and Vial do not support that hypothesis. It is worth noting that Sapelli and Vial are not attempting to estimate peer effects and that their results do not imply that the peer effect does not exist. There is still much work to be done in this area.

The most relevant result of the Sapelli and Vial analysis is that we *still* obtain a large and statistically significant TT$_{PEERS}$ in the first transfer quintile (Table 3.3). Thus, we reject the hypothesis that peer

Table 3.4
Regression Results on the Peer Effect

Summary Statistics			
Adjusted R²			0,7154694
Standard error			22,7303576
Sample (number of observations)			4784

	Coefficient	Standard Error	T statistic
Intercept	240,503297	5,00106913	48,0903763
SD of mother education (Sdme)	− 8,19702088	1,07718397	− 7,60967588
Sdme*area	11,1450606	1,15585093	9,64229931
Sdme*type school	− 10,2336465	1,21169257	− 8,44574499
Area (1 rural)	− 41,9295727	3,40121187	− 12,3278333
Type school (1 private subs)	39,463109	3,54973345	11,1172035
Ln mean mother education	11,4796853	1,63808043	7,00801077

effects explain the results in the previous section. The direct effect of PS schools on educational outcomes is positive, and this estimate is not greatly affected by removing the effect of changing to a class with better peers when transferring to a PS school. The better peers are not the reason for the improvement in scores, Sapelli and Vial find.

Peer Effect: Results

Another way of examining the peer effect is to test whether schools with a higher dispersion of ability, all else being equal, perform better than those with a smaller dispersion of student ability per class. We use data from the 1999 SIMCE results for students in the fourth year of primary school and from a survey of their parents. We use mothers' education as a proxy for student ability. The distribution of scores and student abilities in schools is such that PS schools have both lower ability dispersion and a lower dispersion of results.

We investigated the relation between the average math score and the dispersion of mothers' education by school, including a series of other controls. The results of the analysis are shown in Table 3.4.

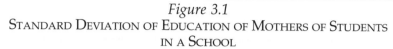

Figure 3.1
STANDARD DEVIATION OF EDUCATION OF MOTHERS OF STUDENTS
IN A SCHOOL

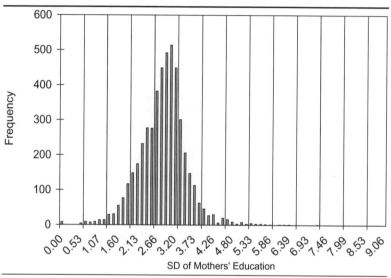

The results in Table 3.4 imply that school results are better when the dispersion of ability is low (except for rural municipal schools). That is, achievement results are better when the class is more homogeneous with regard to ability. In this respect, it is worth mentioning that urban private schools stand out since their achievement results are better than those of other types of schools (urban rural, municipal urban, and municipal rural) for a very wide range of peer characteristics. In fact, urban PS schools perform better than all other types for students with a broad range of abilities (using mother's education as a proxy for student ability). The regression includes two multipliers, "Sdme*area" and "Sdme*type school," which result from the multiplication of the standard deviation of mothers' education and the dummy area (rural = 1, urban = 0) and type of school (private subsidized = 1, municipal = 0), respectively. Those are introduced to detect whether schools differ in the way they are affected by the homogeneity or heterogeneity of the student pool. That is effectively true. For example, even though urban private schools are better for a wide range of student pools, rural municipal schools tend to perform better in the case of very heterogeneous groups. What the data from

53

the regression in Table 3.4 say is that PS urban schools achieve 40 points more (than municipal schools) in standardized tests when the dispersion of student ability is zero (i.e., the class is completely homogeneous regarding student ability) and becomes worse only for levels of dispersion as high as four standard deviations (a level that is very rare, as can be seen in Figure 3.1).

In sum, the data show that sorting and the peer effect are not the reason why PS schools are better. PS schools are more effective even after taking into account sorting and the peer effect. The data also allow us to refute the widely held conviction that a reduction in the dispersion of peer characteristics worsens test performance. That conviction is more often expressed the other way around: reducing the heterogeneity of a class causes deterioration in performance; it is good for students to have a wide range of peers. As can be seen from the empirical study, we find that just the opposite is true: that lower dispersion (more homogeneous classes) improves performance.

Even if it were found that in the Chilean case reducing the dispersion of peer characteristics worsened performance, that could not be generalized to all possible designs of voucher systems. The effect could stem from the specific design of the voucher system in Chile. This is a key point I want to make in this chapter: we need to understand not only the effects of a universal voucher system but also how the results depend on the design of the system. In that way we learn from the experience and can advance to a better-designed voucher system. Such considerations are the subject of the next section.

Issues in the Design of the Chilean Voucher System

Much of the literature describes the Chilean voucher system as a "textbook" voucher case.[22] By characterizing the Chilean system in that way, observers forgo the opportunity to understand how the specific design of the Chilean voucher system influences its results.

The "textbook" case is one in which schools with different internal incentive structures (public and private) function under the same external rules and with the same budget (for which they compete). But in Chile the external rules differ. To begin with, public schools have to abide by the Teachers Labor Statute whereas private voucher schools (at least officially) do not. No public schools have closed their doors as a consequence of a student exodus, and that is because all the schools that have lost students to private voucher schools have received subsidies to pay the teachers' salaries when needed. Hence public schools work within a system of "soft budget constraints" and are thus protected from the consequences of competing with private voucher schools. Even more important, given this incentive structure, schools that face vigorous competition from private voucher schools may actually want some students to leave—the teachers' jobs are not at risk—allowing them to teach smaller classes. Thus, in reality, the incentives faced by municipal schools in the Chilean voucher system are often at odds with the intentions of the designers.[23]

A pattern of results compatible with the existence of those two conflicting incentive structures is shown by Sapelli and Vial[24] where the ATE is positive for private voucher schools with up to 25 percent less funds than public schools (i.e., PS schools are better in this range despite lower or at most similar funding) and negative when public schools have funds that are more than 25 percent above those used by private schools. That result contradicts Hanushek's view that additional funding has little or no effect on productivity of public schools, though clearly the incentive structure here is more complicated than that faced by the typical public school.[25]

Thus, there is a key difference between the Chilean and the "textbook" case: the incentives for municipal schools differ from those they face in the "textbook" voucher system. Public schools do not have to choose between supplying an education that attracts enough students to allow the school to pay its wage bill and laying off staff. The choice those schools actually face is whether public school teachers are to be paid to teach large or small classes.

Recognizing that perverse incentive, the Ministry of Education in Chile has constructed an incentive system to supplement those provided by the vouchers. The parallel system is a second deviation from the "textbook" case, in which supply subsidies (additional ministry funding) were added to demand subsidies (the vouchers). Several programs have been created to fund schools in certain situations (for example, when students are predominantly poor), but those subsidies are designed as supply subsidies (paid directly to the school, not tied to students) and not as demand subsidies and hence operate as a tax on students who move to another school[26]: if students leave a school, they lose the funding associated with the ministry program, thus reducing the amount spent on their education. That is known as "nonportable" funding.

Also, the Ministry of Education in Chile is moving toward standards-based evaluation of public schools. There is also a scheme to reward schools that achieve large increases in test results. In sum, it is a patchwork system of incentives.

Are Vouchers of Equal Value the Appropriate Policy?

Another issue of importance is whether what is considered the textbook case is an appropriate benchmark. One key question is whether the value of the vouchers should vary with the child's characteristics. If the cost of educating students to a certain level falls as the initial human capital of the children rises (a plausible hypothesis), and the level of initial human capital is positively correlated with income and parental education, then that should affect the way we subsidize students.[27] That is, if it is cheaper to teach children who arrive at school with higher initial human capital (generally children of more educated and higher-income parents), then we should take that into account when we set the value of the voucher. On the other hand, if all students, independent of their socioeconomic background, receive a voucher of the same value, then private voucher schools will compete for students who cost less than the value of the voucher to educate (those with the highest initial human capital), and competition between schools for those students will dissipate the "economic rent" (profit) in providing higher-quality education. However, with vouchers of equal value, there is no incentive for schools to compete for students who are costly to educate (those with low human capital), and those students will not see any improvement in the education they receive as a result of the voucher system. Hence, in a system where all children receive vouchers of equal value, children who come to school with less human capital may not receive the higher-quality education they need to catch up with other children.

In summary, the Chilean voucher system is one in which, on both the demand and the supply side, incentives differ for MUN and PS schools. Groups of schools work with different budgets and incentives, and groups of students face different choice sets. Poor students receive the same level of subsidy as wealthy students (even though they are more costly to educate) and hence are more prone to remain captives of the public education system. Public schools do not in general face the incentives of competition, since they work with soft budget constraints; and when extra funding is channeled to poor students, schools receive it in the form of supply subsidies, which merely accentuates the dependence of poor students on public schools.

Regulation of Private Schools

An issue not yet well researched is how PS schools are regulated in Chile and how current regulation may be thwarting the effects of a voucher system. It is clear that an overregulated private system results in private enterprises offering what the regulator requires rather than what consumers want. This is an issue not much discussed in the literature, with the exception of Gauri. According to Gauri:

> All told, the government monitors private schools more closely and frequently than at any other time in Chilean history, a surprisingly paradoxical outcome. . . . The inspections and central government rules raise the costs of innovation for both municipal and private schools. . . . After the reform process was well underway the ministry continued to act as if it were running schools. . . . [Hence] the neoliberal reforms . . . have in fact brought more state controls to private education, arguably even increasing homogeneity in an already uniform system.[28]

A promising hypothesis about how, in such a regulated environment, PS schools have effectively managed to differentiate themselves from MUN schools and obtain better test results is that they have specialized in an area where municipal schools are performing poorly and the government meddles less: discipline. Given that detailed regulation prevents much academic innovation, it is possible that PS schools have concentrated on delivering student discipline. That is a trait that opinion polls show is in high demand, and the superior test results of PS schools may be a byproduct of superior discipline (i.e., there are economies of scope in the production of discipline and academic achievement).

Summary and Conclusions

All voucher systems imply that parents are largely able to choose the school their children attend. The influence of a voucher system on the operation and quality of an educational system will vary in proportion to the amount of money vouchers represent (the smaller the amount relative to total spending per capita, the more limited the extent of parental choice) and also with the number of schools allowed to receive the vouchers (the more restricted, the less effective the system). It is always possible to design a voucher system so restricted that nobody could reasonably expect it to have any effect whatsoever. In the case of Chile, the way in which the value of the voucher is determined limits the choices of poor students. Subsidies net of costs are lower for children from poorer households. The problem of providing them with better education could be addressed more effectively by increasing the value of the vouchers they receive. Also, the proliferation of nonportable funding for schools diminishes competition between them. That contributes to neutralizing the incentives of the voucher system.

Empirical results show that significant gains in test scores are associated with attending private subsidized schools. Those differences are significant when we consider the average gain in test scores for a randomly chosen individual (ATE) but are even greater when we consider the expected gain for those students who actually attend private subsidized schools (TT). In contrast with some previous estimates, the latter gains do not disappear when we control for personal and family characteristics of the students tested, and they increase when we correct for self-selection.

In short, after controlling for budget differences and for the socio-economic characteristics of the students and their peers, we find a new treatment parameter that is positive, large in magnitude, and statistically significant. Taking into account peer effects does not invalidate that outcome. Thus, the superior test results (positive treatment effects) of PS schools do not stem from sorting and the peer effect.

A detailed discussion of the hindrances to the operation of the voucher system on the supply side (such as the soft budget constraint and the Teachers Statute) has been left for another occasion, but it is imperative that they be addressed if the quality of education in municipal schools is to improve. Until the problem is resolved, one can expect competition with PS schools to have little effect on the efficiency and quality of education at MUN schools.

In conclusion, further development of the voucher system is to be recommended. The policy mix is not yet right; some current policies hinder or neutralize the operation of the voucher system. At some point, a redesign of the Chilean voucher system can, and should, be undertaken to better achieve the objectives of the policy.

Notes

1. Hence the empirical literature developed to evaluate the voucher system in Chile faced, for many years, methodological and/or data limitations. Only the most recent literature does not suffer from such limitations. See, for example, Dante Contreras, "Evaluating a Voucher System in Chile: Individual, Family and School Characteristics," Working Paper no. 175, Facultad de Ciencias Económicas y Administrativas, Universidad de Chile, March 2001; Andrea Tokman, "Is Private Education Better? Evidence from Chile," Working Paper no. 147, Central Bank of Chile, 2002, http://ideas.repec.org/p/chb/bcchwp/147.html; Claudio Sapelli and Bernardita Vial, "The Performance of Private and Public Schools in the Chilean Voucher System," *Cuadernos de Economía* (Latin American Journal of Economics), no. 118 (December 2002): 423–54, http://volcan.facea.puc.cl/economia/publicaciones/cuadernos/cuadernos118.htm; Claudio Sapelli and Bernardita Vial, "Peer Effects and Relative Performance of Voucher Schools in Chile," Paper presented to the AEA meetings in San Diego, January 2004; and Claudio Sapelli, "The Chilean Voucher System: Some New Results and Research Challenges," *Cuadernos de Economía*, no. 121 (December 2003): 530–38, http://volcan.facea.puc.cl/economia/publicaciones/cuadernos/cuadernos118.htm. For a discussion of the prior empirical literature in Chile, see Sapelli and Vial, "The Performance of Private and Public Schools in the Chilean Voucher System."

2. Sapelli and Vial, "Peer Effects and Relative Performance of Voucher Schools in Chile"; and Sapelli and Vial, "The Performance of Private and Public Schools in the Chilean Voucher System."

3. See ibid.

4. Sapelli and Vial, "Peer Effects and Relative Performance of Voucher Schools in Chile."

5. This discussion in many respects parallels the discussion between proponents of free markets and proponents of central planning, which occurred during much of the 20th century, in which many participants asserted that the performance of public enterprises was no worse than that of private enterprises and that externalities were significant, thus requiring substantial government intervention.

6. Called the System of Measurement of the Quality of Education (SIMCE) for the Spanish *Sistema de Medición de la Calidad de la Educación*.

7. Bernardita Vial, "Financiamiento Compartido de la Educación," *Cuadernos de Economía*, no. 106 (December 1998): 325–42.

8. However, analysts such as Mizala and Romaguera argue against these results being read as implying that the voucher system failed. They argue that freedom of choice should be factored in as an advantage of the voucher system, even if there is no change in test results. Also, the fact that test results are the same may imply that *both* MUN and PS school results may have increased pari passu as a result of competition. See Alejandra Mizala and Pilar Romaguera, "Determinación de Factores Explicativos de los Resultados Escolares en Educación Media en Chile," Serie Economía no. 85, Centro de Economía Aplicada, Departamento de Ingeniería Industrial, Facultad de Ciencias Físicas y Matemáticas, Universidad de Chile, August 2000.

9. See Francisco Gallego, "Competencia y Resultados Educativos: Teoría y Evidencia para Chile," *Cuadernos de Economía*, no. 118 (December 2002): 309–52; Sapelli and Vial, "The Performance of Private and Public Schools in the Chilean Voucher System"; Contreras; Mizala and Romaguera; and Tokman.

10. See, for example, P. McEwan, and M. Carnoy, "Competition and Sorting in Chile's Voucher System," mimeo, Stanford University, 1998; and C. Hsieh and M. Urquiola, "When Schools Compete, How Do They Compete? An Assessment of Chile's Nationwide School Voucher Program," NBER Working Paper no. 10008, 2003. Those studies purport to present evidence in favor of the importance of sorting and the peer effect in Chile, but they face a key problem with causality. For example, if higher enrollment in private schools coexists with lower test scores in public schools in the same municipality, is that proof of the peer effect or proof that entry is endogenous and occurs first where municipal schools are doing a poor job? See Caroline Hoxby, "School Choice and School Productivity (Or Could School Choice Be a Tide That Lifts All Boats?)" NBER Working Paper no. 8873, 2001.

11. E.g., Hsieh and Urquiola.

12. Gallego.

13. Gallego obtains the Hsieh and Urquiola results when not controlling for endogenous entry.

14. Contreras.

15. Tokman.

16. Sapelli and Vial, "The Performance of Private and Public Schools in the Chilean Voucher System."

17. Those variables are obtained from the answer given by the student tutor to the following question: "What educational level do you believe that the student will attain?"

18. Sapelli and Vial have a variable indicating the county where the school is located, not the county of residence. They believe that there is important mobility across counties but not across provinces (provinces are groups of counties). For that reason, they use dummies for province.

19. See Jay P. Greene, Paul E. Peterson, and Jiangtao Du, "Effectiveness of School Choice: The Milwaukee Experiment," Occasional Paper 97-1, Harvard University, Department of Government, 1997.

20. Sapelli and Vial, "Peer Effects and Relative Performance of Voucher Schools in Chile."

21. Other specifications were used, obtaining similar results.

22. For example, "Chile's government established a 'textbook' voucher scheme." Hsieh and Urquiola, p. 1.

23. It must be noted, however, that some public schools *are* faced with the right incentives. The existence of additional subsidies, quite large in rich municipalities, can present schools in those municipalities with the incentive to improve, attract more students, and thus receive even more subsidies.

24. Sapelli and Vial, "The Performance of Private and Public Schools in the Chilean Voucher System."

25. These results are obtained using 1999 fourth-year primary school data. Preliminary work with data for the second grade of secondary school replicates this pattern: schools in the first quintile of transfers (those that work with 25 percent less funding) have a TT effect of 42 and an ATE not significantly different from zero. As with the

results for primary schools, the TT becomes lower as transfers increase, becoming negative for higher levels of transfer.

26. For an estimation of how the food program operates as a tax on mobility between schools, see Claudio Sapelli and A. Torche, "Subsidios al Alumno o a la Escuela: Efectos Sobre la Elección de Colegios," *Cuadernos de Economía* 39, no. 117 (2002): 175–202.

27. See Hoxby or C. Aedo and Claudio Sapelli, "El Sistema de Vouchers en Eucación: Una Revisión de la Teoría y Evidencia Empírica para Chile," *Estudios Públicos*, Autumn 2001.

28. Varun Gauri, *School Choice in Chile* (Pittsburgh: University of Pittsburgh Press, 1998), p. 28.

4. The Special Education Scare: Fact vs. Fiction

Lewis M. Andrews

An increasing number of states have enacted school choice as a way to improve schools and increase options for parents. As a result, the national debate over school choice has turned to the likely impact on learning disabled students. Research continues to demonstrate the success of school choice programs, and the U.S. Supreme Court recently upheld school choice as constitutional, even when parents choose religiously affiliated schools. Now opponents of parental freedom are trying to raise the concern that children with learning disabilities will somehow be harmed.

The nation's two largest teachers' unions repeatedly warn that making private education more accessible to the poor and middle class will cause good students to flee to independent and parochial schools, leaving behind those kids who are physically and emotionally handicapped, hyperactive, or have been involved with the juvenile justice system.[1] Reinforcing the notion that choice will turn public schools into "special education ghettos," NAACP president Kweisi Mfume argues that, even if parents of kids with "personal, behavioral, or educational challenges" wanted to take advantage of a voucher system, no government could afford to supply private schools with all the support services they would need.[2]

Advocates of choice counter with the argument that giving parents the financial ability to select their children's schools actually helps the learning disabled, freeing them from poorly performing remedial programs and related administrative wrangling. They point to the popularity of Florida's McKay Scholarships Program, passed in 2000, which allows parents of special education students to receive a voucher worth between $6,000 and $20,000 to cover tuition at a private school. According to a 2003 study of the McKay program, published by the Manhattan Institute, 92.7 percent of parents of children on Florida scholarships are "satisfied" or "very satisfied"

63

with their private placements, as compared with a 32.7 percent satisfaction level with their child's previous experience in public school. The study also indicates that learning disabled children in private school exhibit fewer than half the behavioral problems they had in public school.[3]

Defenders of choice can also turn to persuasive data showing that the supposedly high cost of teaching mild and moderately disabled students alongside normal pupils in public schools—a practice called "inclusion"—is grossly inflated by needless paperwork. The American Institutes for Research study *What Are We Spending on Special Education Services in the United States, 1999–2000?* estimates that U.S. public schools spend more than $4 billion annually on elaborate assessments, procedural monitoring, record keeping, and litigation with unhappy parents. Some large school districts spend as much as $28 million annually on activities related to compliance with special education regulations, while teachers themselves spend 50 to 60 percent of their time filling out required forms.[4]

How do we resolve this important debate over the impact of universal school choice on hyperactive, autistic, blind, deaf, and other disabled pupils who are sufficiently functional to receive an education with some assistance at mainstream public schools? How can we know what would happen to more than five million physically and emotionally handicapped children in America, if all pupils—not just special needs children benefiting from something like Florida's McKay bill—could freely switch between public and private schools?

Fortunately, there are some telling indicators from abroad. Today more than 20 countries, including Germany, France, Spain, England, and Poland, have some form of school choice. More important, five advanced industrial countries have adopted some degree of school choice as national policy: New Zealand, Australia, the Netherlands, Sweden, and Denmark.

The Truth about New Zealand

New Zealand is interesting, because it has the only foreign school choice program regularly mentioned by opponents of choice in the United States. In 2000 Edward Fiske and Helen Ladd published *When Schools Compete: A Cautionary Tale*, which made much of a flaw in New Zealand's original school choice legislation. When first drafted, the law provided supplemental funding to every public and private school accepting special needs students, but the amount was not proportional to the actual number of learning disabled students admitted.

That, in turn, led some schools to reject students who would be very costly to educate or whose admission would boost the special needs census to a point that would overtax limited resources. Fiske and Ladd erroneously concluded that the resulting discrimination against some special education students, which did in some cases unfortunately occur, is an inevitable consequence of *any* school choice program, a conclusion widely publicized to this day as "skimming" by American teachers' unions.

What today's critics of school choice fail to point out is that New Zealand has largely remedied its 1980s' legislation with two amendments: one that establishes an elastic supplemental funding formula for public and private schools, based on the actual number of special needs students admitted, and another that provides even greater funding to help educate those students with the most severe kinds of learning disabilities. The revised Special Education 2000 Policy also gives school principals and the parents of special needs children considerable latitude in determining what they believe to be the most appropriate special education services. Furthermore, if a learning disabled child leaves his or her school for any reason, the supplemental funding follows the child to the new placement.

As a result of those modifications to the initial law, school choice enjoys widespread and enthusiastic public support, says Roger Moltzen, director of special education programs in the Department of Education at New Zealand's University of Waikato, and "is unlikely to be repealed."[5] Other local experts, such as David Mitchell, also of the Education Department at the University of Waikato, record significant progress in the treatment of learning disabilities. In recent years, Mitchell notes, New Zealand's special education system has moved "from being relatively ad hoc, unpredictable, uncoordinated and nationally inconsistent to being relatively coherent, predictable, integrated, and consistent across the country. It is moving away from . . . seeing the reasons for failure at school as residing in some defect or inadequacy within the student to seeing it as reflecting a mismatch between individual abilities and environmental opportunities."[6]

The Case of Australia

Australia has also had a good experience with school choice, especially as it affects special education. A 1998 study funded by the national Department of Education, Training, and Youth Affairs found that many intellectually and physically disabled students who received an inclusive education under the nation's school choice program were "achieving in literacy and [math skills] at the same levels as their peers and, in some cases, much better than their classmates."[7]

The only problem with using Australian choice legislation as a model for the United States is that it contains redistributionist elements, which cloud the impact across socioeconomic groups. School choice was adopted in that country as a populist reform in 1973 by a liberal-leaning Labour government, seeking to subsidize private education along the lines of what it called a Social Economic Status model. Students attending private schools from poorer areas in the western part of the country can be reimbursed up to 97 percent of tuition, but students from wealthier towns receive assistance amounting to less than 25 percent of tuition.[8]

The Netherlands and Sweden

To see clearly the impact of school choice on the treatment of learning disabilities, it is perhaps most useful to compare the experience of three northern European countries: the Netherlands, Sweden, and Denmark. Each has adopted school choice as part of its national education policy, but with instructive variations in the area of special education. Consider first the Netherlands, where since 1917 the national government has promoted parental choice by allowing educational funding to follow the child to a private school. Today, almost two-thirds of Dutch students attend private or religious schools.

Until about 17 years ago, the Netherlands had a two-track educational system. A guarantee of school choice for mainstream students coexisted with a separate and complex arrangement for educating the learning disabled. The country actually funded 14 separate school systems, each geared to a particular learning disability—mild mental retardation, severe mental retardation, deafness, physical handicaps, multiple disabilities, and so on—and each mimicking as closely as possible the grade levels of conventional public and private schools.

But by the late 1980s people in the Netherlands noticed a disturbing trend in special education. Although the absolute number of learning disabled had remained constant for many years, it was effectively a sharp percentage increase, since the overall number of school-age children had been on a steady decline.[9] Many observers suspected that the special education bureaucracy was preserving its size by attempting to serve children with mild to moderate learning problems, who in fact could have been well educated in mainstream public and private schools. The solution, it turned out, was to create a financial structure that gave parents of special needs children the same educational choices as other parents.

Under a Going to School Together policy adopted by the Netherlands in 1990, the Ministry of Education declared that "parents of children with disabilities should . . . be able to choose between [any] ordinary or a special school for their child." Dutch children who required additional services for serious learning disabilities were given a "personal budget" that, under the new policy, parents could spend at any school they wished. To ensure equality of opportunity for all students, supplemental funding was provided to both public and private schools in economically depressed districts, where the percentage of learning disabled students tends to be higher.

Today the Dutch educational system enjoys strong popular support, especially from advocates of greater inclusion for special needs students. At the same time, the number of separate school systems for the learning disabled has been reduced from 14 to just 4.

Compare the development of special education in the Netherlands with what has happened Sweden, which in March 1992 adopted a Freedom of Choice and Independent Schools bill. That policy gives parents "the right and opportunity to choose a school and education for one's children" by granting all private and religious schools a municipal subsidy equal to 85 percent of the public school per pupil cost multiplied by that independent school's enrollment. All schools funded in this way are free to emphasize a particular teaching method such as Montessori, an ethnic affiliation, or even a religious affiliation; but they must be licensed by *Skolverket*, the national education ministry.

Like the Dutch, the Swedes have adopted a policy of universal school choice, but with one important exception: the parents of special needs students are not granted the same freedom as parents of normal children. That limitation was probably due to Sweden's long history of educational paternalism, which for decades had low-ered testing standards, altered textbooks, and micromanaged both classroom and extracurricular activities—all in an effort to avoid making the learning disabled feel in any way inferior.[10] When the Swedes finally adopted school choice for normal students, they were reluctant to risk letting the learning disabled "flounder" in a differ-ent, more competitive educational marketplace.

The upshot is that Sweden does not do well on international comparisons of inclusion. The majority of Sweden's deaf students, for example, are still educated in segregated schools. Other learning disabled students continue to suffer under a centrally managed sys-tem, where support services are negotiated between school princi-pals and their respective municipal finance offices, with parents having little input. In theory, all conventional schools are supposed to have an Action Plan outlining a program of support for their special needs students; but according to a 1998 study by Sweden's National Agency for Education (NAE), only half of the country's schools had any such plans and fewer than 20 percent of affected parents felt they are able to participate.[11]

The result of this lingering paternalism is that the number of Swedish children classified as requiring special education services is high, compared with other industrial countries, and is continuing to grow at a disproportionate rate. Between academic years 1992–93 and 1996–97, according to the NAE, the number of students regis-tered in schools for the mentally impaired rose by 20 percent. Fur-thermore, the percentage of students with severe (as opposed to mild or moderate) dysfunctions is consistently higher across categories of disability. For example, only 25 percent of Sweden's mentally retarded are considered mild cases, while 75 percent are labeled moderate to severe. Contrast that with the United States, where the proportions are exactly reversed.[12] To what extent this reflects the failure of Sweden's bureaucratic control of special education (or simply the tendency of public service employees to expand their client base) is unclear, but the failure of Sweden to make school choice truly universal has clearly undermined the government's stated goal of promoting greater inclusion.[13]

The World's Oldest School Choice Policy

Finally, we come to Denmark, which has the world's oldest school choice program. The home of Kierkegaard and Hans Christian Ander-sen has allowed students to freely choose among public and private schools for more than a century and a half—and in 1915 enshrined this right in its constitution. Today, 12 percent of all Danish students attend more than 470 private schools with municipal governments covering 80 to 85 percent of the cost.

The example of Denmark gets even more interesting, when we discover that in May 1969 its parliament passed a resolution declaring that "handicapped pupils" be instructed "in a normal school environment," effectively granting special education students the same right to attend private schools as mainstream students. Since then, parents have had the final say over what school their special needs son or daughter attends; and, if an independent school is chosen, the Ministry of Education pays a sum per pupil to the receiving school (with the student's home town ultimately reimbursing the ministry). Supplemental resources, such as classroom aids, extra courses, and after-hours tutoring, are made available through grants on a case-by-case basis, but as a practical matter this procedure has not proved an impediment to parents placing their special needs child in a private school.

The Danish Ministry of Education is the first to admit that its initial impulse to give learning disabled students equal access to all schools was a bow to the then–politically correct fashion of treating any difference between pupils as if it didn't or shouldn't matter. Official publications now concede that a realistic integration of the handicapped is not just "the omission of segregation." It must also involve some adaptation of the ordinary school environment to cater to the development of impaired pupils.[14] But the inclusive spirit of the original policy has remained unchanged for more than 30 years, making Denmark a uniquely instructive example of how well special needs students can fare under any policy approximating the freedom of a voucher system.

Judged purely on statistics, the Danish system of universal school choice would appear to benefit the vast majority of handicapped pupils. Only .5 percent of Denmark's learning disabled students are confined to specialized institutions, compared with five times that percentage in the United States, and both public and private schools are committed to the philosophy of including special needs children in regular classrooms. The Paris-based Organisation for Economic Co-operation and Development (OECD), which tracks education statistics internationally, has praised the Danes for their exceptionally "strong commitment to inclusive education" and for years has held up Denmark's approach to schooling as a model to the rest of the world.[15]

The seeming success of school choice in Denmark has been accomplished with some interesting economies. While the cost of educating the average pupil in Denmark is one of the highest in the world—due in part to powerful unions that limit a teacher's annual working hours to two-thirds of the American average but also to generally small class sizes—the actual administrative cost for supervising the program that funds students in independent schools is remarkably low. In Denmark it takes only five people in the Ministry of Education to oversee all 82,000 private school students.[16] Compare that with California, where close to half of every public education dollar goes to bureaucratic oversight.[17]

According to Beatrice Schindler Rangvid, an education researcher at Copenhagen's Institute of Local Government Studies, the regulatory burden on Denmark's independent schools is both light and reasonable. Apart from requirements to teach certain basic subjects and vaguely "live up to the standards of public education," each independent school is governed by its own board of administrators, parents, and teachers.[18]

As for the fear that choice might encourage mainstream students to flee public schools, turning them into special needs ghettos, Professor Niels Egelund, a prominent researcher on learning disabilities at the Danish University of Education, notes that "the percentage of pupils in private and parochial institutions is actually quite small" (about 12 percent) in spite of the low supplement required to attend one. "Any parent, who really wanted to," he says, "could manage to send his child to an independent school, but most are satisfied not to." Egelund's observations support the argument that having a private option, instead of consigning the most vulnerable students to failing schools, tends to make all schools more accountable to parents.[19]

Indeed, one of the striking aspects of private education in Denmark is that it is not seen as particularly elite. According to experts throughout that country, the choice of an independent school in Denmark is based far less on academic status than on a school's denominational affiliation; its political or social leanings; the mix of instructional languages; or, increasingly, the desire of some parents for old-fashioned discipline.[20]

The decline of private school snobbery appears to be the common outcome in every country that adopts school choice. Sweden saw a large increase in the number of private and religious schools after legalizing choice in 1992, an average of 15 percent per year; but that increase was from an extraordinarily low base created by a steeply progressive tax code that, prior to 1992, had made private education prohibitively expensive for all but the wealthiest families. Australia has a number of elite private boarding schools, which cater to parents of children from Hong Kong, Singapore, and Malaysia, but domestically nearly half the enrollment in Australia's nongovernment schools is from families with a combined annual income of less than US$27,000.[21]

If school choice in Denmark has not led to the segregation of the learning disabled into inferior public schools, neither does it tolerate the practice sometimes seen in America of giving special needs students the mere appearance of an adequate education. Although the Danish Ministry of Education recognizes that some students need "to follow different tracks in order to reach desirable academic goals," says Per Kristensen, chairman of the umbrella organization for Danish private schools, special education in his country "does not exempt the learning disabled from having to attain [those goals]." To the contrary, Kristensen believes that the existence of independent schools, which are freer to experiment with innovative teaching techniques, actually improves the quality of instruction for the learning disabled throughout Denmark.[22]

Some Conclusions

What does all this tell us about the impact of universal school choice on special needs students? One obvious conclusion to be drawn from this three-way comparison of the Netherlands, Sweden, and Denmark, as well as from the experience of Australia and New Zealand, is that inclusion not only is possible under school choice but may succeed to an extent not even imagined by American educators.

The critical variable appears to be the willingness of legislators to extend freedom of choice to all parents, including the parents of the learning disabled. In Australia—a school choice country where individual territories or states have wide discretion in directing how the money is spent—the regions that provide the most flexibility for parents of the learning disabled also have the best record of mainstreaming. Between 1990 and 1995, the percentage of special needs students successfully integrated into schools in New South Wales more than doubled, while the number of Schools for Special Purposes (the Australian euphemism for segregated special needs schools) declined sharply. By contrast, western Australia retained most of its separate schools during that period.[23]

A second conclusion we can fairly draw is that the financial mechanisms for providing services to the learning disabled may be just as important to their intellectual and social development as any known teaching technique. In fact, that is just what the European Agency for Development in Special Needs Education reported in its *Seventeen Country Study of the Relationship between Financing of Special Needs Education and Inclusion*. Agency researchers found that monopolistic public school systems that simply upped the budget for every increase in the number of learning disabled students produced the least desirable outcomes, no matter what the educational philosophy or curriculum.[24]

Why Choice Benefits Special Needs Children

The interesting question, of course, is Why? Why has school choice proved such a successful policy in helping the learning disabled in foreign countries, when the intuitive judgment of so many American educators has been negative?

One difficulty in answering that critical question is a lack of detailed research from the country with the longest and most successful experience in mainstreaming learning disabled children. "Denmark has been so successful in this area that it never felt it had a problem it needed to understand," says Dan Terkildsen, a Danish politician and lawyer active in promoting free-market reforms. The result is that Denmark has never deeply analyzed how autistic, blind, and other special needs students adapt to its system. The Danish Ministry of Education in its own published evaluation of the nation's schools simply observes that its method of serving handicapped pupils has "often succeeded in practice in cases where it has been deemed impossible in theory."[25]

Nevertheless, as we study school choice worldwide, at least two reasons for the beneficial impact of school choice on the learning disabled suggest themselves. The first comes from the United States where well-researched experiments with both publicly funded and privately financed voucher programs show that parents of learning disabled children not only take advantage of choice but often do so at a higher rate than parents of mainstream students. This result has been known since the late 1990s when Children First America Foundation and James Leininger organized the CEO Horizon Scholarship Program, which provides private school subsidies to virtually all families in the Edgewood Independent School District of San Antonio, Texas.[26]

On reflection, the particular enthusiasm of parents of special needs children for school choice should not surprise us, since those parents are often the most dissatisfied with public education. Their concerns include both the failure of teaching staffs to adequately implement agreed-upon plans for remedial instruction and lax disciplinary rules, which allow frequent teasing and even bullying of their children. Parents of the learning disabled are also attracted to private and parochial schools by their generally lower class sizes, which provide the opportunity for more individualized instruction.

It is not a coincidence that Florida's McKay Scholarships Program, mentioned earlier, has become the fastest-growing school choice program in the United States, serving more than 12,185 children in 749 private and parochial schools after just three years. In spite of the fact that the state subsidy is sometimes less than the amount needed to cover independent school tuition, increasing numbers of parents seem eager to pay the difference in return for the financial wherewithal to remove their child from the local public school. That eagerness is even more telling when we realize that 50 percent of students using McKay scholarships are from families poor enough to qualify for free or reduced federally funded lunches in their former public schools.[27]

The second answer comes from Danish teachers, parents, and political leaders, who, while lacking an empirical explanation for the connection between school choice and successful inclusion, have definite opinions about why the connection exists. Indeed, the one phrase that consistently crops up in all discussions of special education in Denmark is "similarity of values."

The Danes recognize that a learning disability is not synonymous with stupidity and that many special needs students are exceptionally strong in math, science, and the arts. "In public schools many of these talented children are outcasts," says Terkildsen, "but private schools have the flexibility to appreciate their condition." Because Danish parents are free to place their children in a school with a compatible pedagogical, philosophical, or academic emphasis, Terkildsen adds, the learning disabled youngster can not only learn but often thrive.[28]

The suggestion that school choice benefits special needs students by allowing parents to take advantage of the power of shared values gains added credibility from studies in the United States on the relationship between education economics and the well-being of another vulnerable group—minority students. Until the late 1990s most educators just assumed that public schools were better integrated than private institutions, largely because the average public school had a greater percentage of black and Hispanic students.

But in 1998 two American education researchers, Jay Greene and Nicole Mellow, posed a provocative research question: Does the fact that public schools have a larger percentage of minorities really mean that the children inside are mixing on a friendlier basis, or does it just mean that fewer minority children can afford private or religious schools? To develop a more meaningful indicator of racial integration that takes into account the quality of a minority child's daily experience, Greene and Mellow decided to observe public and private school lunchrooms and watch where students sat by race. By this measure, independent schools turned out to be much better integrated than public schools. Furthermore, choice programs, giving poor black and Hispanic parents the freedom to choose among a variety of placements, promoted racial harmony much more effectively than simply assigning students to public schools on the basis of where they happened to live.[29]

What makes the Greene and Mellow study so relevant to our discussion of special education is that, when they attempted to discover the reasons why choice promotes racial integration, an increasingly obvious answer was *values*. Because all the parents at a freely chosen school shared a similar educational philosophy, their children were attracted to each other by interests and beliefs that transcended racial differences. In the case of religious schools, mission appeared to be a particularly "important component of school success in promoting integration."[30]

All this is not to suggest that allowing parents to choose their children's schools on the basis of shared values is a panacea for treating all special needs students. Nor does it suggest that, in the case of special education, principles and philosophy are a substitute for remedial instruction. But, if anything is clear from looking at how special needs children prosper in school choice countries, it is that the effectiveness of any remedial program is modulated by the context in which it is used.

It would appear that the people in the United States who are now attempting to discredit school choice by suggesting that it would harm learning disabled children are committing the intellectual error of equating statutory declarations of good intentions with de facto accomplishment. In their warning to parents of learning disabled children on the dangers of school choice, People for the American Way and the Disability Rights and Education Defense Fund caution that "once parents use a voucher to transfer their children to private schools, they have effectively opted out of the legal rights and educational services guaranteed under [federal law]."[31] The implied premise of that argument is that only a legal compliance model of education can help special needs children get through school.

If the world's experience with choice has demonstrated anything, it is that a school's accountability to a financially empowered parent is infinitely more helpful to that parent's learning disabled child than any book of rules and procedures. The formal legal guarantee of a particular level of service in public schools has proved a weak substitute for the synergies of voluntary association.

At the very beginning of this chapter, I noted that two of the most common objections to school choice—allegations that it is an academically inferior educational system and that it violates the constitutional separation of church and state—have been disproved in recent years. On the basis of the experience of special needs students in Denmark and many other countries, we must now add a third objection to the list of groundless accusations—namely, the suggestion that school choice is in any way a threat to American children who require special education services.

Notes

1. Howard Fuller and George Mitchell, "Selective Admission Practices? Comparing the Milwaukee Public Schools and the Milwaukee Parental Choice Program," *Current Education Issues 2000–01* (Marquette University, Milwaukee, WI), January 2000.

2. http://www.rethinkingschools.org/special_reports/voucher_report/vquotes. shtml.

3. Jay Greene and Greg Forster, *Vouchers for Special Education Students: An Evaluation of Florida's McKay Scholarship Program*, Civic Report no. 38, Manhattan Institute, Center for Civic Education, 2003.

4. Jay Chambers, Thomas Parrish, and Jenifer Harr, *What Are We Spending on Special Education Services in the United States, 1999–2000?* American Institutes for Research, Center for Special Education Finance, 2004 (update).

5. Personal conversation with Roger Moltzen during the International Association of Special Education Conference, Warsaw, Poland, July 23–26, 2001.

6. David Mitchell, "Paradigm Shifts in and around Special Education in New Zealand," mimeo updating an earlier paper with the same title in *New Zealand Journal of Educational Studies* 34, no. 1 (2000): 199–210.

7. C. E. van Kraayenoord et al., *Students with Disabilities: Their Literacy and Numeracy Learning*, Australia, Commonwealth Department of Education, Training and Youth Affairs, 2000.

8. Australian National Council of Independent Schools' Association, "Funding of Independent Schools," September 2001, p. 9.

9. http://www.european-agency.org/national_pages/netherlands/national_overview/no07.html.

10. A "handicap," as defined by official publications of the Swedish National Agency for Special Needs Education, "is not tied to an individual but is created by the demands, expectations, and attitudes of the environment."

11. Skolverket, *Students in Need of Special Support* (Stockholm: 1998), pp. 18–20.

12. Ibid., p. 9.

13. Ibid., p. 16.

14. "Section 9. Prerequisites of the Integration," *Integration of Handicapped Pupils in the Mainstream School System*, Undervisnings Ministeriet, http://www.uvm.dk/gammel/handicap.htm.

15. OECD, *Special Needs Education: Statistics and Indicators* (Paris: OECD, 2000).

16. Personal conversation with Niels Egelund, Institute of Psychology and Special Education, Copenhagen, Denmark, October 14, 2003.

17. Lewis Andrews, "Magic Bullet," *American Enterprise*, October–November 2003, pp. 42–43.

18. Personal conversations with Beatrice Schindler Rangvid at the Institute of Local Government, Copenhagen, Denmark, April 14, 2004.

19. Ibid.

20. Personal conversations with Egelund; with Beatrice Schindler Rangvid; and with Dan Terkildsen, partner at Osborne, Clarke in Copenhagen, Denmark, and lecturer at the University of Copenhagen, April 14, 2004.

21. Bill Daniels, "NCISA Opinion Piece," Australian National Council of Independent Schools' Association, 2000.

22. Personal conversation with Per Kristensen, secretary general of ECNAIS, October 14, 2003.

23. Kevin Wheldall, "Barbie in a Wheelchair? Progress towards Inclusive Education in Australia with Particular Reference to New South Wales," address to International Conference in Inclusive Schooling and Communities, Malta, July 23–26, 1997.

24. *A Seventeen Country Study of the Relationship between Financing of Special Needs Education and Inclusion* (Copenhagen: EADSNE, 2000).

25. "Section 15. Limits to Integration," *Integration of Handicapped Pupils in the Mainstream School System*.

26. Robert Aguirre, *Report on the First Semester of the Horizon Voucher Program* (Bentonville, AR: CEO Foundation, 1999); and Robert Aguirre, *Power to Choose: Horizon Scholarship Program Second Annual Report* (Bentonville, AR: CEO Foundation, 2000).

27. Lewis Andrews, "End State and Local Budget Deficits with School Choice," Yankee Institute Public Policy Report, http://www.yankeeinstitute.org/papers/budeget_deficits.php.

28. Personal conversation with Terkildsen.

29. Jay Greene and Nicole Mellow, "Integration Where It Counts: A Study of Racial Integration in Public and Private School Lunchrooms," paper presented at the American Political Science Association meeting, Boston, September 1998.

30. Ibid., p. 6.

31. "Executive Summary," *Jeopardizing a Legacy: A Closer Look at IDEA and Florida's Disability Voucher Program* (Washington, and Berkeley, CA: People for the American Way and Disability Rights Education and Defense Fund, 2003).

5. What the United States Can Learn from Other Countries

Charles L. Glenn

The title of this chapter may fall in an unfamiliar way upon the ear; Americans are usually quite reluctant to concede that they have anything to learn from experience elsewhere. That is especially true with respect to education. The exceptions are periods of short-term panic, such as when the Soviet example was anxiously studied after the launching of *Sputnik* or the Japanese example in the 1980s.

Other countries, it seems, are more open to ideas from abroad as exemplified by a questionnaire I recently received on Dutch education to which I and a few other foreigners were asked to reply. The first question, for example, was "In Dutch elementary schooling there is too little attention given to [fill in the blank], because [fill in the blank]. In this respect, the Netherlands could learn [fill in the blank] from abroad." A second set of questions asked the foreign observers our considered judgment about the achievements of Dutch schools in comparison with those of other countries (seeking to go beyond test score results). The third section asked how adequately Dutch education meets a series of challenges: integration of minorities, responding to individual needs, and so forth. A final section provided a series of open-ended questions to which the foreign observers were asked to respond. The first question was "What, in your opinion, should be done concretely about Dutch education?"

American educators and policymakers, in my experience, are generally far less curious about how others assess the strengths and weaknesses of our schools. Too often we use some version of "American exceptionalism" to deny that we could in fact learn anything from experience elsewhere. We are told that the United States is a uniquely diverse society (not true), or that we continue the schooling of a higher proportion of our youth than do other countries (not true) as though such distinctiveness meant that it is not possible to use the successes and failures of other countries as natural experiments that might inform what we should or could be doing.

There is, by contrast, significant interest in Europe about what can be learned from America's educational successes—and how to avoid America's mistakes. I'm frequently asked to speak or write for European audiences on one of two themes: the schooling of immigrants and other minority groups and the role of educational standards in promoting school reform. Those are considered domains in which the American experience offers important examples, though not always successful ones. It is much more unusual for an American audience to invite European speakers to explain what we can learn from their countries.

Family choice of schools is undoubtedly an area where we have a great deal to learn. As my colleagues at OIDEL (the Geneva-based organization promoting educational freedom around the world) have shown in a comprehensive report, virtually every country in the world with a well-developed educational system allows parents, at their own expense, to choose alternatives to state-operated schools (the exceptions are Cuba and Vietnam). In China, indeed, there are reportedly tens of thousands of private schools that respond to the new prosperity of many families.

In addition, governments in most Western democracies provide partial or full funding for nongovernment schools chosen by parents; the United States (apart from a few scattered and small-scale programs) is the great exception, along with Greece.

Ten years ago, when I wrote "School Choice and Privatization" for the *International Encyclopedia of Education*, it was sufficiently noteworthy to point out the widespread existence of policies permitting and even supporting parental choice of schools. Today, we need to look at that issue in a more detailed and critical way. Hoover Institution economist Eric Hanushek has pointed out that "the term choice conveys about the same information as saying that I just ate in New York City. There are a wide variety of places to eat in New York City. Some of them are good. Some of them are okay. Some of them are dreadful. And that is my view of what we will see in a number of these choice plans."[1]

What can we learn from the experience of other countries about how to make American education more effective, more equitable, and more consistent with a free society? Here are four possible lessons:

1. The right of families to choose schools for their children is first and foremost a question of freedom of conscience. It is a fundamental injustice to make the exercise of that right contingent upon the financial resources that each family has at its disposal.
2. The existence of some sort of market in educational services requires that schools be allowed to differ in ways that are meaningful to families. There is good reason to believe that distinctive schools are likely to be more effective educationally.
3. Experience in this and other countries demonstrates consistently that allowing schools to be educationally and philosophically distinctive does not lead to weird or damaging results or to segregation and social division.
4. Close attention should be given to the framework of policies and procedures within which school distinctiveness and family choice function. Finding the right balance between public accountability and the private educational objectives of families is difficult but essential.

Children Are the Responsibility of their Families

Of course there are parents who abuse or neglect their children, and in such cases society has an obligation to intervene. But public policy should not be based on a mistrust of families—as some progressives as well as some conservatives seem to wish. The primacy of parents in making decisions about the education and other aspects of the welfare of their children is firmly established in international law as well as in that of the United States. For example, the *Universal Declaration of Human Rights* (1948) states that "parents have a prior right to choose the kind of education that shall be given to their children" (article 26, 3).[2] According to the *International Covenant on Economic, Social and Cultural Rights* (1966),

> the States Parties to the present Covenant undertake to have respect for the liberty of parents . . . to choose for their children schools, other than those established by public authorities, which conform to such minimum educational standards as may be laid down or approved by the State and to ensure the religious and moral education of their children in conformity with their own convictions (article 13, 3).[3]

Similarly, the First Protocol to the *European Convention for the Protection of Human Rights and Fundamental Freedoms* provides that "in the exercise of any functions which it assumes in relation to education and teaching, the State shall respect the right of parents to ensure such education and teaching in conformity with their own religious and philosophical convictions" (article 2).[4]

Unfortunately, discussion of school choice in the United States has often been dominated by arguments about the virtues or potential dangers of markets. Although those arguments deserve thoughtful consideration, we should not allow questions about the virtues of markets versus government provision to define the debate. The bottom line is whether we will operate a system of mandatory schooling that denies to some parents, because of their relative poverty, the right to make important decisions about what is in the best interest of their children.

Schools Should Be Allowed to Differ in Significant Ways

Schools that differ in ways that are meaningful to families not only are more satisfactory to those families but also are more likely to be effective educationally. Commonly, those are schools founded on the basis of and seeking to express an alternative, religious, understanding of life that is not reflected in the public schools.

The reason is not mysterious. Schools whose staffs are clear and in agreement about what they are seeking to accomplish are more likely to be successful than schools whose staffs are responding only to procedural requirements, as is too often the case in public schools. A study conducted for the National Center for Education Statistics found that 46.4 percent of central-city public secondary teachers reported serious apathy among their students. That was true of only 10.7 percent of the central-city private secondary teachers. Also, 32.5 percent of the public school teachers but only 5.4 percent of the private school teachers complained of "disrespect for teachers." Motivated students, a relatively safe and undistracting environment, and a school size that allows the students and adults to know one another well more than offset the public school advantage in resources such as computers and teachers with master's degrees. Most important is the clarity that private schools—particularly faith-based private schools—commonly have about their goals and shared values. The NCES study found that 71.4 percent of the teachers in the small (fewer than 150 students) private schools agreed that "colleagues share beliefs and values about central mission of school" compared with 40.8 percent of those in small public schools. For large schools with more than 750 students, the numbers dropped to 49.4 percent in the private and 26.2 percent in the public schools.[5]

As University of Washington professor Paul Hill has pointed out, under conditions of family choice,

> a school will be stabilized by its commitments and respond to the needs of a group of students and parents to whom it is committed rather than to the politically bargained preferences of society as a whole. . . . Social trust and community feeling are higher when schools are distinctive and families have choices. In an ongoing study, the author has found that students in schools based on a clear set of common premises are more likely than students in less well-defined schools to engage in vigorous discussion of values and social policy. In schools that throw together students from different races and social classes without creating a common intellectual and values framework, students are likely to resegregate socially and academically along racial and class lines.[6]

It is important to point out that the educational advantages noted here cannot be attributed to market forces alone or primarily. Coleman and Hoffer, for example, did not find any significant advantage for youth attending nonreligious private schools. It appears to be the functional community that faith-based schools commonly create and their concomitant clarity of educational focus that make the difference. Structural factors, such as a significant measure of autonomy and public funding for parental choice, are primarily significant because they allow that clarity to emerge and to be sustained.

Research in France, England, Belgium, and the Netherlands supports the evidence from U.S. research that schools with a distinctive identity—often but not always religious—offer educational advantages deriving from their clarity of focus.

Most schools that operate under deliberate choice programs (such as magnet schools, charter schools, and private schools receiving vouchers) are educationally distinctive and are chosen at least in part for that reason. However, it is difficult to determine whether their greater effectiveness is the result of the market or simply of the way in which the market has allowed them to occupy a special-ized niche that produces better results. Thus, for example, Peter Mortimore and his colleagues found in their careful study of effective schooling in London that Church of England and Catholic "volun-tary aided" schools had a definite advantage in producing good educational outcomes. There was

> a consistent pattern of associations between voluntary status and schools' effects upon a number of the cognitive and noncognitive outcomes. . . . It is likely that schools which were chosen for very specific reasons may have had the advantages of greater parental support for their educational aims and, because of such support, were helped to be more effective. [And, again,] voluntary schools, based on denomi-national membership, may also elicit a greater commitment from both parents and pupils, which may act as a strong cohesive force.[7]

Distinctive Schools Do Not Harm Children or Create Social Divisions

Experience in other countries demonstrates that the concerns expressed by opponents of family choice of schools in the United States (that it will lead to various harmful side effects) are unfounded. The Dutch example is particularly telling since there is a constitutional guarantee of freedom of the religious or philosophical character of schools—their *richting*—and two-thirds of pupils in the country attend nonpublic schools. Surely in the Netherlands, if anywhere, we might expect to find weird or divisive education. But in fact the rich variety of publicly funded schools—including Catholic, five varieties of Protestant, Anthroposophic, Orthodox and Reform Jewish, Rosicrucian, Hernhutter, Platonic, several varieties of Muslim, several varieties of Hindu, Montessori, Dalton, Freinet, Jenaplan—has neither divided Dutch society nor resulted in groups of children being poorly educated.

The idea that bizarre or extremist schools would flourish unchecked under a well-designed school voucher program is a sort of ghost story to frighten the gullible. University of Amsterdam professor Ben Vermeulen's study of how the Dutch system has accommodated and regulated some 40 Islamic (and several Hindu) schools shows that such issues can readily be addressed through sound policies and oversight.[8]

On the other hand, it is true that family choice of schools can reduce the extent of social and ethnic integration even below the low level that already results from residential segregation. Dutch and other European educational authorities are concerned about educational segregation but have been less effective than have many U.S. cities in putting school choice to work as a means of promoting integration.

During the turbulent 1970s and 1980s, I was the state official responsible for educational equity in the state of Massachusetts. One of the lessons we learned during that period was that well-designed programs of parental choice could promote stable racial and social class integration more successfully than did mandatory reassignments. That required listening carefully to what parents wanted in the schools their children attended and then encouraging the staff of each school in a district to identify one segment of the "educational market" to which they would make a special appeal, seeking to please some parents very much rather than (as is often the case) offering a lowest-common-denominator education. By the time I left government, there were 180,000 pupils attending integrated public schools that their parents had chosen under such explicit policies.

It was not good enough, however, and the year I left my government job and went to Boston University I published an article in the *Public Interest* calling for charter schools and vouchers because the rigidity of the public school system was preventing parental choice from having its full effect. In too many schools, the old habits persisted; teachers and principals were afraid to create schools that were really distinctive or were unwilling to admit that there were some families for whom they did not have the right sort of program. Unfortunately, bureaucracy is not simply a set of rules; it can sink deep into the hearts of those who have come to take it for granted and prevent them from responding creatively to the challenges of education. My current nightmare is that we will manage at last to achieve a system of universal vouchers and find that educators have grown unable to respond to the opportunities it offers.

And those opportunities need to come with financial incentives to concentrate the minds of those who might otherwise fall into the complacency that has proven so damaging for American public education. Just yesterday (as I write this) I came upon a good illustration of this point in a book on schooling in Renaissance Italy. Town councils, we learn, "fixed the teacher's salary and authorized him to collect supplementary fees from his students at rates established by the commune." The theory was that "if part of the master's income depended on student fees, he would have to teach well in order to attract the number of pupils needed to augment his income significantly."[9]

The wisdom of those town councils still applies. Schools and teachers should be at least somewhat dependent on tuition paid by parents and the school's ability to attract pupils. Only then do teachers and school operators have a financial incentive to be creative and to improve. German economist Ludger Woessmann, who conducted a multinational survey of private and public schools, found that math achievement in private schools was less positive in its effect when private schools received all their funding from government sources. The most positive effects were in private schools that received less than half their core funding from government.[10] In other words, students do better in private schools that obtain at least part of their funding directly from tuition paid by parents.

Regulations Should Allow School Distinctiveness and Family Choice

Unsatisfied with generalizations about family choice of schools, Belgian legal scholar Jan De Groof and I set out, a few years ago, to document the specific ways in which different Western nations permit, support, and regulate school distinctiveness and choice. I will not attempt here to summarize what we describe in detail in the 1,500 pages of our three volumes, but we found significant variations that were often consequential for how real the choices are and how coherent and mission driven schools are allowed to become.[11]

The most crucial issue—beyond the fundamental right of parents to choose a school for their children—was the right of the school or its sponsoring board to select staff on the basis of criteria specific to the distinctive mission of the school rather than to some universal standard established for all schools. Also very important was the right to select the academic and other outcomes for which the individual school (or group of schools in a network) would be held accountable. Other issues that we found significant included the right to establish open and mission-related criteria for the selection of pupils and to provide character education based on a school-specific understanding of the nature of a good life.

That leads to my advice to all those concerned about educational freedom: that we need to move beyond singing the praises of parental choice of schools and think very seriously about the terms on which and the constraints within which such choice is exercised. There are those who argue that government should simply cease to concern itself with education, but I am convinced that that is profoundly unrealistic and possibly not even desirable. Our goal should be to limit the role of government to setting the ground rules within which schools as institutions of civil society provide education and providing the public funding that makes education universally and adequately available.

Conclusion

Educational freedom, then, requires more careful legal and policy design and less enthusiastic rhetoric. Those of us who believe that freedom is not only necessary to promote effective schools but also required by the respect that we owe to the convictions of families and individuals must be willing to engage in the difficult task of crafting laws and procedures.

It is much too easy, as we have seen in the case of some state charter school laws, to give lip service to school distinctiveness and parent and teacher choice but then surround schools with so many procedural requirements that creative problem solving at the school level is frustrated. No wonder many strong supporters of nonpublic schools are suspicious of vouchers as a tempting trap.

Forty-five years ago, when France adopted legislation allowing the government to contract with Catholic and other schools to provide instruction at public expense, some observers warned that it could lead to the nationalization of private schools. They were at least partly correct, and the intervening decades have seen an ever-renewed struggle to protect the freedom of schools under contract to maintain and continue to develop their distinctive character (*caractère propre*). In 1984 more than a million parents and other supporters rallied in Paris to protest an attempt by a Socialist government to bring private schools into the public system, leading to the fall of that government. Eternal vigilance is the price of liberty. That is particularly true in education. For that reason, we must undertake

the difficult task of finding the right balance between public accountability and private school autonomy.

Notes

1. Quoted in Andrew Nikiforuk, *School's Out* (Toronto: Macfarlane Walter & Ross, 1993), p. 99.

2. *Universal Declaration of Human Rights* (1948), article 26.3, in *International Declarations and Conventions on the Right to Education and the Freedom of Education*, ed. Alfred Fernandez and Siegfried Jenkner (Frankfurt am Main: Info3-Verlag, 1995). Cited hereafter as *International Declarations*.

3. *International Covenant on Economic, Social and Cultural Rights* (1966), article 13.3, in *International Declarations*.

4. Found in ibid.

5. Susan P. Choy, *Public and Private Schools: How Do They Differ?* NCES 97-983 (Washington: National Center for Education Statistics, 1997), pp. 19–22.

6. Paul Hill, "The Supply-side of School Choice," in *School Choice and Social Controversy*, ed. Stephen D. Sugarman and Frank E. Kemerer (Washington: Brookings Institution, 1999), p. 151.

7. Peter Mortimore et al., *School Matters* (Berkeley: University of California Press, 1988) pp., 221, 273.

8. See Ben P. Vermeulen, *Witte en zwarte scholen* (The Hague: Elsevier, 2001). For a discussion in English, see Charles L. Glenn, *Educating Immigrant Children* (New York: Garland, 1996).

9. Paul F. Grendler, *Schooling in Renaissance Italy: Literacy and Learning, 1300–1600* (Baltimore: Johns Hopkins University Press, 1989), p. 22.

10. Ludger Woessmann, "Why Students in Some Countries Do Better," *Education Next*, Summer 2001, http://www.educationnext.org/20012/67.html.

11. Charles L. Glenn and Jan De Groof, *Balancing Freedom, Autonomy, and Accountability in Education*, 3 vols. (Tilburg: Wolfe, 2004).

6. Private Education for the Poor: Lessons for America?

James Tooley

In April 2004, the Global Campaign for Education launched its self-styled "World's Biggest Ever Lobby," where "politicians and leaders in 105 countries came face to face with children." Nearly one million people joined in "to speak out for the right to education." Nelson Mandela added his voice to the "millions of parents, teachers and children around the world," "calling on their governments to provide free, good quality, basic education for all the world's children."[1]

However well-intentioned, the Global Campaign for Education is overlooking something rather important that is happening in developing countries today: the phenomenal growth of private schools for the poor. In this chapter, I outline what is taking place and discuss how it is received in development circles, before asking if it has any relevance to the school choice debate in the United States.

Seven Features of Private Education for the Poor

I first discovered for myself the phenomenon of private schools for the poor while doing consultancy for the International Finance Corporation, the private finance arm of the World Bank, in Hyderabad, India, in 2000. I'd just published an argument for privatization of education, *Reclaiming Education*,[2] and was wrestling with the criticism from even sympathetic readers that what I'd argued might be good for the middle classes, or richer countries, but what about the poor, especially in poor countries? That criticism bothered me. I knew from my reading of E. G. West[3] that historically the poor in Victorian England were largely provided for by private education, before the state got involved. Why wouldn't the same be true of the poor today? Out of curiosity, I left my work—looking at private schools for the elite and middle classes—and took an auto-rickshaw into the slum areas behind the imposing 16th-century Char-minar in the center of the Old City. And to my surprise, I found private schools on almost every street corner. Inspired by that, I grew to know many of the school owners, teachers, parents, and children; I learned of their motivations and difficulties and their successes and requirements. I raised funds to conduct research on their work, first in a small-scale study looking in detail at 15 of the schools funded by the British education services company CfBT,[4] then extending the research further in India and into Africa and China with a grant from the John Templeton Foundation.

I have found private schools in battle-scarred buildings in Somali-land and Sierra Leone; in the shanty town of Makoko built on stilts above the Lagos lagoons in Nigeria; scattered among the tin and cardboard huts of Africa's largest slum, Kibera, Kenya; in the teem-ing townships perched on the shoreline of Accra, Ghana; in slums and villages across India; among the "floating population" in Beijing; and in remote Himalayan villages in China. Indeed, I have yet to find a developing country environment where private schools for the poor don't exist, and I doubt that I will. My teams have combed poor areas—slums or shanty towns in and around the major cities and villages inhabited by peasant farmers and fishermen—going down every lane and alleyway, asking people in market places and on the streets where the poor are sending their children to school.

And while we've been conducting the censuses, we've been find-ing out as much as possible about the schools, what their facilities are like, whether teachers are teaching, building up a comprehensive picture of the private schools and comparing them with the govern-ment alternative. Then, most important of all, we've been comparing the achievement of students in the private and public schools serving the poor areas; testing a stratified random sample of 4,000 children in each country, chosen equally from registered private, unregistered private, and government schools; and using advanced statistical techniques to control for as many background variables as we can, to find out whether the poor are better served by public or private education. Although the study is ongoing and additional findings are anticipated, there are seven themes that have emerged from the data that I can report on in general terms.

First, there are startling facts about the private-sector provision of schools for the poor. In each of the poor areas studied in detail, in Ghana, Nigeria, Kenya, and India (we've not yet analyzed the results of the China study), we've found that a large majority of the schools serving the poor are private, with either a large majority or a substantial minority of poor parents taking the private option.

Second, contrary to expectations, we find that the majority of private schools are run not as philanthropic endeavors but as businesses. Those private schools are created largely by local entrepreneurs responding to the needs in their communities. In general, after studying the reported income and expenditure of the private schools, we can see that they are profitable institutions—which of course helps explain why there are so many of them—with the vast majority of income coming from school fees rather than, as some might expect, philanthropic donations. Even in our studies of Africa, where a minority of the private schools are linked to churches or mosques, we find that, if anything, the school subsidizes the church rather than the other way around!

Third, there are large differences between the pay and commitment of the teachers in public and private schools serving the poor. Private school teachers are recruited locally from the communities served, unlike public school teachers who are bussed in from outside. Teachers in private schools are paid considerably less than are teachers in the government schools. Yet the private schools do not in general suffer from teacher shortages, suggesting that the market rate for teachers is considerably lower than that set by teachers' unions in the public schools. When our researchers have called unannounced in the classroom, in every case they have found significantly more absenteeism among the public school teachers than among those in the private schools. And when teachers are present, the researchers have found much higher levels of teaching activity in the private than in the public schools. That is true even of the unregistered, hence illegal, private schools, which are outperforming the public schools in this respect.

Fourth, we have found considerable statistically significant differences in inputs between the public and private schools. The pupil/ teacher ratio is lower in the private than in the public schools—with the unregistered private schools usually having the lowest of all— and school facilities such as libraries, toilets, and drinking water are usually better provided in the private than in the public schools.

Fifth, there are differences between countries in the relative costs of public and private schooling. In countries where public schooling is entirely free at the point of delivery—India for instance—clearly, the private schools cost more for parents. But in other countries— China and Ghana, for instance—where public schools charge low fees or "levies," we find that sometimes the private schools are undercutting public schools, because the really poor can't afford the public option. What makes the private schools financially attractive is that they allow the parents to pay on a daily basis—perhaps 10 cents a day—rather than to pay the full term levy up-front as they must for the public schools, even though this might work out more cheaply if they could afford to pay it. In Kenya, the government has recently introduced "free primary education," but our interviews with parents point to many "hidden costs" of public schools, such as the requirement for full uniforms, which mean that, in practice, private slum schools often turn out to be less expensive.

Fees charged are typically about $3 per month in India, although this might amount to up to 10 percent of a rickshaw puller or market trader's expected monthly income. Parents report that they value education highly and will scrimp and save to ensure that their children get the best education they can afford—which means, it seems, pulling them out of public schools.

Sixth, private school owners themselves are very much aware of the plight of the poorest of the poor: for those parents who are too poor to send their children to private school, or as an aid to those children who have been orphaned or who are from large families, the school entrepreneurs themselves offer free or subsidized scholarships. That was true of nearly 20 percent of all places in one Indian sample and nearly 10 percent in the Nigerian sample.

Finally, our first results on the achievement of pupils show that the private schools substantially outperform the public schools in mathematics and English, after controlling for the school choice process and for a range of background factors. All this is for considerably lower per pupil costs. If our results withstand scrutiny, then it would seem that the poor are making sensible choices by sending their children to private, rather than public, schools.

Three Surprising Areas of Agreement with Development Experts

The odd thing is, it turned out that my "discovery" was not a discovery at all but a phenomenon that was actually quite widely known, at least by some key figures in development circles. But although many knew about the ubiquity of private education for the poor, no one seemed to be drawing what seemed to me to be the obvious conclusion. Instead, those influential in development circles seemed to be engaged, if not in a conspiracy of silence, then at least in a refusal to explore the implications of where the evidence seemed to lead. In development circles, as the quotes from the Global Campaign for Education cited earlier reveal, all were repeating the same refrain that "education for all" required government intervention, assisted by international agencies; the presence of private schools for the poor was irrelevant.

Many development experts seem to have no problem at all accepting three propositions that seem to me to lead in an altogether different direction from the one in which the experts see them heading:

First, it seems to be widely accepted that private schools for the poor are burgeoning. The *Oxfam Education Report,* for instance, the Bible of many development education experts, looking at evidence from a range of developing countries, challenges the "misplaced" notion that private schools service only the needs of "a small minority of wealthy parents" and points to the "lower cost private sector" that has emerged to "meet the demands of poor households."[5] One of its sources of evidence is the *Probe Report* on education in villages in five northern Indian states. That report says that "even among poor families and disadvantaged communities, one finds parents who make great sacrifices to send some or all of their children to private schools, so disillusioned are they with government schools."[6]

Second, among the same experts, it seems to be common currency that the reason why poor parents are sending their children to private schools is, at least in part, the gross inadequacies of state education, especially teacher absenteeism. The *Oxfam Education Report* states clearly that it is the "inadequacies of public education systems" that have "driven many poor households into private systems." Those inadequacies include "inadequate public investment," causing staff and pupil demoralization and the provision of poor facilities.[7] Most important, however, says the *Oxfam Education Report,* is the problem of teacher absenteeism and commitment.[8] The Probe Team reported that when their researchers called unannounced on their large random sample of government schools, in only 53 percent was there

93

any "teaching activity" going on at all! In fully 33 percent the head teacher was absent.[9] The investigators found a particularly alarming pattern of systematic neglect of first grade children in those schools: "When teachers are unable or unwilling to teach all the children, they typically concentrate their efforts on the older children" because such children are easier and less demanding to teach. The report gives some touching examples of parents who are struggling against the odds to keep children in school but whose children are clearly learning next to nothing. Children's work is "at best casually checked."[10] The team reported

> several cases of irresponsible teachers keeping a school closed or non-functional for several months at a time; a school where the teacher was drunk . . . a headteacher who asks the children to do domestic chores, including looking after the baby; several cases of teachers sleeping at school . . .; a headteacher who came to school once a week . . . and so on down the line.[11]

The Probe Team observed that in the government schools, "generally, teaching activity has been reduced to a minimum, in terms of both time and effort." Significantly, "this pattern is not confined to a minority of irresponsible teachers—it has become a way of life in the profession."[12]

Those problems were not found in private schools serving the poor. When visiting one such school in Uttar Pradesh, researchers found it

> packed with enthusiastic children (boys as well as girls) while the local government school exudes a familiar atmosphere of desertion, apathy, and decay.[13]

The Probe Team also agreed that the same problems are not inherent in the private sector; when researchers called unannounced on their random sample of private unaided schools in the villages, "feverish classroom activity" was taking place.[14] Indeed, private schools for the poor, the Oxfam report says, sometimes "offer cheaper and better-quality alternatives to State provision."[15]

So what is the secret of success in the private schools? A third proposition seems to gain widespread agreement among the development experts. The *Probe Report* put it succinctly:

> In a private school, the teachers are accountable to the manager (who can fire them), and, through him or her, to the

parents (who can withdraw their children). In a government school, the chain of accountability is much weaker, as teachers have a permanent job with salaries and promotions unrelated to performance. This contrast is perceived with crystal clarity by the vast majority of parents.[16]

Indeed, such was the view of the relative merits of public and private schools that "most parents stated that, if the costs of sending a child to a government and private school were the same, they would rather send their children to a private school."[17]

Accountability is also the factor highlighted by Drèze and Saran, who note of one government primary school that, "since the salary of the teacher was not related to his work performance, and since his appointment was technically a 'permanent' one, he had little incentive to take his job seriously. In fact he rarely took the trouble of turning up at all." And again, they note that such problems are not found in the private sector:

> Private schools have the advantage of being "incentive compatible," in the sense that it is in the interest of the parents to keep an eye on the teacher, and in the interest of teachers to be responsive to parental demands (unlike in the government primary school, where the teacher is paid irrespective of his performance).[18]

That poor parents in some of the poorest countries on this planet are flocking to private schools because state schools are inadequate and unaccountable seems to be hugely significant territory for these development experts to concede. The more I read of this evidence, the more it seems that these development experts are missing the obvious conclusion to be drawn from it. If we are concerned with reaching the "education for all" target of all children in quality primary education by 2015, surely we should be looking to the private sector to play a significant role here. Surely we should be trumpeting its successes and seeking ways of helping its improvement as a major response to the needs of education for all—that is, to go with the grain of current parental choice and think about the potential of private education to meet the educational needs of all.

Four Areas of Substantial Disagreement

Curiously to me, however, that is not a possibility currently being explored by development experts: Oxfam's report, for instance, is typical. Although, as noted, it is quite explicit that private schools for the poor are emerging and that those schools are superior to government schools for the poor, its fallback position is that "there is no alternative" but blanket public provision to reach education for all. The *Probe Report* arrives at the same conclusion: we must not be misled into thinking that there is a "soft option" of entrusting elementary education to private schools.[19] The only message from the development experts appears to be that parents are misguided in making choices in favor of the private sector and that their progeny should be dragged back into government schools. Why is that the case?

The *Probe Report* gives four reasons, which seem to be shared by the mainstream development view. It concedes that, although it has painted a "relatively rosy" picture of the private sector, where there is a "high level of classroom activity, . . . better utilisation of facilities, greater attention to young children, responsiveness of teachers to parental complaints," this does not mean that private education is an answer to the problem of providing education for all, because

- private schools are out of reach of the vast majority of poor parents;
- private schools "often take advantage of the vulnerability of parents," which they do by maintaining "appearances without imparting much education to the children";
- private teachers' "overwhelming objective is to cram the heads of the pupils, so that they may pass the relevant tests and examinations," rather than engage in wider educational activities; and
- if poor parents support private education, this "carries a real danger of undermining the government schooling system."[20]

The first objection is about fees. Certainly the schools we've examined, while charging low fees, are out of the reach of some of the poorest parents. But why is that seen as an objection to a greater role for private education? Clearly, there is the possibility of creating targeted vouchers or scholarships for the poorest, which would overcome the objection. Indeed, as noted above, the private schools themselves are aware of the needs of the poorest and provide scholarships for them. So surely a way around the first objection is to follow the lead of the private schools by providing public or private targeted vouchers, or both, for the poorest.[21]

The second and third criticisms are of the quality of private education. But on closer reading, they did not themselves seem to be based on the evidence in the *Probe Report* but at best were subjective judgments about the schools. Our research is suggesting that these are not valid criticisms. In our detailed study of private schools in Hyderabad, for instance, the schools were clearly not simply "teaching to the test" but were engaged in teaching the whole curriculum and a multiplicity of extracurricular activities. We saw first hand the range of interschool sports competitions, science fairs, general knowledge, singing, drama, and sporting activities. Where they were teaching "to the test," this seemed primarily because the government curriculum required them to do so. Parents were not as ignorant of what was happening in the schools as the *Probe Report* suggests. On the contrary, parents reported to us that they were active choosers, keen to move their children if the quality of the school was not what they wanted. The majority surveyed several schools before they chose the one to which to send their child.[22]

In any case, even if the quality was poorer than considered desirable, that wouldn't necessarily lead to a wholesale dismissal of the private schools—for there is, as noted, widespread acknowledgment that the government schools have poor-quality provision, and the development experts are looking to improve them. So even if the Probe Team were right, that would at most imply looking at ways of improving the private schools, not of abandoning them as an option for education for all.

But the fourth point seems the oddest to make. What it seems to be saying is that poor parents will just have to wait until "things get better." By removing your children from the totally inadequate state school, imply development experts, you are jeopardizing the state system. It doesn't matter that you are poor yourself and that your children's education may be the only viable vehicle out of poverty; you'd better stay in the state sector and hope that something happens to make things better. Meanwhile, your children can irrevocably suffer from teachers who don't turn up, or who don't teach if they do turn up, until governments learn the lessons from experiments elsewhere. But don't, whatever you do, send your children to private school!

It seemed to me that parents in the slums and villages may be less sanguine and more impatient. Parents may not feel they have any impact on distant or corrupt political processes. They may not believe in any case that politicians can or will effect solutions to their problems. Their only realistic alternative might be to exit the state system. Increasingly, it seems to me that progress toward accountable education might not necessarily involve complex political processes and the realignment of power relationships. Instead, the lessons coming loudly and clearly from parents using the private system might be that accountable education involves a very simple and easy transfer of power from the politician to the parent, and that can be done now. And for those who are unable to make that move for financial reasons, there are other ways of helping that do not involve wholesale change through the political process—through targeted nongovernmental financial assistance and microfinance, for instance.

Two Lessons for School Choice in America

Clearly, the evidence and discussion presented here have implications for U.S. development policy. It might make Americans think again about the way in which aid from USAID and the World Bank is typically aimed at public, rather than private, education, for instance, and raise questions about the apparent denial on the part of those development agencies of the range and usage of private education among the poor. It can lead to sophisticated challenges from Americans to the glib certainties of the Global Campaign for Education and the "World's Biggest Ever Lobby."[23] But does it have any implications for the school choice debate for Americans themselves? I believe it does, that the growing body of evidence of school choice among some of the world's poorest people could bring new inspiration and vitality to the school choice movement in the United States.

Certainly, the research evidence from developing countries can put the American experience into a wider context, further undermining the claims of those who seek to portray the school choice movement as the bastion of only the privileged. Innovative models from around the world of the way private education enhances choice and improves opportunities for the most disadvantaged, evidence concerning the effectiveness of those models in raising standards, and stories highlighting the creativity and entrepreneurship of concerned educationists can all play an important role in helping buttress calls for school choice in America.

There is an obvious precedent for this ambition. Perhaps the evidence of private education for the poor can do for the school choice debate what E. G. West did for the same debate, using evidence from history. In his pioneering study of the origins of state education, *Education and the State,* West argued that, prior to the major state involvement in education in England and Wales in 1870, school attendance rates and literacy rates were above 90 percent, and state intervention, far from being required to ensure universal attendance and literacy, merely reinforced a process that had been developing for some time.[24] That historical work was influential around the world. Notably, the leading school choice advocates Milton and Rose Friedman relate how they changed their minds about government compulsion after reading West.[25] Writing to West on being honored with the De Tocqueville Award for the Advancement of Education Freedom, Milton Friedman said, "I am only one of many who has had his views changed by your pathbreaking work."[26]

Moreover, going back to the press clippings[27] around the first publication of West's work, we can see how his historical evidence transformed the school choice debate in the United Kingdom and beyond. The *Sunday Times* described *Education and the State* as "perhaps the most important work written on the subject this century. . . . Any rich benefactor . . . could hardly do better than to present Dr. West's book to every Member of Parliament." Similarly, the *Times Educational Supplement* challenged: "If working-class parents were prepared to back the choice they then possessed with money, why should they be presumed unfit to choose today when they are so much richer?" That is a question that the current research raises in a new and fresh context. Finally, the *Times* noted that West's historical argument raised the question "why the state, in preference to individuals, should provide the bulk of a country's education . . . as more people are critical of the deficiencies of state schools and frustrated that for those with even moderate incomes there is no way of opting out it becomes increasingly important that alternatives should be politically voiced. . . . The most promising proposal put forward so far is that of the education voucher. . . ."

What West did for the school choice debate in the 1960s and 1970s, influencing key figures like Milton Friedman and the policies of

Margaret (now Lady) Thatcher, I believe the evidence of private education for the poor can do for the school choice debate now. West used the history of Victorian England to show how the poor could manage educationally on their own without the state—leading to calls for increased school choice in Britain and America. The mounting evidence summarized here can have a parallel impact: if the evidence reveals that the poorest people worldwide are achieving better educational outcomes without the state, then this must help inspire and buttress appeals for increased school choice in rich countries too.

However, perhaps the new evidence from developing countries can go even further than that. Many participants in the school choice debate in the United States currently seem to limit their ambitions to the possibility of vouchers in education—that is, where government taxes you, then allows some part of your own money to be transferred to a school of your choice within strict constraints set by government. Here it seems to be assumed that public funding of education at least is a nonnegotiable requirement. Or those advocating school choice propose "charter school" legislation as the way to help the disadvantaged, to permit independent schools to opt into state funding and regulation. Both presuppose that the only way of solving the problems of the educationally disadvantaged is through some form of government intervention.

But two far more radical lessons are suggested by the evidence emerging from developing countries, which might imply that such voices in the American school choice debate are not being bold enough.

The first radical lesson concerns the spirit of self-help. Here, if a public school is failing in the ghettoes of New York or Los Angeles, we assume that the only way in which the disadvantaged can be helped is through some kind of public intervention—through vouchers, or charter schools, or some other "school choice" proposal. But the poor in Asia and Africa don't sit idly by, dispossessed and disenfranchised—adjectives used by the liberal elite to describe the disadvantaged in America—acquiescent in their government's failure until outsiders propose some such reform. Instead, some of the most disadvantaged people on this planet engage in self-help, vote with their feet, exit the public schools, and move their children to private schools set up by educational entrepreneurs from their own communities to cater to their needs, without any outside help. Could the experiences of parents and educational entrepreneurs from those poor countries inspire a similar response among disadvantaged communities in America too, and among those who purport to help them?

Second, and perhaps most important, a lesson we can learn from the poor in Asia and Africa is that not only can a majority of the poor that we've researched afford private education themselves, without state intervention, but it is precisely their payment of fees that appears to keep the schools accountable to them. And the schools' accountability to parents through fees is the key difference, noted even by the critics of private education, that keeps standards higher than in the public alternative. If the private schools were to be brought into a universal voucher system, as might be the ambition of many American proponents of school choice, with state funds provided for them on a per capita basis, then this may drastically undermine or remove altogether the ability of parents to ensure essential accountability.

There is an important precedent from India that we should learn: government subsidy to private schools through "grant-in-aid" was introduced in 1882 and has remained intact to the present day.[28] The partnership, proposed in the famous Wood's Despatch of 1854, reportedly written by John Stuart Mill, aimed in a way somewhat parallel to today's voucher proposals, to "combine with the agency of the government ... the exertions and the liberality of [private enterprise]."[29] It experienced considerable early success, "encouraging educational entrepreneurship ... initially inspired by patriotic and service motives."[30] But nowadays, the private aided schools are virtually indistinguishable from their government counterparts—with all the disadvantages listed above.[31] It is argued, for instance, that if private unaided schools receive the public subsidies, teachers become less accountable to school management and parents since they become "employees paid by the state, ... sheltered from disciplinary action on the part of local managers."[32]

The most important lesson from what is happening in developing countries today may be that public funding can be part of the problem, not part of the solution. One parent in our Kenya study put it succinctly. He had taken advantage of free public education when it was introduced, taking his child from a private school in the slums to a public school on the outskirts of town. However, quickly disillusioned by what was offered, he transferred her back to the private school. He told us: "If you go to a market and are offered free fruit and vegetables, they will be rotten. If you want fresh fruit and vegetables, you have to pay for them." That parent knew that the school's accountability to him depended on his paying fees. Perhaps that is a lesson that could be of use to proponents of school choice in America.

Notes

1. See www.campaignforeducation.org/actionweek.

2. James Tooley, *Reclaiming Education* (London and New York: Continuum, 2000).

3. E. G. West, *Education and the State* (London: Institute of Economic Affairs, 1965; Indianapolis: Liberty Fund, 1994).

4. See J. Tooley and P. Dixon, *Private Schools for the Poor: A Case Study from India* (Reading: CfBT, 2003); P. Dixon and J. Tooley, "The Regulation of Private Schools Serving Low-income Families in Andhra Pradesh, India: Pattern-matching with Austrian Economic Principles," *Review of Austrian Economics* (forthcoming 2005); and J. Tooley and P. Dixon, "An Inspector Calls: The Regulation of Private Education for the Poor in Andhra Pradesh, India," *International Journal of Education and Development* (forthcoming 2005).

5. K. Watkins, *The Oxfam Education Report* (London: Oxfam GB, 2000), pp. 229–30.

6. Probe Team, *The Probe Report* (Oxford and New Delhi: Oxford University Press, 1999), p. 103.

7. Watkins, p. 6.

8. Ibid., p. 230.

9. Probe Team, p. 47.

10. Ibid., p. 48.

11. Ibid., p. 63.

12. Ibid.

13. J. Drèze and H. Gazdar, "Uttar Pradesh: The Burden of Inertia," in *Indian Development: Selected Regional Perspectives*, ed. J. Drèze and A. Sen (New Delhi: Oxford University Press, 1997), p. 72.

14. Probe Team, p. 102.

15. Watkins, p. 207.

16. Probe Team, p. 64.

17. Ibid., p. 102.

18. J. Drèze and M. Saran, "Primary Education and Economic Development in China and India: Overview and Two Case Studies," Discussion Paper no. 47, Development Economic Research Programme, London, 1993, pp. 36, 39–40.

19. Probe Team, pp. 136–37.

20. Ibid., pp. 105–6.

21. For discussion of targeted vouchers, see James Tooley, Pauline Dixon, and James Stanfield, *Delivering Better Education: Market Solutions to Education* (London: Adam Smith Institute, 2003).

22. See Tooley and Dixon, *Private Schools for the Poor.*

23. The American lobby group's website is http://www.campaignforeducationusa. org/.

24. West.

25. M. Friedman and R. Friedman, *Free to Choose* (New York: Harcourt Brace Jovanovich, 1980), p. 162 and n. 15.

26. Personal communication in E. G. West Archives, E. G. West Centre, University of Newcastle Upon Tyne, England.

27. All quoted in *New Statesman*, December 20, 1965, p. 925.

28. Geeta Kingdon and Mohd Muzammil, *The Political Economy of Education in India: Teacher Politics in Uttar Pradesh* (New Delhi, Oxford, New York: Oxford University Press, 2003), p. 100. See also J. Tooley, "Management of Private-aided Higher Education in Karnataka, India: Lessons from an Enduring Public-Private Partnership," *Educational Management and Administration* (forthcoming 2005).

29. Sir Charles Wood, president of the Board of Control of the East India Company, Despatch of 1854, quoted Kingdon and Muzammil, p. 138.

30. Ibid., p. 139.

31. The examples given above from India are about private unaided schools, not subject to these public subsidies.

32. Kingdon and Muzammil, pp. 203–4.

7. School Choice: Lessons from New Zealand

Norman LaRocque

New Zealand's experience has been a topic of much discussion in educational policy circles since the introduction of national school reforms, known as Tomorrow's Schools, in the late 1980s and early 1990s.[1] The focus of this chapter is on extracting some of the broader policy lessons that can be drawn from the New Zealand experience with school reform, as well as on highlighting some of the policy innovations introduced as part of the New Zealand reforms.

The New Zealand School Sector

The New Zealand school sector is predominantly "public" in nature. That is true in terms of both the provision and the funding of school-level education. The vast majority of schools and enrollments are in the state sector. The state funds a significant proportion of the operating costs of state and state-integrated schools and a smaller, but still significant, share of the operating costs of private schools.

The regulatory framework that governs schools varies with the type of school. There are three major types of school in New Zealand:

- State schools. These are state-owned schools that receive "full" state subsidies and are extensively regulated by the state.
- State-integrated schools. These are privately owned schools that have "integrated" into the state system. They are funded at the same per pupil level as state schools and are subject to many of the regulations that apply to state schools.
- Independent schools. These are privately owned schools. They receive lower government funding and are subject to fewer regulations than state or state-integrated schools.

As of July 1, 2003, there were around 761,000 students enrolled in 2,692 schools in New Zealand. Europeans made up around 60 percent of the student population, with Maori, Pacific, Asian, and other students making up 21 percent, 8 percent, 7 percent, and 4 percent, respectively. In recent years, enrollments have grown more strongly at state-integrated and independent schools than at state schools.

Around 86 percent of students were enrolled in publicly owned and funded state schools in 2003. There were 2,256 state schools in that year. State schools are governed by parent-run boards. They cannot charge fees but can and do seek donations from parents. Those fees are typically quite low relative to private school fees. State schools are subject to the national teachers' contract, must follow the national curriculum, and must hire registered teachers.

Within the public system, there is some choice in schooling. Although school zoning based on geographic area has been reintroduced progressively since the mid-1990s, it is generally less restrictive than the system of attendance zones that operates in most jurisdictions in the United States. Students in New Zealand have the right to attend the local school for which they are zoned. However, students are also free to attend out-of-zone schools if those schools have the capacity to accept them. Where there is an excess demand for places at a particular school, the criteria for determining priorities for allowing children into schools are set in legislation. Schools have no discretion in selecting students.[2]

School zoning is a more significant issue in the main cities of New Zealand—Auckland, Christchurch, and Wellington—although it has increased in importance in regional centers in recent years. In July 2003, 36.6 percent of schools in Auckland, 18 percent of schools in Canterbury, and 17.1 percent of schools in Wellington were limiting enrollments through the use of attendance zones (called enrollment schemes in New Zealand) because there was an excess demand for places at those schools. However, the proportion of public enrollments in "zoned" schools is larger than these figures suggest, given that zoned schools tend to have higher enrollments than nonzoned schools and that these figures include both state and nonstate schools.

State-integrated schools, which had around 10 percent of enrollments in New Zealand in 2003, provide some choice within the public sector. These are predominantly formerly independent schools that were "integrated" into the state system but were allowed to retain their special character. The special character generally, though not always, relates to some sort of religious or philosophical belief. The integration of independent schools was not motivated by a desire to broaden the state sector but was a response to the financial problems that beset many Catholic schools in the mid-1970s.

State-integrated schools receive the same per pupil level of subsidy as state schools. However, they face different regulations. In particular, state-integrated schools are not subject to geographic attendance restrictions although they are subject to restrictions on the number of "nonpreference" students (i.e., non-Catholic students in a Catholic school) they can enroll. They can charge attendance fees that are intended to cover capital financing costs. Attendance fees are typically quite low, although there are some exceptions. Integrated schools are also subject to the national teachers' contract and must follow the national curriculum. Enrollment data for state, state-integrated, and independent schools are summarized in Table 7.1.

Further diversity is provided in the public system through the creation of Kura Kaupapa Maori (schools where teaching is in the Maori language and based on Maori culture and values) and designated character schools. There are, however, only a small number of such schools. Alternative Education (explained in the accompanying box) is available to students aged 13 to 15 who have become alienated from the regular school system.

New Zealand has a very small independent school sector, with around 4 percent of enrollments in 111 schools in 2003. Independent schools are privately owned and largely privately funded but receive government subsidies that are estimated at 25 to 35 percent of the average per pupil cost of educating a child in a state school, depending on grade level.[3] They are the least regulated of all schools as they can charge whatever fees the market will bear, are not part of the national teachers' contract, and do not need to follow the national curriculum (though most do).

Independent schools must be registered; that requires satisfying the Education Review Office (ERO) that a school is "efficient," that is,

Table 7.1
Enrollments by School Type and Governing Authority, New Zealand, July 2003

School Type	State		State-Integrated		Independent		Total	
	Number	%	Number	%	Number	%	Number	%
Primary/intermediate	411,850	90.2	38,826	8.5	6,106	1.3	456,782	100.0
Secondary	215,155	83.5	33,613	13.0	8,818	3.4	257,586	100.0
Composite (combined primary and secondary)	15,447	41.9	7,527	20.4	13,936	37.8	36,910	100.0
Other	10,477	100.0	0	0	0	0	10,477	100.0
Total	652,929	85.7	90,443	10.5	39,337	3.8	761,755	100.0

Source: www.minedu.govt.nz.

Alternative Education

Alternative Education (AE) is a program that funds the delivery of education in nonschool settings for students aged 13 to 15 who have become alienated from the regular school system. The program was instituted in 1997.

Students must be enrolled at a school in order to attend AE. The AE program may be delivered on or off the school site. Schools may deliver the AE program themselves or contract providers to offer it. The aim of the program is that students will either return to mainstream education or move to tertiary training or employment at the appropriate age. Programs for these students may be delivered either on or off the school site. Off-site programs may be delivered by community-based organizations or private training establishments.

In 2003, there were just over 3,000 students and more than 200 providers participating in AE. The government subsidizes each student to the tune of $NZ11,000—well above the average cost of a student in primary or secondary education.

SOURCE: Education Review Office, *Alternative Education Report*, Wellington, 2004, p. 1.

- has suitable premises, staffing, equipment, and curriculum;
- provides tuition for nine or more students between the ages of 5 and 15;
- provides suitably for the inculcation in the minds of students of sentiments of patriotism and loyalty; and
- provides education of a standard no lower than that provided to students enrolled at a state school of the same type.

Independent schools can seek provisional registration and can operate for 12 months with that status. The ERO must inspect the school within the first 6 to 12 months after it has begun operating. An independent school receives no funding while only provisionally registered, and it is up to the school to book an ERO inspection in order to gain full registration. Once the ERO is satisfied that the school is efficient in relation to the standards set out in the Education

Act, full registration will be recommended to the Ministry of Education. Regulatory requirements for state, state-integrated, and independent schools are summarized in Table 7.2.

The school sector has much lower private participation than the early childhood and postsecondary education sectors in New Zealand. In July 2003, 14 percent of postsecondary students and 100 percent of early childhood enrollments were in nongovernment centers (although 28 percent of all enrollments were in kindergartens that are considered by some to be government owned). Both the postsecondary and the early childhood sectors are funded through what is, in many respects, a voucher program.

School Choice in New Zealand: Recent History

The Tomorrow's Schools reforms of 1989 ushered in a new era of self-managing schools and increased choice and competition in schooling through changes to school zoning laws and the creation of new avenues for establishing schools.

In addition, earlier policy reforms, such as the introduction of the Private Schools Conditional Integration Act of 1975 (which "integrated" a number of private schools into the state system) and government funding of independent schools, especially from 1970 onward, played key roles in the development of school choice in New Zealand.

It is important, however, to emphasize that the Tomorrow's Schools reforms are only part of the recent New Zealand school choice story. Subsequent reforms, including the abolition of school zoning laws in 1991, successive changes to government funding of independent schools, and the introduction in 1996 of the Targeted Individual Entitlement (TIE), a small-scale voucher program targeted at poor families, are an important part of the school choice canvas (see box).

As Table 7.3 shows, there have been some significant swings in regulatory and funding policies that have affected the degree of choice available in schooling in New Zealand—both within and outside the public sector. School choice policies have had more ups and downs than Disneyland's Thunder Mountain rollercoaster. In the case of independent school funding, subsidies were increased in the mid-1970s, abolished in the mid to late 1980s, reintroduced in the early 1990s, and capped in 2000. The school zoning story is

Table 7.2

KEY FEATURES OF THE REGULATORY FRAMEWORK FOR NEW ZEALAND SCHOOLS

Aspect of Regulation	State Schools	State-Integrated Schools	Independent Schools
Private financing	Schools can ask for donations, but cannot charge fees	Schools can ask for donations and charge attendance fees to cover capital costs such as leases/mortgages	Schools can charge fees and ask for donations
Government funding	"Fully" subsidized. Funding covers • teacher salaries • operating costs • capital works	Schools receive the same per pupil funding as state schools	Subsidy estimated at 25–35% of the average cost of educating a child in a state school, depending on grade level Subsidy rate is declining as a result of cap imposed on independent school subsidies Subsidy is paid on a per student basis
Equity funding for students in low-income communities	Subsidy includes equity funding aimed at reducing barriers to learning for students in low-income communities	Subsidy includes equity funding aimed at reducing barriers to learning for students in low-income communities	Schools do not receive equity funding for students in low-income communities

(continued next page)

Table 7.2
KEY FEATURES OF THE REGULATORY FRAMEWORK FOR NEW ZEALAND SCHOOLS (*continued*)

Aspect of Regulation	State Schools	State-Integrated Schools	Independent Schools
Centralized enrollment restrictions	Schools required to set geographic school zone. Enrollment scheme set in place when the school is at maximum enrollment. Students have right to attend school for which they are zoned	Not required to set geographic school zone. Centrally determined limit on proportion of "nonpreference" enrollments	No
Other enrollment restrictions	Yes. Maximum school roll	Yes. Restrictions on "nonpreference" students	No
Subject to national curriculum	Yes	Yes	No
Subject to national teacher contract	Yes	Yes	No
Subject to teacher registration requirements	Yes	Yes	Yes

The Targeted Individual Entitlement

The Targeted Individual Entitlement (TIE) program was introduced in 1996 as a three-year pilot scheme. In 1998, it was given indefinite funding. The TIE program was designed to assist children from low-income families to attend a private school, to give choice to families whose education options were limited and to lift educational achievement among low-income families.

Under the scheme, the Government funded a small number (160) of children per year to be educated in private schools. Private schools received 110% of the average cost of education at a state school for each TIE student accepted (equal to approximately $NZ4,000 to $NZ7,000 per student in 1998). Families also received an allowance of $NZ900 to $NZ1,100 to cover nontuition costs.

To be eligible for the TIE program, students had to come from families earning less than $NZ25,000 per year. Students were eligible to receive funding for up to six years. Participating schools had to be registered and had to offer the National Curriculum. The application process was managed by the organization representing independent schools in New Zealand.

An evaluation of the TIE program conducted in the late 1990s by the Children's Issues Centre at the University of Otago concluded that the scheme was "successful in facilitating access to private schooling for a small group of students from low income New Zealand families." Participating families tended to be headed by a single parent, were relatively well educated, and of low-income and middle-income socio-economic status. The evaluation found that both parents and students were highly satisfied with the scheme and that most parents felt their children were better off educationally in the private school than in their previous school. Satisfaction with the scheme significantly outweighed any concerns that parents or students

(continued next page)

(continued)

had with it. Participating schools also showed a high degree of satisfaction with the TIE program.

Despite its success, the TIE scheme was abolished by the incoming Labour government and no new students were allowed into the program from the year 2000.

SOURCE: Michael Gaffney and Anne B. Smith, "New Zealand's Targeted Individual Entitlement Scheme," in *Can the Market Save Our Schools?* ed. Claudia Hepburn (Vancouver: Fraser Institute, 2001).

somewhat different. Although school zoning was abolished in the early 1990s, it has since been gradually reimposed by successive governments.

Policy support for school choice in New Zealand reached its peak in the mid to late 1990s when private school subsidies were increased and before a mild form of school zoning was reintroduced. Since then, it has all been downhill, with the progressive tightening of zoning, the capping of independent school subsidies, and the abolition of the TIE program.

The New Zealand Experience with School Choice: Some Observations

New Zealand is often held up—by both proponents and opponents of school choice—as an example of large-scale introduction of market competition and choice in schooling. The New Zealand education reform experience is often said to hold many lessons for other countries that might be thinking of pursuing a similar reform path. On the one hand, proponents argue that New Zealand's market reforms have led to improved educational performance and lower costs; on the other, opponents argue that the reforms have led to, among other things, increased segregation of the rich and the poor.[4]

The Tomorrow's Schools and subsequent reforms did a number of things right and undoubtedly were a significant advance over the centralized system that existed until the late 1980s. In particular, the reforms created a more competitive environment for schools (at

Table 7.3
SCHOOL CHOICE POLICIES IN NEW ZEALAND: A CHRONOLOGY

Year	Description
Pre-1970	Small subsidy provided to independent schools in the form of goods and services provided in kind and some operational expenses. Subsidy amount varied over time.
1970	Independent schools became eligible for a subsidy equal to 20% of teachers' salaries.
1975	Private Schools Conditional Integration Act of 1975 passed. It allowed private schools to "integrate" into the state system while retaining their special character. Teachers' salary subsidy increased to 50% for independent schools.
1985	Private school subsidies gradually reduced to zero by 1990.
1989	Tomorrow's Schools reforms introduced self-governing schools and amended school zoning laws. Under the new law, students could attend any school, but students had the right to attend their local school.
1991	School zoning abolished. Under the new law, students could attend any school, and there was no right to attend the local school. Schools were responsible for determining enrollment schemes to limit enrollments in cases where the school was at capacity. Teacher salary subsidy (20%) for independent schools reintroduced.
1996	New formula for calculating subsidy to independent schools implemented. Provided subsidy to independent schools equal to 25% of state school costs. Targeted Individual Entitlement (TIE) program introduced. It provided a small number of vouchers for low-income children to attend private schools.

(continued next page)

115

Table 7.3
SCHOOL CHOICE POLICIES IN NEW ZEALAND: A CHRONOLOGY
(continued)

Year	Description
1997	Alternative Education program introduced.
1998	School zoning rules amended. Under the new law, students could still attend any school. They had no right to attend the local school, and enrollment schemes continued to be developed by schools. However, enrollment schemes now had to be approved by the secretary for education and ensure that students could attend a "reasonably convenient" school. Independent school subsidy reached 25% for students in years 1–10 and 40% for upper secondary students. Ministry of Education began review of the policy and regulatory framework for schools. Discussion paper released in October 1999.
1999	Independent school subsidy increased from 25% to 30% for year 1–10 students. Pilot program for schools to self-manage their school property funding introduced.
2000	School zoning rules amended. All discretion removed from schools in setting criteria for enrollment schemes. Right to attend local school reintroduced. Overall budget for independent school subsidies capped at year 2000 levels (around $NZ38 million). Review of policy and regulatory framework for schools cancelled. TIE program cancelled—no new admissions to program from the year 2000. Bulk funding of teacher salaries abolished.

least within the public sector), increased choice for all and particularly for students from low-income families, eliminated an entire level of education bureaucracy, provided communities with greater voice in schooling, and gave schools the freedom and autonomy to better meet the needs of local communities. Good principals were given the freedom to turn around failing schools. In many respects, the New Zealand reforms were world leading.

This positive assessment of the Tomorrow's Schools reforms is supported by New Zealand economist Mark Harrison in his book *Education Matters: Government, Markets and New Zealand Schools,* where he argues:

> The reforms introduced competition between government schools, increased parental voice, gave many parents (particularly the poor) increased choice and gave schools more autonomy. Substantial numbers of parents gained from being able to move their children to good schools. . . .[5]

Demand for School Choice

The New Zealand reform experience revealed a clear demand for choice in schooling among New Zealand families. Following the removal of zoning in 1991, the proportion of students who were not attending their local school rose from 24 percent in 1990 to 31 percent in 1991 (and reached 35 percent in 1995).[6]

The phenomenon of attending schools outside a student's "home" zone continues today, despite the tightening of zoning since the late 1990s. In Porirua, a city just north of Wellington, 40 percent of secondary school students attend schools outside the city, despite the existence of several local high schools.[7] The TIE program was popular and was seen as highly successful by parents, students, and schools (see previous box).

Traditionally disadvantaged groups such as Maori and Pacific families made particular use of their increased ability to choose a school when zoning was removed (Table 7.4). In 1990, only 21 percent of Maori and 18 percent of Pacific families attended "nonlocal" schools. By 1995, those figures had increased to 39 percent and 38 percent, respectively, for Maori and Pacific families.

Not only did choice increase following the market reforms of the early 1990s, but research carried out for the Ministry of Education showed that income segregation in state schools fell when zoning was abolished in 1991 (Table 7.5) and that ethnic residential segregation was greater than school segregation in all years.[8] Some schools halved their student intake between 1990 and 1993.[9] The reforms have also provided scope for the Ministry of Education to enter into

Table 7.4
PROPORTION OF STUDENTS NOT ATTENDING LOCAL SCHOOL BY
ETHNICITY, SMITHFIELD PROJECT, 1990, 1991, AND 1995

	Percentage of Students Not Attending Their Local School			
	1990	1991	1995	Change: 1990–95
Maori	21	30	39	+18
Pacific	18	28	38	+20
Pakeha (Europeans)	26	32	33	+7
Other	24	32	35	+11

SOURCE: David Hughes et al., "Markets in Education: Testing the Polarization Thesis," Report Four, Smithfield Project, 1996, Table 9, p. 14.

Table 7.5
SOCIOECONOMIC SEGREGATION IN STUDENT INTAKE,
NEW ZEALAND, 1990–93

	Degree of Socioeconomic Segregation in Student Intake*			
	1990	1991	1992	1993
	For 6 Local Schools			
Socioeconomic status	69.7	49.2	54.9	63.6
Unemployed	59.3	44.2	57.2	61.6
	For All 11 Schools			
Socioeconomic status	58.3	48.1	49.3	53.4
Unemployed	58.2	51.6	52.6	55.2

SOURCE: Hugh Lauder et al., "The Creation of Market Competition for Education in New Zealand," Report One, Smithfield Project, 1994, Table 3, p. 27, and Table 5, p. 29; reprinted in Mark Harrison, *Education Matters: Government, Markets and New Zealand Schools* (Wellington: Education Forum, 2004), p. 227.

*Higher number means greater segregation.

innovative educational partnerships with local *iwi* (Maori tribes) to improve educational outcomes for Maori children.[10]

The Catholic school sector is growing, with existing schools expanding, new ones being built, and many having waiting lists.

Enrollments in both the independent and the state-integrated sectors have grown more quickly than in the state sector in recent years. Between 1997 and 2003, independent school rolls grew by 29.5 percent (albeit from a low base), while state-integrated school rolls grew by 12.4 percent. That compares with growth of 5.5 percent in the state sector over the same period.[11] Between July 2002 and July 2003, independent school rolls increased by 4.8 percent—more than two and a half times the growth in overall school enrollments over the same period.[12]

The reintroduction of tighter school zoning rules is estimated to have increased the price of houses by up to $50,000 as families have responded by shifting into "desirable" school zones. A 2003 survey found that 52 percent of people surveyed thought private schools were better than state schools, and 47 percent said that they would send their children to a private school if money were no object.[13]

Impact of School Choice on Educational Outcomes

There is no evidence on the impact of school choice on educational outcomes in New Zealand—either in aggregate or for those at the bottom end of the performance scale. That is due in part to the fact that there is no system of national testing in New Zealand, as there is in other countries. Indeed, the concept of benchmarking performance through such tests has long been resisted by many education stakeholder groups.

Some evidence on education outcomes is available from the National Education Monitoring Project (NEMP), an annual survey that samples the performance of year-four and year-eight primary school children. Each curriculum area is assessed every four years. NEMP results showed substantial gains in oral reading between 1996 and 2000 for year-four students and smaller gains for year-eight students.

Further evidence comes from international surveys of educational performance, in which New Zealand's performance has been mixed. New Zealand students performed well in the OECD's Programme for Student Assessment (PISA) survey of educational performance. The PISA survey, which was conducted in 2000, involved 32 countries and looked at whether young adults have the ability to use

Table 7.6
RANKINGS OF NEW ZEALAND STUDENTS ON INTERNATIONAL
SURVEYS OF EDUCATIONAL PERFORMANCE, 1994–2001

Subject Area	International Rankings on			
	PIRLS (2001)	PISA (2000)	TIMSS-Repeat (1998–99)	TIMSS (1994–95)
Reading	13	3	N/A	N/A
Math	N/A	3	21	15
Science	N/A	6	19	15

SOURCE: Constructed using data from Alan Smithers, "England's Education: What Can Be Learned by Comparing Countries," University of Liverpool, Centre for Education and Employment Research, 2004; and OECD, "Knowledge and Skills for Life: First Results from PISA 2000," Paris, 2001.

their knowledge and skills to meet real-life challenges, rather than at whether they have mastered a school curriculum. As Table 7.6 shows, New Zealand students ranked third, third, and sixth in the PISA survey and scored well above the OECD average in reading literacy, mathematical literacy, and scientific literacy.

More recent evidence is available from the Progress in International Reading Literacy Study (PIRLS), which measured literacy levels among some 2,500 nine- and ten-year-olds from 35 countries. The study was conducted in 2001 by the International Association for the Evaluation of Educational Achievement (IEA). New Zealand students ranked just 13th in overall reading comprehension among PIRLS countries—near the bottom among English-speaking countries and behind countries such as the Czech Republic, Bulgaria, and Lithuania.

Earlier surveys such as the IEA's Third International Math and Science Study (TIMSS) of 1994–95 and the follow-up TIMSS-Repeat study of 1998–99, yielded mixed results. As shown in Table 7.6, New Zealand students ranked 15th in both math and science on TIMSS and 19th in science and 21st in math on TIMSS-Repeat. In the original TIMSS, New Zealand students generally scored below the international average in math and above the international average in science.

New Zealand's overall performance on international surveys masks significant differences in educational outcomes across students from different societal groups. Indeed, a 2002 UNICEF study found that New Zealand had one of the highest proportions of "bottom-end inequality"—a measure of the difference in achievement between children at the bottom and middle of each country's achievement range. Only Belgium ranked below New Zealand among the countries examined.[14]

While interesting and useful in their own right, these surveys provide little guidance as to the impact of school choice or competition on student outcomes in New Zealand.[15] There have been no "U.S.-style" controlled studies of the impact of school choice on educational outcomes in New Zealand, such as have been conducted in Milwaukee, Cleveland, and elsewhere.[16]

The Role of the Education Review Office

The creation of the Education Review Office, whose role is to undertake regular reviews of, and report on, school performance, played an important part in supporting the introduction of school choice (see box). Despite lacking some of the tools needed to properly carry out its task—such as nationally benchmarked assessment data—the ERO nonetheless played an important role in highlighting widespread educational failure in areas such as South Auckland, the Far North, and the East Coast—all areas with high concentrations of Maori or Pacific families, or both.

The combination of school choice and the work of the ERO brought to light educational underperformance that had remained hidden and motivated actions to address that underperformance. It also allowed students from poor families to escape underperforming schools that had remained resistant to previous school improvement efforts. A good example is provided by South Auckland, where the quality of schooling had been a cause for concern as far back as the 1970s. Despite its lengthy history of educational underperformance and various efforts to address it, a significant proportion of children in South Auckland continued to receive substandard schooling in the mid-1990s. According to a 1996 ERO report, 42 percent of the schools in the South Auckland suburbs of Mangere and Otara were performing very poorly or underperforming.[17]

The Education Review Office

The Education Review Office (ERO) is a New Zealand government department whose purpose is evaluating and reporting publicly on education in schools, early childhood centres. . . . ERO's findings inform decisions and choices made by parents, educators, managers and others, at the individual school and early childhood level and at the national level by government policy makers.

ERO carries out reviews of individual schools and groups of schools, conducts homeschool reviews, provides contract evaluation services and undertakes national evaluations of education issues. ERO publishes national reports which evaluate specific education issues using its inspection evidence.

Reviews of schools and centres are scheduled on the basis of prior performance, current risk appraisal and general review frequency. Schools and early childhood centers are reviewed on average every three years. Reviews are more frequent in particular cases where the performance of a school or center is poor and there are risks to the education and safety of the students.

ERO reports on individual schools and centers are freely available to the public. They are available on ERO's website, or can be obtained from the individual school or center or from any ERO office.

SOURCE: Education Review Office, *The Role of the Education Review Office in New Zealand Education,* http://www.ero.govt.nz/about/roleleaf.htm.

Implications for Future Reform Efforts

One of the key lessons from the New Zealand experience with school reform is that we should be careful about drawing too many lessons from it. The experience is neither a ringing endorsement of market competition, nor is it a "cautionary tale" for countries considering similar moves. The New Zealand reforms, although "more complete and far bolder than is typically the case for major educational reforms,"[18] were, at best, only partial. As a result, they provide few lessons on the desirability of introducing school choice but many on how to do it better.

A major weakness in the New Zealand reforms is that, although they facilitated greater competition and choice in the education system, they did little to create the conditions under which market competition could work. For example:

- New Zealand never had a voucher system per se. The state continued to fund inputs such as property, teacher salaries, and operating costs instead of funding outputs, and hence funding was not fully demand driven (although some of the underlying components of the funding system were). In that sense, the funding system lacked an essential characteristic of a voucher.
- The accountability measures included in the Tomorrow's Schools reforms had only limited effect. In that sense, New Zealand schools are more appropriately considered "schools with charters" than "charter schools" in the American sense.
- Effective choice was limited to state-owned schools because private schools received a much lower subsidy than state schools and could not access equity funding aimed at helping schools overcome barriers to learning for students from low-income communities. Both of those factors limited access to independent schools, especially for those on low incomes.
- The lower subsidy and the failure to provide equity-related subsidies discouraged independent schools from expanding and discouraged the establishment of new independent schools.
- Teacher pay and conditions continued to be set centrally through negotiations between the Ministry of Education and the relevant teachers' union.
- Legislative restrictions limited the degree to which schools could be restructured, merged, or taken over by other schools.
- The Ministry of Education retained control of the allocation of school property and, beyond a certain point, refused to allocate new classrooms to expanding schools when neighboring schools had excess capacity.
- It proved difficult to close schools whose rolls were falling. School closures consumed significant amounts of bureaucratic effort and took a long time to carry out.
- The governance structure for state and state-integrated schools was centrally determined, leaving little scope for diversity in

governance structures, especially in communities where parent-dominated boards were unsuitable. Although the government has introduced some flexibility in governance structures, it too is centrally controlled and only a handful of schools have made use of such arrangements.

- A new centrally determined national curriculum was introduced.
- The vast majority of new teachers were taught at a small number of state-owned colleges of education.

As noted above, the New Zealand reforms did little to open up the supply side of the education market. The central government retained control over virtually all supply-side decisions in the public school sector, including the creation of new schools and the expansion or restructuring of existing ones. The introduction of school choice was a demand-side reform that could succeed only if it was accompanied by freeing the supply side of the school market.

In many cases, the mechanisms existed to allow more flexibility and diversity in the provision of schooling, but they went largely unused. For example, the Tomorrow's Schools reforms provided an avenue for the creation of designated charter schools. Although the legislative requirements for establishing such schools are not onerous, the first one was not approved by the minister of education until 1999—fully 10 years after the legislation came into effect. Even now, there are only a small number of such schools.

Critics such as Edward B. Fiske and Helen F. Ladd, authors of *When Schools Compete: A Cautionary Tale*, have raised a number of criticisms of the New Zealand reforms. Broadly speaking, their concerns are that the reforms have increased ethnic polarization of enrollments, have led to the emergence of loser schools, and have failed to balance the interests of competing education sector stakeholders.[19]

Some observers have challenged many of the criticisms of the reforms advanced by Fiske and Ladd and others. For example, Mark Harrison argues that socioeconomic polarization actually decreased after dezoning took effect in 1990, citing evidence from the Ministry of Education–funded Smithfield Project to support his contention. He has also argued that

- some ethnic polarization observed after the removal of zoning may have resulted from "positive" factors, such as the establishment of Maori education options like Kura Kaupapa Maori, and
- critics are overly focused on the impact of dezoning on schools, rather than its impact on students and student achievement. As a result, roll declines at schools are seen as necessarily a bad thing, when in fact they may be a good thing if students are leaving inferior schools for better ones.[20]

Merrifield argues that stratification is a predictable result of parental choice among highly regulated, relatively uniform schools because it means that remaining differences like student body composition dominate school choices.[21]

Researchers Mark Harrison, Ron Crawford, and Woodfield and Gunby all raise a number of technical and policy issues relating to the Tomorrow's Schools reforms and the criticisms leveled at them. Interested readers should refer to their publications for a more detailed discussion of the reforms and a more thorough assessment of the work by Fiske and Ladd.[22]

An additional point is that many of the cautionary tales told by Fiske and Ladd are in fact criticisms of other elements of the New Zealand school policy environment, not of school choice itself. Those criticisms include

- the reluctance on the part of authorities to close failing schools,[23]
- the failure of the Ministry of Education to address the problems of failing schools,[24]
- the failure to retain central control over some operational functions such as combating truancy,[25]
- the one-size-fits-all school governance structure,[26] and
- limits on the establishment of schools.[27]

Fiske and Ladd also highlight a number of positive points about the Tomorrow's Schools reforms—something that other critics of the New Zealand experience with school choice routinely ignore. For example, Fiske and Ladd argue that

- "there is little doubt that parental choice made it possible for many students to escape from low-performing schools and thereby improve their educational experiences";[28]

- "one potential benefit of the new governance arrangement is that the failures of such schools are more visible and less easily ignored than under the old system";[29]
- "the country's experience with Tomorrow's Schools provides considerable vindication for the notion of self-governance in and of itself";[30]
- "such dramatic transformations of whole schools would not have been possible under the system that Tomorrow's Schools replaced"; [31] and
- "we have little doubt that the system has been beneficial for many students and schools."[32]

There is no question that the reforms could have been better designed and better implemented, as supporters and opponents have both pointed out. Such is the benefit of hindsight and the relaxation of political constraints. Yet, despite weaknesses in the design and implementation of the Tomorrow's Schools reform program, Fiske and Ladd conclude:

> For those who oppose such reforms, these policy conclusions may provide additional ammunition against them. We would argue, though, that none of the negatives is devastating. What matters is that these issues are addressed, not that they arise. Moreover, just because New Zealand implemented these ideas one way need not mean that other countries would have to follow the same course.[33]

Fiske and Ladd also note that there is little desire in New Zealand to reverse the Tomorrow's Schools reforms:

> In the course of our travels and research for this book, we encountered literally no one, not even the most vocal critics of the new fiscal and enrolment policies, who wanted to go back to the old highly regulated system.[34]

The policy reversals introduced to date—the abolition of bulk funding, the reintroduction and subsequent tightening of zoning, and the abolition of the TIE program—have all been politically motivated, instead of reflecting evidence of policy failure.

Although the issue of whether the New Zealand reforms were successful is of interest, what is of greater interest looking forward is whether a better-designed school choice policy would yield better outcomes. For the reasons cited above, New Zealand may not provide much of a guide. The cautionary tale from New Zealand's experience is that the introduction of school choice needs to be done right. Not all school choice policy frameworks are created equal. Like U.S. charter school laws, there can be good and bad ones. Half measures cannot be expected to yield the full demand- and supply-side response needed to generate the benefits expected from the introduction of choice. A more comprehensive reform is required to drive the transformation of the education system. The New Zealand choice reforms would not meet the minimal criteria for school system transformation set out by Merrifield in this volume, namely:

- minimal regulation of private schools beyond what applies to all entities serving the general public (i.e., few formal entry barriers, allowing opportunities for schools to specialize); and
- keeping informal entry barriers low (i.e., nondiscrimination in funding between public and private schools), minimizing uncertainty about the scope of the market, avoiding controls on tuition fees, and allowing private tuition copayments.

Looking internationally, many countries operate demand-side financing policies—on both a large and a small scale. However, the degree of regulation of private schools differs markedly across countries, with some placing a significant amount of regulation on schools and others less.[35] Despite the differences in regulatory environments, one stylized fact emerges: higher funding of private schools tends to be associated with increased regulation of private schools (see Table 7.7).

For that reason, the issue of government funding of private schools is controversial among supporters of educational freedom. Although the concern that government assistance leads to government regulation and control is real, it need not be that way. Funding and regulation are two separate policy instruments, and there is no reason why a well-designed funding policy that funds students in public and private schools in a neutral fashion must necessarily be accompanied by bad regulation.

Conclusion

The Tomorrow's Schools and subsequent reforms ushered in a new era of choice, competition, and self-managing schools for New

Table 7.7
DEGREE OF REGULATION AND FUNDING OF PRIVATE SCHOOLS,
VARIOUS COUNTRIES, 1999

		Degree of Regulation		
		Low	Medium	High
Level of Public Funding	High	Australia	Denmark	Austria, Belgium, France, Germany, Luxembourg, Netherlands, Norway, Portugal, Spain
	Medium	New Zealand		British Columbia (Canada)
	Low	United Kingdom		Greece Italy

SOURCE: Adapted from Nancy Kober, "Lessons from Other Countries about Private School Aid," Center on Education Policy, Washington, 1999, pp. 10–11.

Zealand. The reforms were by no means perfectly designed or flaw-lessly implemented. The impact of the Tomorrow's Schools and subsequent reforms has not been formally examined by researchers and is therefore unknown. Nonetheless, the reforms created a more competitive environment for schools (at least within the public sector), increased choice for all, eliminated an entire level of education bureaucracy, provided communities with greater voice in schooling, and gave schools freedom and autonomy to better meet the needs of local communities. The reforms revealed a significant demand for educational choice—particularly among students from low-income families who were being badly served by the centralized education system.

So what is the outlook for the global school choice movement? In my view, there is reason to be optimistic. The choice movement, for want of a better phrase, is large when measured on a global scale. It comprises a range of policies that include the removal of school zoning restrictions, charter schools, demand-side financing initiatives such as student-based funding, scholarships and vouchers, management of public schools by the private sector, and home schooling.

In the United States, existing voucher programs in places such as Cleveland, Milwaukee, and Florida are relatively small and provide little indication of what could be expected under a significant market-based reform. Nonetheless, the No Child Left Behind Act (NCLB) and the 2002 Supreme Court decision in *Zelman v. Simmons-Harris* have both provided renewed impetus to the school choice movement in the United States. In 2003, Colorado governor Bill Owens signed into law the Colorado Opportunity Contract Pilot Program, which provides vouchers to low-income students in low-performing school districts (currently being challenged in the courts). The first federally funded school voucher program recently took effect in Washington, D.C. Response to the program has been overwhelming, with the number of applications more than double the places available.[36] The Supplemental Education Services (SES) provisions of the NCLB have led to the development of a significant tutoring market, with more than 1,000 providers delivering SES services.

Although much of the discussion of school choice focuses on developments in the United States, the reality is that school choice is a global phenomenon. Demand-side financing programs such as vouchers and subsidies to private schools operate in many countries—often with far less fanfare and far less controversy than in the United States and New Zealand. Many of those school choice programs are large relative to current U.S. initiatives. They are not simply voucher programs. For example, the Educational Service Contracting program in the Philippines finances private school attendance for around 280,000 students annually. In Côte d'Ivoire in the late 1990s, more than 40 percent of all students in private schools (some 160,000 students) were there under a government sponsorship scheme. National voucher-type programs operate in the Netherlands, Denmark, and Chile. The Netherlands provides equivalent funding to state and nonstate schools, while Denmark funds private schools at around 80 percent of state school levels.

Other choice-based policies are also significant and growing. More than 900,000 students from poor communities attend Fe y Alegría schools operated by the Jesuits in Latin America. The city of Bogotá, Colombia, contracts for the private management of 25 public schools with more than 26,000 students. The number of public schools managed by private education management organizations in the United States stood at 463 in 2003–04—more than three times the number in 1998–99. More than one million children were being home schooled in the United States in 2003—up 29 percent since 1999. In the United Kingdom, academies and specialist schools are providing increased choice for families, and local education authorities have been contracting out some of their services to the private sector since the late 1990s.[37]

The road to school choice is, and no doubt will continue to be, marked by setbacks. Choice-based reform efforts will need to be sustained if they are to overcome the agenda-driven "No Teachers' Union Left Behind" policies favored by many opponents of school choice. The changes to zoning, the abolition of the TIE program in New Zealand, and the abolition of the private school tax credit in the province of Ontario (Canada) are good examples of politically motivated reversals of school choice policies.

What of the future for New Zealand? The Tomorrow's Schools and subsequent reforms were world leading. One can only hope that New Zealand can shake off the ideology-driven reversals of the recent past. The future may be uncertain, given the recent setbacks, but supporters remain optimistic that progress can be made on the school choice front. There are several reasons for that. First, there was no policy or research basis for the post-1999 reversals of market-based policies in New Zealand. They were purely political decisions to please vested interests. Second, the need for reform has not gone away. International surveys suggest that, although the school system delivers a good education to many in New Zealand, it continues to fail far too many families—especially those in lower socioeconomic groups. Third, the primary and secondary school sector in New Zealand remains the "outlier," with both the early childhood sector and the tertiary education sector being much more choice based.

Finally, opponents of school choice in New Zealand—well-funded teachers' unions, parts of the education academic community, and the government—are finding themselves increasingly isolated from the mainstream of thinking on school reform. Support for choice-based reforms spans the political spectrum, including think tanks such as the Cato Institute and the Heritage Foundation in the United States, "third-way" Democrats in the United States, the "new" Labour Party in the UK, and organizations such as the Black Alliance for Educational Options and the Hispanic Council for Reform and Educational Options.

Notes

I would like to thank Martin Connelly, Roger Kerr, John Merrifield, Joy Quigley, David Salisbury, and Sue Thorne for helpful comments. The views expressed and any errors are mine.

1. See, for example, Alan Woodfield and Philip Gunby, "The Marketization of New Zealand Schools: Assessing Fiske and Ladd," *Journal of Economic Literature* 41 (September 2003): 863–84; *The Tomorrow's Schools Reforms: An American Perspective,* ed. Edward B. Fiske and Helen F. Ladd, Institute of Policy Studies Policy Paper no. 6, Wellington, 2000; and Mark Harrison, *Education Matters: Government, Markets and New Zealand Schools* (Wellington: Education Forum, 2004), www.educationforum. org.nz.

2. For a more detailed description of the existing school enrollment scheme legislation and its recent history, see Norman LaRocque and Jonathan Kaye, "Enrolment Scheme Provisions in New Zealand," Education Forum Briefing Paper no. 3, Wellington, 2002, www.educationforum.org.nz.

3. The average state per pupil cost equals the average per pupil cost of operational grant funding, teacher salaries, and an estimate of the cost of capital.

4. Matthew Ladner and Hon Maurice McTigue, "School Choice, Kiwi-style," Frontier Public Policy Institute, 1999, http://www.fcpp.org/pdf/kiwistyle.pdf; and David Hughes and Hugh Lauder, "School Choice Equals Greater Disparity in New Zealand," *Teacher Newsmagazine* 14, no. 7 (May–June 2002), www.bctf.ca.

5. Harrison, p. 233.

6. David Hughes et al., "Markets in Education: Testing the Polarisation Thesis," Report Four, Smithfield Project, 1996, p. 13.

7. Matt O'Sullivan, "Student Exodus Hurting Business," *Dominion Post*, January 22, 2004, p. A6.

8. Hugh Lauder et al., "The Creation of Market Competition for Education in New Zealand," Report One, Smithfield Project, 1994, p. 28.

9. Ibid., p. 44. For a fuller discussion of dezoning and its impact, see Harrison, pp. 219–33.

10. Education Forum, "Ministry's *iwi* Partnerships: A Flagship for Education," *Subtext*, November 2002, www.educationforum.org.nz.

11. Ministry of Education, Data Management and Analysis Division, *Education Statistics of New Zealand for 2003* (Wellington: Ministry of Education, 2004), p. 69.

12. Data for independent schools are for the period July 2002 to July 2003 and are from www.minedu.govt.nz. Catholic school data are from New Zealand Catholic Education Office, "Catholic Schools Continue Their Upward Roll Trend," news release, July 8, 2003.

13. Deborah Hill Cone, "Private Schools Hold Sway but the State Gets a Tick," *National Business Review*, June 13, 2003, p. 16.

14. UNICEF, *A League Table of Educational Disadvantage in Rich Nations*, Innocenti Report Card, no. 4, November 2002.

15. This point is supported by Woodfield and Gunby, p. 880.

16. For an overview of several of those studies, see Jay P. Greene, "A Survey of Results from Voucher Experiments: Where We Are and What We Know," in *Can the Market Save Our Schools?* ed. Claudia R. Hepburn (Vancouver: Fraser Institute, 2001), pp. 121–49.

17. Education Review Office, *Improving Schooling in Mangere and Otara*, Wellington, 1996, www.ero.govt.nz.

18. Fiske and Ladd, "The Tomorrow's Schools Reforms," p. 1.

19. For a summary of the book, see ibid.

20. See Harrison, pp. 219–33.

21. John Merrifield, "Parental Choice as an Education Reform Catalyst: Global Lessons," Education Forum, Wellington, forthcoming 2005.

22. Harrison, pp. 219–33; Ron Crawford, "Commentary," in *The Tomorrow's Schools Reforms;* and Woodfield and Gunby, pp. 863–84.

23. Edward B. Fiske and Helen F. Ladd, *When Schools Compete: A Cautionary Tale* (Washington: Brookings Institution Press, 2000), p. 288.

24. Ibid., p. 289.

25. Ibid., p. 295.

26. Ibid.

27. Ibid., p. 303.

28. Ibid., p. 288.

29. Ibid., p. 288.

30. Ibid., p. 292.

31. Ibid., p. 292.

32. Ibid., p. 304.

33. Ibid., p. 281.

34. Ibid., p. 72.

35. Pauline Nesdale, "International Perspectives on Government Funding of Non-government Schools," Briefing Paper no. 7, Education Forum, Wellington, 2003.

36. "Huge Demand for School Vouchers in Capital City," *USA Today,* June 11, 2004, www.usatoday.com.

37. For a summary of private participation in education, see Norman LaRocque, *Private Participation in Education*, Speech delivered to the Rotary Club of Palmerston North, Education Forum, Wellington, 2004, www.educationforum.org.nz.

8. Evidence on the Effects of Choice and Accountability from International Student Achievement Tests

Ludger Woessmann

Many scholars have long argued that institutional setups that ensured choice and accountability in the education system might improve students' learning opportunities.[1] However, evidence on such effects is hard to come by, particularly because systemic features such as choice and accountability usually do not vary much within a single country. For example, central exams, which are one mechanism for introducing accountability, tend to be a national feature (with the exceptions of Canada and Germany, where they are a regional feature), so they are either present in the whole country or not at all. Furthermore, choice and accountability can often be expected to exert their impact in a systemic way, affecting not only individual schools but the whole system. For example, the prevalence of private schools may affect not only the performance of students in those schools but also the performance of students in public schools that are located nearby and exposed to competition from the private schools. Thus, the fact that three-quarters of Dutch students attend privately managed schools may have systemic effects on the whole Dutch school system, relative to school systems with small shares of private schools.

Another problem with evidence from within single countries is that where within-country institutional variation exists, it is often not random but purposefully introduced by choices of individuals who may also differ along other lines, thereby confounding any empirical identification of the actual effects of the institutional features.[2]

Therefore, in this chapter I look at a different kind of variation in the prevalence of choice and accountability—the variation that exists across countries. For example, I ask whether students perform better in terms of their educational knowledge in countries where parents have a lot of choice about sending their children to privately managed schools. To answer that question, I use data from several recent international student achievement tests, which provide information on students' educational achievement that is comparable across many countries. For that reason, the research is truly "looking worldwide," in the sense that it looks at as many countries as possible in order to analyze what countries can learn from each other in terms of the effects of school choice and accountability.

Why Should Institutions Matter?

Why would we expect institutions that introduce choice and accountability to have an effect on student learning? The background of these considerations is that in the private business sector, market competition tends to discipline firms to work effectively because they would otherwise fail to profit. Inefficiency leads to higher costs and higher prices—practically an invitation to competitors to lure away customers.

However, all over the world, countries finance and manage the great majority of their schools publicly.[3] The relative lack of competition in the K–12 education sector tends to dull incentives to improve quality and restrain costs.[4] Moreover, in the public system, the ability of parents and students to ensure that they receive a high-quality education is often constrained by enormous obstacles to leaving bad schools.

That is the reason why institutions that ensure choice and accountability may be expected to improve student performance. Such institutions create incentives for school personnel to use their resources in ways that maximize performance. Therefore, those institutions may ultimately lead to improved student learning.[5]

The choice and accountability that different institutions can introduce are not limited to parental choice of privately managed schools. Choice also includes, for example, choice of schools and teachers in terms of their ability to make autonomous decisions. Likewise, accountability may be aimed at schools or at students, through such institutional features as external exit examinations and regular monitoring of student progress by tests and exams.

How to Get Evidence on the Effects of Institutions

How can we test whether the hypothesized effects of choice and accountability prevail in the real world? And how can we estimate how large the effects are? To get evidence on the institutional effects, one needs *variation* in the institutional factors. For example, you want to learn whether a system with choice performs differently than one that does not have choice. Lacking such variation, one obviously cannot provide evidence on the effects. Comparing two systems that both have choice, or two that do not, cannot tell us whether choice has an effect on performance.

Variation in institutional factors such as choice and accountability are often not found *within a single country*: You either have it or you don't. That is most apparent in the case of system-wide central exams, which are either given to all students in the system or to none. There is no way to provide evidence on the performance effect of this institution from within a country, because one can compare only persons who are all "treated" by central exams or only persons who are all not "treated." Because most of the extant research tends to focus on individual countries, the potentially important effects of choice and accountability tend to be missed in most empirical studies of the determinants of educational performance.

So, how can we get evidence on institutional effects? The method I use is to look at the institutional variation that exists *across countries*. Some countries have central exam systems, others do not. People in some countries are free to choose their schools, while people in other countries are not. I use that kind of variation to see which institutional factors are related to better student learning and which are not. For example, I estimate whether students show better educational performance in countries where parents and schools have certain kinds of choices relative to countries where parents and schools do not have those choices.

The Data: International Student Achievement Tests

The data that enable this cross-country identification of institutional effects are international student achievement tests. Those tests quantify the educational performance of students in subjects such as math, science, and reading by using the same test items in all participating countries. Thus, they provide measures of educational performance that are directly comparable across countries. Furthermore, all the international student achievement tests use random sampling methods to draw representative samples of students in each participating country.

In particular, the research summarized in this chapter uses data from four different recent international student achievement tests. The first one is the Third International Mathematics and Science Study (TIMSS), conducted in 1995 with data released in 1997. TIMSS was conducted by the International Association for the Evaluation of Educational Achievement (IEA), an independent cooperation of national research institutes and governmental research agencies. TIMSS targeted representative samples of students in the two adjacent grades with the largest share of 13-year-olds (usually seventh and eighth grade). For the analyses conducted in this paper, TIMSS yielded internationally comparable data for 266,545 students from 6,107 schools in 39 countries.[6]

The second source of data is the TIMSS-Repeat study. The IEA replicated the TIMSS test in 1999 under the name TIMSS-Repeat, with data released in 2001. TIMSS-Repeat targeted the upper of the two grades tested in TIMSS (usually the eighth grade), covering 180,544 students in 38 countries.[7] The sample of participating countries differed considerably between the two tests, so that the pooled TIMSS/TIMSS-Repeat database contains 54 different countries (447,089 students).

The third source of data is the Programme for International Student Assessment, known as PISA. The Organisation for Economic Co-operation and Development (OECD) conducted PISA in 2000 with data released in 2002, which targeted 15-year-old students. The PISA database covers 175,227 students in reading, 96,855 in math, and 96,758 in science in 32 countries.[8]

Finally, I use data from the Progress in International Reading Literacy Study (PIRLS) conducted by the IEA in 2001 with data released in 2003. While the focus of the previous studies was on secondary schools, PIRLS tested the reading performance of 140,626 primary school students in 35 countries.[9] The target population of PIRLS was the upper of the two grades with the highest share of nine-year-olds of a country (usually the fourth grade).

Table 8.1 is a plot of the aggregate performance of the countries participating in each of the four tests. Each test was scaled so as to yield an international mean performance of 500 among the countries participating in the respective test, with an international standard deviation of 100.[10] As is evident from Table 8.1, the United States performed around the international mean in the secondary school

Table 8.1
AGGREGATE PERFORMANCE ON INTERNATIONAL STUDENT ACHIEVEMENT TESTS

Table 8.1A STUDENT PERFORMANCE ON THE THIRD INTERNATIONAL MATHEMATICS AND SCIENCE STUDY (TIMSS)		Table 8.1B STUDENT PERFORMANCE ON THE THIRD INTERNATIONAL MATHEMATICS AND SCIENCE STUDY-REPEAT (TIMSS-R)		Table 8.1C STUDENT PERFORMANCE ON THE PROGRAMME FOR INTERNATIONAL STUDENT ASSESSMENT (PISA)		Table 8.1D STUDENT PERFORMANCE ON THE PROGRESS IN INTERNATIONAL READING LITERACY STUDY (PIRLS)	
Country	Score	Country	Score	Country	Score	Country	Score
Singapore	599	Singapore	586	Japan	543	Sweden	561
Republic of Korea	571	Taiwan	577	Hong Kong	542	Netherlands	554
Japan	570	Republic of Korea	568	Republic of Korea	541	England	553
Belgium, Flemish	551	Japan	565	Finland	540	Bulgaria	550
Czech Republic	549	Hong Kong	556	Canada	532	Latvia	545
Hong Kong	542	Belgium, Flemish	547	New Zealand	531	Canada	544
Bulgaria	538	Netherlands	543	Australia	530	Hungary	543
Netherlands	534	Hungary	542	United Kingdom	528	Lithuania	543
Slovenia	532	Slovakia	535	Austria	514	**United States**	**542**
Austria	531	Australia	533	Ireland	514	Italy	541
Hungary	528	Slovenia	532	Sweden	513	Germany	539
Slovakia	527	Canada	532	Belgium	508	Czech Republic	537
Australia	519	Czech Republic	530	France	507	New Zealand	529
Ireland	515	Russian Federation	528	Switzerland	506	Hong Kong	528
Russian Federation	515	Finland	528	Iceland	506	Russian Federation	528
Switzerland	514	England	517	Norway	501	Singapore	528
Canada	513	Bulgaria	515	Czech Republic	500	Scotland	528
England	512	**United States**	**509**	**United States**	**499**	France	525
Thailand	509	Morocco	506	Denmark	497	Greece	524
Germany	506	Latvia	504	Liechtenstein	491	Slovakia	518

(continued next page)

137

Table 8.1 continued

Table 8.1A
STUDENT PERFORMANCE ON THE THIRD INTERNATIONAL MATHEMATICS AND SCIENCE STUDY (TIMSS)

Country	Score
Israel	505
Sweden	505
United States	**505**
New Zealand	497
France	495
Norway	494
Belgium, French	487
Scotland	487
Spain	482
Iceland	476
Denmark	471
Latvia	469
Romania	469
Greece	468
Cyprus	451
Lithuania	446
Portugal	446
Iran	434
Kuwait	397
Colombia	388
South Africa	336

Table 8.1B
STUDENT PERFORMANCE ON THE THIRD INTERNATIONAL MATHEMATICS AND SCIENCE STUDY-REPEAT (TIMSS-R)

Country	Score
New Zealand	501
Italy	486
Lithuania	485
Thailand	475
Romania	472
Cyprus	468
Israel	467
Moldova	464
Macedonia	453
Jordan	439
Tunisia	439
Iran	435
Turkey	431
Indonesia	419
Chile	406
Philippines	345
Morocco	330
South Africa	259

Table 8.1C
STUDENT PERFORMANCE ON THE PROGRAMME FOR INTERNATIONAL STUDENT ASSESSMENT (PISA)

Country	Score
Hungary	488
Germany	487
Spain	487
Poland	477
Italy	474
Russian Federation	467
Greece	461
Portugal	461
Latvia	460
Luxembourg	443
Israel	440
Bulgaria	436
Thailand	433
Mexico	410
Chile	403
Argentina	401
Macedonia	385
Indonesia	377
Albania	369
Brazil	368
Peru	317

Table 8.1D
STUDENT PERFORMANCE ON THE PROGRESS IN INTERNATIONAL READING LITERACY STUDY (PIRLS)

Country	Score
Iceland	512
Romania	512
Israel	509
Slovenia	502
Norway	499
Cyprus	494
Moldova	492
Turkey	449
Macedonia	442
Colombia	422
Argentina	420
Iran	414
Kuwait	396
Morocco	350
Belize	327

Note: For all four parts of Table 8.1, mean = 500; standard deviation = 100.

tests of TIMSS, TIMSS-Repeat, and PISA and substantially above the international mean in the primary school PIRLS test.

The question addressed in this chapter is whether, on average, the countries performing better than the United States on these tests feature an institutional setup of their education systems that gives a bigger role to choice and accountability, after holding constant other influence factors such as parental background, the development level of a country, and the mean educational expenditure per student of a country. Given that the Netherlands (the country with the largest share of privately managed schools) and Japan (the country with the largest share of private schools that are financially independent from government funding)[11] are two countries that perform consistently better than the United States, there seems to be some preliminary indication that choice might matter for student performance.

However, the research presented in this chapter goes far beyond comparing aggregate performance across countries. It analyzes performance at the level of the individual student, using individual student-level data not only on educational performance in math, science, and reading but also combining those data with extensive background information on other potential influence factors. Those include dozens of indicators of family background, mostly taken from student background questionnaires (and parental background questionnaires in the case of primary school PIRLS); several indicators of the resource endowment of the specific class or school, mostly taken from teacher and school background questionnaires; and several indicators of institutional features of the school systems, mostly taken from school background questionnaires. Among the latter are several indicators of the extent of choice and accountability in the specific school of each tested student.

Although the topic of this chapter is the effect of the latter institutions, the general pattern of results on the effect of family background and resource endowments should be briefly mentioned. All studies find very strong family background effects on educational performance, with students from better-educated homes with a higher socioeconomic status performing substantially better.[12] By contrast, most studies usually find no consistent effect of resource endowments.[13] Students in countries with higher spending levels or smaller classes do not tend to perform better than students in less well-equipped countries.

Private School Management: Choice for Parents

To estimate the effects of institutions that introduce choice and accountability, the research summarized in this chapter employs econometric techniques that control for differences in family background and the level of resources devoted to education.[14] What do the summarized studies find in terms of the effects of institutions? The first institutional feature analyzed is the availability of private schools, which provide choice for parents.[15]

The bottom line of the results on private schools is that students perform better in countries where more schools are privately managed. For example, among the OECD countries participating in TIMSS, students scored 11 test score points better in math and 9 in science if the share of enrollment in privately managed schools of a country was 1 standard deviation (or 14 percentage points) higher. Considering that one grade-level equivalent (the unconditional performance difference between seventh and eighth grade) in the U.S. school system was roughly equal to 25 points on the TIMSS test, that is a very large effect indeed. Put differently, students in countries that had a private school sector that was 35 percentage points larger (as measured by the enrollment share) on average performed better by the equivalent of a whole year's learning. The effect was even larger when only those private schools were considered that were financially independent from government funding, in the sense that they received less than half of their core funding from government agencies.

Also, students from countries with a higher share of public educational spending going to private institutions performed better. If the share of public funds going to independent private schools rose by 7 percentage points (or 1 standard deviation), there was a 20-point increase in math achievement. In sum, student performance is higher in education systems where taxpayers' money is allocated by private schools rather than by the public schooling system.

The evidence discussed so far, using TIMSS data, is based on country-wide measures of the extent of private schooling. This does not allow for a direct assessment of the relative performance of public and private schools, because TIMSS does not provide school-level data on whether individual tested schools are public or private.

However, measuring the system-level effect of private school management may be the appropriate way to estimate the general systemic effect of the competitive environment prevailing in the different education systems, because increased competition from private schools may also positively affect the effectiveness of resource use in nearby public schools.

By contrast, PISA for the first time provides specific school-level data on public versus private management and financing. In particular, in PISA there is information for each tested school both on whether the school is privately or publicly managed and on how large its share of public funding is. Public school management is defined as schools managed directly or indirectly by a public education authority, government agency, or governing board appointed by government or elected by public franchise, whereas private school management is defined as schools managed directly or indirectly by a nongovernmental organization, for example a church, trade union, business, or other private institution. The share of public funding is defined as the percentage of total school funding coming from government sources (at different levels), as opposed to such private contributions as fees and donations.

Looking across all countries, the result is that students perform better if their specific school is privately managed. The size of the performance difference between privately and publicly managed schools is between 16 and 20 PISA test score points in the three different subjects. Once the mode of management is held constant, though, the share of public funding does not show an impact on student performance in math and science. In reading, it shows a positive impact.

That means that it seems to be good for students' educational performance if schools are privately operated but mainly publicly financed. The latter effect might be explained by financial constraints for children from poor families. Poor families may be constrained in their choices if there is no working voucher system. In such a case, some public funding may help those families to exert their choices for privately managed schools, thereby helping the educational achievement of their children.

School Autonomy: Choice for Schools and Teachers

The second set of institutional features analyzed is the extent of autonomy that schools have, which indicates the extent to which schools and teachers can make their own choices.

141

The general pattern of results on school autonomy is that students perform better in schools that have autonomy in process and personnel decisions. Those decisions include such things as deciding on the purchase of supplies and on budget allocations within schools; hiring and rewarding teachers (within a given budget); and choosing textbooks, instructional methods, and the like. That is, there are positive performance effects of choice not only for parents but also for schools in those specific decisionmaking areas.

Similarly, students perform better if their teachers have both incentives and power to select appropriate teaching methods. In this sense, there are also positive performance effects of choice for teachers—as long as they are held accountable for what they are doing.

Holding Schools and Students Accountable

In addition to the effects of choice, it has been argued that institutional features that introduce accountability into education systems may also affect their performance. The challenge for the institutional setup of school systems is to create a set of incentives that encourage school personnel to behave in ways that do not necessarily further their own interests but rather the interest of student learning. For instance, without the right incentives, teachers may avoid using the most promising teaching techniques, preferring to use the techniques they find most convenient. In terms of the institutional setup of the school system, one might speculate that if a nation assesses the performance of students with some sort of national exam and uses this information to monitor teachers, teachers will put aside their other interests and focus mainly on raising student achievement.

The evidence from the international student achievement tests shows exactly that. Students perform substantially better in countries that have external exit exam systems than in countries without external exit exam systems. That is true in TIMSS, in TIMSS-Repeat, and in PISA, as well as in other previous international achievement tests.[16] By and large, the evidence suggests that the effect is at least as large as a whole U.S. grade-level equivalent. That is, student performance is immensely higher where schools and students are held accountable by external exams.

Similarly, students perform better where parents take an interest in teaching matters, suggesting positive effects both of parental choices and of parents holding schools and children accountable.

Also, students perform better where teachers place a lot of emphasis on monitoring student progress by regular tests and exams. That is additional evidence that accountability for students increases their educational performance. Furthermore, that is the case in primary school (PIRLS) as well as in secondary school.

External Exams as the "Currency" of Choice-Based School Systems

So far, the institutions of school autonomy (choice for schools) and external exams (accountability for schools) have been considered as unrelated institutional features. However, there are reasons to expect that there is a complementarity between external exams and school autonomy, in the sense that the one is particularly effective if the other is also in place. Put differently, external exams are a prerequisite for decentralized, choice-based school systems to function properly. In this sense, external exams are the "currency" of decentralized school systems.

In the economic system, money is an institutional feature that allows one to value and compare different objects. As is well known, this kind of price system creates knowledge that no single person can gather. External exams can provide such "price information" to the education system. As long as they are instituted as standardized tests by independent institutions, it is probably not key whether the tests are publicly or privately provided, whether they are regional or national in coverage, or whether they are comprehensive or specific for certain school types. What is key is that the examinations are external to the individual school, providing independent and comparable information on how the school performs.

Parents can use the information provided by external exams to make proper choices. That is the core of the idea of accountability: It creates real competition where before no uniform yardstick was available for making informed choices. Once this "price system" is in place, one can leave schools as much autonomy as possible, and the system of decentralized, autonomous schools can be expected to work much better than any centralized system could.

That assertion can be corroborated by evidence from the cross-country pattern of student performance. The results show that external exit exams improve educational performance and that school

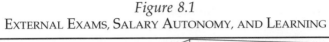

Figure 8.1
EXTERNAL EXAMS, SALARY AUTONOMY, AND LEARNING

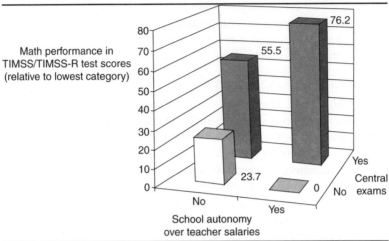

SOURCE: Ludger Woessmann, "The Effect Heterogeneity of Central Exams: Evidence from TIMSS, TIMSS-Repeat and PISA," CESifo Working Paper 1330, Munich, 2004.

autonomy is better in systems with external exams. In several decisionmaking areas, external exams even turn an initially negative autonomy effect around into a positive effect.

One such case is depicted in Figure 8.1, which plots students' math performance in TIMSS and TIMSS-Repeat under the four conditions resulting from the presence and absence of central exams and school autonomy about teacher salaries: the performance of students in schools without salary autonomy in systems without central exams, with autonomy but without central exams, without autonomy but with central exams, and with both autonomy and central exams. Performance is depicted relative to the condition with the lowest performance, which is the condition of salary autonomy without central exams in this case.

As Figure 8.1 shows, school autonomy regarding teacher salaries has a *negative* effect on student performance in systems without central exams. In systems with central exams, student performance is generally higher than in systems without central exams, in both the case with and the case without school autonomy. In addition, however, it is striking that the effect of school autonomy on student performance in systems with central exams is turned completely around: salary autonomy of schools has *positive* effects on student performance in systems with central exams.

That is strong evidence of the complementarity of accountability and decentralized choice. Without the accountability introduced by central exams, schools behave opportunistically because their local opportunistic behavior cannot be externally observed and thus cannot be sanctioned. Hence school decisionmakers do not feel obliged to set teacher salaries so as to contribute to enhancing student performance but can use their decisionmaking autonomy to promote other interests. In contrast, central exams provide information about whether the schools perform well or not, so that parents and supervisory authorities can draw possible conclusions from school behavior that weakens performance. That creates incentives for the decisionmakers in the schools, not to exploit their autonomy in setting teacher salaries in an opportunistic way, but to use it to effectively promote student performance. The benefits of superior local knowledge then come into effect, as school decisionmakers ought to know better than any central authority which teachers deserve to be rewarded for good work.

That is, the accountability introduced by the "price information" of external exams creates real competition, which brings the best effects of local school choices to the fore. The very same effects of school autonomy over teacher salaries with and without central exams are found not only in TIMSS and TIMSS-Repeat but also in PISA. Likewise, similar cases where external exams turn a negative autonomy effect around into a positive effect have been found for such decisionmaking areas as school autonomy in determining course content and teacher influence on resource funding. More generally, for several additional decisionmaking areas the general pattern of the evidence suggests that school autonomy is better for student performance when external exit exams are in place.

In sum, external exams can be regarded as the "currency" of school systems: They are a measure of value that prevents decentralized opportunism. As such, they are a precondition for decentralized education systems to achieve high student performance. Efficient education policies would thus combine external exams with school autonomy, setting and testing standards externally but leaving their pursuit up to schools.

Summing Up

The conclusion that can be drawn from the evidence based on four extensive international student achievement tests is clear: Institutions matter. In particular, institutional features that ensure choice and accountability in the school system are key to high student performance. The different institutional effects add up to a huge aggregate effect. For example, their effects in TIMSS add up to more than 200 test score points, compared with an international standard deviation of 100 test score points and to a U.S. grade-level equivalent of 25 test score points.[17] Similarly, about a quarter of the total international variation in educational performance in PISA can be accounted for by international variation in institutional features.[18] That is, the institutional effects are very large indeed.

The lessons that Americans can learn from the cross-country evidence include that students perform better

- in countries where more schools are *privately managed,*
- in *schools* that have *autonomy in process and personnel decisions,*
- if their *teachers* have both incentives and power to select appropriate *teaching methods,*
- where *parents* take an *interest* in teaching matters,
- where student progress is monitored by regular *testing,*
- where *schools* are held *accountable by external exams,* and
- where external exams and school autonomy are combined.

Clearly, this analysis offers lessons not only for America but for other countries as well. Since the international comparisons across numerous countries allow us to truly "look worldwide," we can all learn something from each other in terms of what works best in education. No single country has the single best education system that does everything right. The cross-country perspective taken in this chapter enables the exploitation of institutional variations between all the participating countries. Thereby, it allows us both to analyze the underlying reasons for differing performance and to learn from each other about revealed best educational practice.

Notes

1. The argument for choice in education goes back at least as far as Milton Friedman's *Capitalism and Freedom* (Chicago: University of Chicago Press, 1962), chap. 6. A collection of recent research on school choice is found in Caroline Hoxby, ed., *The Economics of School Choice*, NBER Conference Report (Chicago: University of Chicago

Press, 2003). Two recent treatments of accountability are *School Accountability*, ed. Williamson Evers and Herbert Walberg (Stanford, CA: Hoover Institution Press, 2002); and *No Child Left Behind? The Politics and Practice of School Accountability*, ed. Paul Peterson and Martin West (Washington: Brookings Institution Press, 2003). Both also contain historical references.

2. For recent examples of research that is based on the kind of variation in choice and accountability that exists within the United States, and that also attempts to make sure that the estimates are not confounded by other effects, see Caroline Hoxby, "Does Competition among Public Schools Benefit Students and Taxpayers?" *American Economic Review* 90, no. 5 (2000): 1209–38; William Howell et al., "School Vouchers and Academic Performance: Results from Three Randomized Field Trials," *Journal of Policy Analysis and Management* 21, no. 2 (2002): 191–217; Eric Hanushek and Margaret Raymond, "The Effect of School Accountability Systems on the Level and Distribution of Student Achievement," *Journal of the European Economic Association* 2, nos. 2–3 (2004): 406–15; and Martin Carnoy and Susan Loeb, "Does External Accountability Affect Student Outcomes? A Cross-state Analysis," *Educational Evaluation and Policy Analysis*, forthcoming.

3. Lant Pritchett, "When Will They Ever Learn? Why All Governments Produce Schooling," Harvard University, Kennedy School of Government, 2002.

4. Eric A. Hanushek et al., *Making Schools Work: Improving Performance and Controlling Costs* (Washington: Brookings Institution Press, 1994).

5. For a more elaborate theoretical model of institutional effects, see John H. Bishop and Ludger Woessmann, "Institutional Effects in a Simple Model of Educational Production," *Education Economics* 12, no. 1 (2004): 17–38.

6. For details see Ludger Woessmann, "Schooling Resources, Educational Institutions and Student Performance: The International Evidence," *Oxford Bulletin of Economics and Statistics* 65, no. 2 (2003): 117–70 and the references therein.

7. See Ludger Woessmann, "Central Exams as the 'Currency' of School Systems: International Evidence on the Complementarity of School Autonomy and Central Exams," DICE Report, *Journal for Institutional Comparisons* 1, no. 4, (2003): 46–56 and the references therein.

8. See Thomas Fuchs and Ludger Woessmann, "What Accounts for International Differences in Student Performance? A Re-examination using PISA Data," CESifo Working Paper 1235, Munich, 2004, and the references therein.

9. See Thomas Fuchs and Ludger Woessmann, "Governance and Primary-School Performance: International Evidence," Ifo Institute for Economic Research at the University of Munich, 2004, and the references therein.

10. In PISA, the mean of 500 was scaled for the group of OECD countries only. As a consequence, the mean of all countries participating in PISA is somewhat lower than 500.

11. Here, financial independence is defined as receiving less than 50 percent of core funding for basic educational services from government agencies.

12. See Ludger Woessmann, "Schooling Resources, Educational Institutions and Student Performance"; Fuchs and Woessmann, "What Accounts for International Differences in Student Performance?" and Ludger Woessmann, "How Equal Are Educational Opportunities? Family Background and Student Achievement in Europe and the United States," CESifo Working Paper 1162, Munich, 2004.

13. See Ludger Woessmann, *Schooling and the Quality of Human Capital* (Berlin: Springer, 2002); Ludger Woessmann and Martin R. West, "Class-Size Effects in School

Systems around the World: Evidence from Between-Grade Variation in TIMSS," Program on Education Policy and Governance Research Paper, PEPG/02-2, Harvard University, 2002; and Eric A. Hanushek, "The Failure of Input-Based Schooling Policies," *Economic Journal* 113, no. 485 (2003): F64–F98.

14. For methodological details, see Woessmann, "Schooling Resources, Educational Institutions and Student Performance"; and Ludger Woessmann, "Central Exit Exams and Student Achievement: International Evidence," in *No Child Left Behind?*

15. The results are only briefly summarized here. For considerably more detail, see Ludger Woessmann, "Why Students in Some Countries Do Better: International Evidence on the Importance of Education Policy," *Education Matters* 1, no. 2 (2001): 67–74; Woessmann, *Schooling and the Quality of Human Capital*; Ludger Woessmann, *Central Examinations Improve Educational Performance: International Evidence*, Kiel Discussion Papers 397 (Kiel: Institute for World Economics, 2002); Woessmann, "Schooling Resources, Educational Institutions and Student Performance"; Ludger Woessmann, "Central Exit Exams and Student Achievement: International Evidence"; Woessmann, "Central Exams as the 'Currency' of School Systems"; Ludger Woessmann, "The Effect of Heterogeneity of Central Exams: Evidence from TIMSS, TIMSS-Repeat and PISA,": CESifo Working Paper 1330, Munich, 2004; Fuchs and Woessmann, "What Accounts for International Differences in Student Performance?" and Fuchs and Woessmann, "Governance and Primary-School Performance."

16. Also see John H. Bishop, "The Effect of National Standards and Curriculum-Based Examinations on Achievement," *American Economic Review* 87, no. 2 (1997): 260–64; and John H. Bishop, "Drinking from the Fountain of Knowledge: Student Incentive to Study and Learn," in *Handbook of the Economics of Education*, ed. Eric A. Hanushek and Finis Welch (Amsterdam: North-Holland, forthcoming).

17. Woessmann, "Schooling Resources, Educational Institutions and Student Performance."

18. Fuchs and Woessmann, "What Accounts for International Differences in Student Performance?"

9. Market Education and Its Critics: Testing School Choice Criticisms against the International Evidence

Andrew Coulson

As school choice programs and proposals have proliferated in the United States over the past generation, so, too, have the criticisms leveled at them. Critics fear that, among other things, markets could never serve more than a small fraction of children, would not improve achievement, and would exacerbate inequalities between haves and have-nots. Those are serious concerns, and should they prove accurate they would call into question the wisdom of moving toward a marketlike system of education in this country.

An effort to validate or invalidate such criticisms of school choice is thus eminently warranted, but that task cannot readily be accomplished using U.S. data alone. The modern U.S. experience with marketlike education systems is limited to just a few programs, most of which are recent and all of which are relatively small. Those programs are a tenuous basis from which to generalize about the likely long-term effects of large-scale education markets. To circumvent the paucity of relevant U.S. evidence, this chapter seeks to vet criticisms of market education against the international evidence.

This endeavor, like any realistic public policy assessment, must have a frame of reference. Should we compare the world's education markets and pseudo-markets with a hypothetical alternative that perfectly fulfills all of the public's aspirations or with the actual state-run school systems that they would supplant? Because the intention of this chapter is to provide guidance to policymakers considering market-based education reforms, I adopt the latter tack. In the evaluation that follows, marketlike school systems from around the world are measured against the performance of traditional public school systems in the United States and abroad.

The concept of a relatively free education market accompanied by some form of financial assistance mechanism has been attacked on many different grounds over the years. Rather than spread itself too thinly, the current investigation will focus on just four of the most serious and most often heard among them. Those four criticisms are as follows:

1. Market education systems could never serve more than a small fraction of the student population, with the majority remaining in traditional public schools; hence "choice" is a distraction from the more important task of improving the public system.
2. Education markets would not provide genuine parental choice because schools, not parents, would do the choosing. Private schools would use their admissions policies to shun the poor, the low achieving, the disabled, and the otherwise difficult to educate.
3. Markets would provide parents with real choice but that would prove socially divisive, undermining democracy.
4. Competition and parental choice would not improve academic outcomes; they would instead widen existing racial and socio-economic achievement gaps.

Assessing the Criticisms

Criticism One

> Market education systems could never serve more than a small fraction of the student population, with the majority remaining in traditional public schools; hence "choice" is a distraction from the more important task of improving the public system.

In an article titled " 'Choice' and Other White Lies," Makani N. Themba warns:

> We need to fight to improve the entire [education] system, not for a better place within it for select individuals. . . . This is not to deny that many [public] schools are in trouble. But the answer lies in wholesale reform, not in a few of us taking the money and running.[1]

That concern is obviously valid when directed at legislatively limited school choice programs: a program specifically designed to serve a tiny percentage of students will serve only that tiny percentage. Case closed. But the concern is actually much broader than that. Many critics of market education believe that the private sector simply could not accommodate more than a small fraction of students under *any* choice plan. The New Jersey Education Association, ostensibly quoting a U.S. Department of Education study, asserts that "private schools can only accommodate 150,000 more students nationwide."[2] In fact, the DOE study in question collected no nationally representative data and did not consider the possibility that a school choice program might spur existing schools to expand their operations or lead to the creation of new schools.[3] What it did was simply to ask *existing* private schools in 22 urban communities how many vacant places they *currently* had. The study's findings are thus incapable of answering the larger question about how the marketplace would respond to the introduction of a universal choice program.

Other critics of market education, from the Clinton administration's education secretary Richard Riley[4] to the solidly anti-voucher Applied Research Center,[5] refer to a study of California private schools commissioned by the Department of Education in 1992. The purpose of that study *was* to determine the likely response of private schools to a proposed voucher plan. Its authors, Marcella Dianda and Ronald Corwin, were unequivocal in their conclusion:

> We estimate that only about 43,000 public school students, or fewer than 1% of California's public school enrollment, can expect to find spaces in private schools. Barring a phenomenal [private sector] expansion . . . a voucher program in California might affect up to 200,000 public school students which is about 4% of the state's enrollment. This upper limit is unrealistic. It would mean increasing current private school enrollment by one-half. . . . Therefore, a statewide voucher program will not significantly effect [*sic*] public school enrollment.[6]

But how did Dianda and Corwin reach that conclusion, and is it consistent with the actual private-sector response in nations that have introduced voucher or voucherlike programs? The methodology used in the study was to mail a written survey to all existing private schools in the state and then extrapolate from the answers received. One problem with that approach is that the 37 percent of schools that responded to the mailing were not necessarily representative of California private schools as a whole. The authors simply did not have the data to convincingly address this problem, which undermined the significance of their conclusions.[7] More fundamentally, they made no attempt to forecast the number of new schools that would enter the market in response to a voucher program, further eroding their conclusions' credibility.

An arguably more conclusive way of finding out how the private sector responds to universal school choice programs is to look at nations that have already implemented them. Many countries provide some form of financial assistance to families choosing private schools. The most established universal choice programs can be found in Chile and Holland. Both of those nations make it possible for families at all income levels to participate in the education marketplace. Chile's nationwide voucher program dates back to 1982 and Holland's to 1917. In 1981, 22 percent of students were enrolled in Chile's nongovernment schools. That percentage more than doubled, to 46 percent, by 1999.[8] Most of that new private-sector enrollment was in private schools created in response to the voucher program. Dianda and Corwin's belief that a 50 percent increase in private school enrollment was "unrealistic" turns out to have been conservative in the face of the Chilean precedent.

Holland's program has followed a similar pattern, but, given its longer history, the private sector has had more time in which to expand. From its small size prior to the voucher system's introduction, the private sector has grown to enroll 76 percent of all primary and secondary students today.[9]

Perhaps more surprising than either of the above choice programs is the large and growing education market that exists in India. Though official government figures have been shown to be grossly inaccurate,[10] and national data are thus hard to come by, studies of individual regions and cities point to a remarkably high consumption of unsubsidized private fee-charging schools. That, moreover, is despite the existence of both public schools and government-funded private schools. Oxford University professor Geeta Gandhi Kingdon estimates that 80 percent of all children in the city of Lucknow are enrolled in unsubsidized private fee-charging schools. That enrollment, as researchers James Tooley and Pauline Dixon have separately shown,[11] extends into even the poorest income brackets.

A similar situation obtains in Pakistan. Families earning $1 per person per day or less in Lahore are about as likely to enroll their children in fee-charging private schools as in public schools. In much of the developing world, private enterprise schools have emerged and grown substantially in the last several decades in response to the very poor quality of government schooling—even without government financial assistance.[12]

Criticism Two

> *Education markets would not provide genuine parental choice because schools, not parents, would do the choosing. Private schools would use their admissions policies to shun the poor, the low achieving, the disabled, and the otherwise difficult to educate.*

People for the American Way, an organization committed to preserving the current public school system, says, "Private Schools Do the Choosing, Not Parents." Under voucher programs, PFAW contends that "many students with vouchers would still be ineligible or unable to attend private schools because of long waiting lists and restrictive admission standards."[13] That assessment is echoed by both of the national teachers' unions. American Federation of Teachers president Sandra Feldman declares:

> A particularly dishonest argument that voucher advocates use in selling "parental choice" is that all parents should have the right to choose a good private school for their children—"the way President and Mrs. Clinton did for Chelsea." The people using this argument conveniently neglect to point out that good private schools generally have many more applicants than places, so it's the schools—not the parents—who do the choosing.[14]

Bob Chase, former president of the National Education Association (NEA), concurred:

> Some people argue that the best solution to low-performing schools is to abandon them. Take away funding and give low-income families vouchers towards private school tuition instead. These so-called reformers claim that vouchers will give families "school choice"—even though it will be private schools—accountable to no one—that will be doing the choosing, not the parents.[15]

In its official position statement on school vouchers, the NEA elaborates, stating:

> Vouchers offer false parental "choice." Vouchers provide no choice for the 90 percent of parents whose children attend public schools, particularly for the parents of children with special needs, low test scores or behavioral problems.[16]

Like all free markets, free education markets are based on voluntary association. A student can enroll in a particular school only with the mutual agreement of the parents *and* the school's directors. Compared with an ideal system in which all students are always admitted to their preferred school, this need for mutual agreement is somewhat limiting. We are, however, comparing markets, not with that nonexistent ideal, but rather with the existing U.S. public school system. Under the current system, most students are assigned to a public school on the basis of their place of residence; they have no choice in the matter. In a minority of jurisdictions, families can choose from among multiple public schools, but those choices are often constrained by racial quotas. The amount of real variation among public schools in curriculum, methods, staffing, and policies is also circumscribed by state-wide regulations, to the point where "public school choice" recalls the "choice" of colors offered on the Model T Ford: "any color you want, so long as it's black."

A clear effect of the current system is thus to concentrate choice in the hands of the wealthy. Wealthier families can most easily afford to purchase a residence in whatever district they perceive to have the highest-quality public schools. Should they be dissatisfied with all the nearby public school districts, they can also most easily afford to pay tuition at a private school. Poor families assigned to low-quality public schools are consigned to stay there. The real question thus becomes Do markets provide greater and more equitable choice than the current public school system?

Consider the case of Chile. Under its national voucherlike program, low-income families are more likely to choose public schools (over private voucher schools) than their higher-income fellow citizens. There are several possible explanations for the difference: private schools are more likely to deny admission to low-income families, low-income families prefer public to subsidized private schools, and subsidized private schools are less likely to exist in poor areas than in wealthier areas. A combination of those factors is of course also a possibility.

Disappointingly, none of the dozens of academic studies performed on the Chilean school system over the past two decades has bothered to ask parents *why* they chose a public or a subsidized private school for their children. As a result, we can only speculate as to the reasons for the relatively higher share of public school enrollment among low-income families.

There are no nationally representative data available on the admissions policies of schools in Chile, so there is no way to know for sure how significant a role they might play. It is also the case that some public schools have selective admissions policies, and so selectivity is not a prerogative reserved to the private sector.

There is good reason for low-income parents to prefer public schools to private voucher schools. First and foremost, government education funding in Chile is higher for public schools than it is for private schools, and that funding advantage would make the biggest difference to the poorest families. Public schools often receive funding from their municipalities in addition to the federal per student voucher payment, a revenue source that is unavailable to private schools. Public schools are also more likely to receive extra funding from the federal government, over and above the voucher, for targeted educational programs. Researchers Sapelli and Vial studied the effect of this extra funding and found that the minority of public schools that received only slightly more government funding than their private competitors did poorly compared with those competitors but that the highest-spending public schools, those receiving between 150 percent and 300 percent of the base voucher amount, performed better than private schools.[17] Low-income families, who can afford to make little extra educational investment of their own, are thus wise to choose the highest-spending public schools.

Finally, poverty and urbanicity are inversely correlated in Chile. In other words, the country's rural areas are also generally its poorer areas. Since urban areas have higher population densities, and hence a larger potential base of customers, they are more appealing from a business standpoint than rural areas. Until the urban market for subsidized private schools is saturated, therefore, it is to be expected that rural areas will attract fewer new schools. It should come as no surprise that families in rural areas (who happen also to be lower-income families, on average) have somewhat less access to private subsidized schools than their urban counterparts. If the experience of Pakistan is any guide, access to private schooling in rural areas is likely to improve over time.[18]

Whichever of the above explanations is most significant, it would be hard to argue that Chilean families at all income levels do not enjoy a greater degree of educational choice today than they did under the earlier state education monopoly.

The evidence from other countries also suggests that parents at all income levels, with children of all descriptions, are readily gaining access to independent schools of their choosing under a wide range of school choice programs. New Zealand, which decentralized its public schools during the 1990s, is a case in point: some control over public schools was handed over to parent/teacher boards, automatic student assignment was replaced with parental choice, and between 1991 and 1999 those semiautonomous public schools were permitted to set their own admissions policies. A recent book on New Zealand's education system by economist Mark Harrison points out that, during the 1990s, low-income families were *more likely* than middle- or upper-income families to have children enrolled in a school outside their former catchment area. New Zealand's unfettered school admissions policy thus does not appear to have prevented low-income families from enrolling their children in schools they preferred to the ones to which they would have been automatically assigned during the days of residential catchment areas.

Under the Dutch voucher program, private schools have long been free to set their own admission criteria. Nevertheless, "most private schools pursue non-restrictive admissions policies,"[19] according to World Bank economist Harry Patrinos. Unlike the Chilean system, the Dutch government system provides larger vouchers for low-income children and for the children of immigrant families it considers disadvantaged.[20] Dinand Webbink of the University of Amsterdam finds that there is "segregation along lines of [religious] denomination [but] not along lines of income/education of parents, [with] some exceptions."[21] The religious segregation results, of course, from the fact that the Dutch voucher system makes it easy for families to choose schools consistent with their religious beliefs, unlike U.S. public schooling. Karsten and Meijer find that there is no evidence that private schools in the Netherlands systematically refuse to serve "students at risk."[22]

Hungary and the Czech Republic introduced voucher programs after the fall of communism, and researchers report that the creation of new private schools has been concentrated in areas of excess educational demand and lower-quality state schools. Since the worst-performing public schools are generally concentrated in poor areas, this would seem to indicate that low-income parents are enjoying the greatest range of choices under those plans.[23]

Some of the most striking examples of how markets serve low-income families come from the developing world and from schools that do not receive government subsidies. The cases of Lahore, Pakistan, and Lucknow, India, have already been discussed, and the latest evidence from the Indian city of Hyderabad is no less stunning. Preliminary data released from an ongoing study by James Tooley of the University of Newcastle reveal that more than two-thirds of poor families in Hyderabad chose to pay for their children to attend low-cost private schools rather than send them to the free government schools. These early data also suggest that the private school students outperform their government school counterparts across a range of academic tests.[24]

Ironically, an unsubsidized for-profit private school chain in Brazil has actually been criticized for *not* imposing a restrictive admissions policy. According to its critics, the fact that Objetivo accepts all comers is evidence that it is in business only to make money.[25] What Objetivo's critics fail to acknowledge is that, as an independent fee-charging school, it can make money only if parents actively choose to enroll their children and to keep them enrolled over time—a constraint that does not apply to monopoly state school systems whose students are automatically assigned to them.

But how well do private schools, compared with public schools, serve disabled students? This is a rare case in which we can begin to answer the question using domestic U.S. evidence. According to a 1997 Mackinac Center study, the public school systems of 22 U.S. states send upwards of 100,000 disabled or otherwise difficult-to-educate students to be educated in private schools at public expense because public schools are incapable of serving those children.[26] That was without any special school choice program. More recently, Florida passed the McKay Scholarships Program, which is specifically targeted to families with disabled children. The McKay program has been found by Manhattan Institute researchers to be extremely popular among its target audience.[27]

In Holland, parents of disabled children can choose to send them either to specialty schools catering to their particular disability or to mainstream schools. Even if they choose to mainstream their children, special assistance and supervision are still provided by the staff of specialty schools.[28] Public funding follows the child to the school of choice.

Denmark and Sweden, both of which have limited school choice programs, demonstrate other approaches.[29] In Sweden, the government was initially reluctant to allow disabled students to participate in the private school choice program, maintaining its own schools that specialized in serving students with particular disabilities. That is now changing, but only slowly. Denmark has taken the opposite course, strongly encouraging the mainstreaming of disabled students into regular government and private schools, with the government picking up the tab for parents who choose private schools.

The manner in which the special needs of disabled children are served thus varies from one school choice program to another, depending on the public policy preferences of the voters and legislatures enacting the programs. There is no question, however, that, when parents are afforded the freedom to choose a school for their disabled child and provided financial assistance to do so, private schools are willing and able to meet their children's needs.

Criticism Three

> *Markets would provide parents with real choice, but that would prove socially divisive, undermining democracy.*

Some critics of market education are worried, not that markets would *fail* to create real parental choice, but rather that they would *succeed* in doing so. Their fear is that, if families are allowed to obtain whatever sort of education they deem best, social conflict will ensue as society is Balkanized into warring factions.

Former secretary of education Richard Riley told reporters at the National Press Club that "private school vouchers are . . . too divisive to have any potential for improving the public school system," adding that "public schools are the foundation of a democracy and a free enterprise economic system."[30] Amy Gutmann, professor of political science at Princeton University, has seconded that position, stating that "support for public education is the last bastion for true democracy."[31] In both of the above contexts, the terms "public schooling" and "public education" refer to schools owned, operated, and funded entirely by the state.

Among the most forceful expositions of those views is the written dissent of Supreme Court Justice Stephen Breyer in the case of *Zelman v. Simmons-Harris* (2002). In *Zelman*, the majority of the Court upheld the constitutionality of the Cleveland school voucher program. Several justices dissented, and Breyer joined them, but in a written dissent of his own he declared that

> I write separately, however, to emphasize the risk that publicly financed voucher programs pose in terms of religiously based social conflict. . . .
>
> How will the public react to government funding for schools that take controversial religious positions on topics that are of current popular interest—say, the conflict in the Middle East or the war on terrorism? Yet any major funding program for primary religious education will require criteria. And the selection of those criteria, as well as their application, inevitably poses problems that are divisive. Efforts to respond to these problems not only will seriously entangle church and state . . . but also will promote division among religious groups, as one group or another fears (often legitimately) that it will receive unfair treatment at the hands of the government.[32]

Once again, the first step in assessing this criticism is to set the context in which school choice programs must be evaluated. There is a widespread assumption among market critics, evident in some of the above quotations, that public schooling not only fosters social harmony and vibrant democracy but that it is the single education system capable of doing so. It is difficult to reconcile that assumption with reality.

Public schools are today, and have been since their inception, a source of considerable conflict in American society. Because they are the official state organ of education, for which all taxpayers must pay, different constituencies within the general public have fought to control their curricula. Initially a sectarian Protestant institution, U.S. public schooling openly discriminated against Catholics. In the late 1800s, when Catholics in Philadelphia managed to get the local public schools to adopt their version of the Bible instead of the Protestant one, the infamous Bible Riots erupted in which 13 people were killed and St. Augustine's Church was burned to the ground.

Today, there are ongoing battles between parents of different religious and ideological stripes on a wide range of issues, including the phrase "Under God" in the Pledge of Allegiance, school prayer, evolution vs. creation/intelligent design, sex education, U.S. history, early reading instruction techniques, mathematics instruction techniques, book censorship, and on and on. Those battles are sometimes highly acrimonious, and they inevitably have winners and losers. Because there is only one official public school system, it cannot cater simultaneously to families with incompatible views and preferences.

So how have the world's parent-driven, marketlike education systems performed by comparison? Interestingly, the Dutch voucher program was a direct response to mounting social conflict over that nation's conventional public school system. Dutch society was highly "pillarized," or segmented, into four groups: Catholics, Protestants, socialists, and (classical) liberals. As a result, a fierce battle had been going on for generations over what should be taught in the official public school system, and the voucher program was introduced as a way of diffusing those tensions by allowing all parents to obtain the kind of education they preferred for their children without having to force their choices on their neighbors.

In the view of critics of market education, vouchers should have exacerbated the preexisting pillarization of Dutch society, Balkanizing it into antagonistic factions. That didn't happen. In fact, by the 1960s, pillarization was receding rapidly, and today only vestiges remain. The Dutch became increasingly secular over the years despite easier access to religious schooling, and barriers to interactions between the different communities diminished substantially. Not only did the critics' feared social Balkanization fail to materialize, vouchers in the Netherlands have been contemporaneous with a reduction in social polarization.

Still, modern Dutch society is not a paradise of individual freedom, harmony, and integration. Although vouchers effectively defused the preexisting tensions among the nation's native groups, recent waves of Muslim immigrants have created new ones. Some of this uneasiness can be attributed to xenophobia on the part of some Dutch citizens who want immigrants to abandon any traditions they deem to be inconsistent with the views of the native Dutch majority. Such xenophobia exists, to a greater or lesser extent, in every nation and has little to do with the presence or absence of a state education monopoly. In fact, as I documented in *Market Education: The Unknown History*, one of the driving forces behind the U.S. "common school" campaign of the mid–19th century was a desire on the part of the Anglo-Saxon Protestant majority to inculcate their own views into immigrant children, with no regard for parents' preferences.[33]

There is, however, another aspect to the Dutch debate over Muslim schooling that is directly related to vouchers: the opposition of some citizens to being compelled to support instruction that violates their convictions. This concern leapt into the media spotlight when the BVD (the Dutch internal security agency) reported that about one in five government-funded Islamic schools "receives money from the radical Islamic organisation Al Waqf al Islami, or has members of the [board of] school governors who are allied to radical Muslim organizations."[34] Staff members from the government Schools Inspectorate subsequently arranged to visit those schools, and upon doing so did not find any militant teaching or incitement to violence, although the inspectorate acknowledged that the schools could have softened their rhetoric in the inspectors' presence.[35]

In other words, the belief that some government-funded Muslim schools might be promoting an agenda that is militant or anti-Western, or both, causes just the sort of controversy in the Netherlands that Justice Breyer predicted would follow government funding of religious schools in the United States.

Such controversies are not limited to systems in which sectarian schools are paid for at public expense. Many American conservatives strongly object to subsidizing what they see as the one-sided secular humanist agenda of U.S. public schools. For generations they have battled, with varying degrees of success, to have their own views reflected in the public schools. In March 2004, for example, the Ohio State School Board voted to have the deistic belief in "intelligent design"[36] taught alongside the theory of evolution. A similar campaign is under way in Montana. Many high school biology textbooks no longer have the word evolution in their indexes. Most scientists and adherents of evolutionary theory have vigorously opposed these changes, and there is no sign that an amicable resolution to this dispute is possible within the current structure of U.S. public schooling.[37] As already noted, such secular issues as sex education and the teaching of history, reading, and mathematics in public schools are also frequent sources of social conflict.

In investigating the causes of education-related social conflicts, we thus quickly discover that not all such conflicts stem from the extension of government funding to sectarian schools. It is also not obvious whether choice programs that extend such funding precipitate a higher overall level of social conflict than state-run secular education monopolies. There is, however, one thread that does tie together virtually all such conflicts: compulsion. School systems in which citizens are forced to pay for teaching that violates their deeply held convictions, whether religious or otherwise, consistently lead to conflict.

That is true in nations with relatively diverse societies such as England and the United States and also in more homogeneous ones such as Japan and Israel. In both of the latter countries, there have been ongoing disputes, for instance, over the teaching of national history. In Japan, the portrayal of that country's actions during World War II is often at issue, and in Israel the treatment of the conflict with the Palestinians is the most common curricular lightning rod. France is currently suffering from precisely the sort of social conflict Justice Breyer warned of in his *Zelman* dissent, but the controversy is over that nation's prohibition of religious clothing and accessories in its forcibly secular public schools, not its funding of religious Catholic schools. Ironically, France's private Catholic schools continue to permit Muslim girls to wear headscarves—the specific item of religious clothing that motivated the blanket proscription of religious attire in the nation's public schools.

Criticism Four

> *Competition and parental choice would not improve academic outcomes; they would instead widen existing racial and socioeconomic achievement gaps.*

On its website, the National Education Association makes the unequivocal assertion that "there is no evidence that vouchers improve student learning. Every serious study of voucher plans has concluded that vouchers do not improve student achievement."[38]

Although there is certainly ongoing controversy over the significance and validity of the U.S. school voucher research, the NEA's assertion is patently mistaken. Many sophisticated statistical analyses of U.S. voucher programs have found that enrollment in private voucher schools has led to student achievement gains in one or more

162

subject areas.[39] Nevertheless, the NEA's view on this subject is widely shared. An on-line article by the managing editor of the public school advocacy publication *Rethinking Schools* is titled "Vouchers and the False Promise of Academic Achievement." In this piece, editor Barbara Miner writes:

> Conservatives have spinned [*sic*] vouchers as a way to increase achievement for low-income minorities. And clearly, reducing the Black/white academic achievement gap is one of this country's highest educational priorities. But the academic case for vouchers rests on rhetoric, not reality.[40]

The Applied Research Center goes one step further, asserting that "a voucher system in California would only exacerbate educational inequity. The primary beneficiaries of vouchers are people who already have resources."[41] That is also the view of Stanford University professor Bruce Fuller, whose "results suggest that school choice may inadvertently exacerbate stratification and inequality."[42]

One of the most thoroughly researched and argued presentations of this criticism is a paper by World Bank researchers Chang-Tai Hsieh and Miguel Urquiola. Hsieh and Urquiola examined data from the first eight years of the Chilean voucher program and concluded that it succeeded only in redistributing wealthier and higher-achieving students to the private sector and not in improving overall student performance.[43]

In weighing those criticisms, context, once again, is key. We must keep in mind that wealth and academic achievement are already correlated under the current U.S. public school system. In fact, among the education systems of all 27 nations belonging to the Organization for Economic Cooperation and Development (OECD), U.S. public schools show the single strongest correlation between wealth and achievement.[44]

So how would the introduction of a universal school choice program likely affect overall student achievement and the distribution of student achievement? An obvious jumping-off point for answering those questions is to review the conclusions of Hsieh and Urquiola. They rest their case, essentially, on five findings:[45]

- In 1988 achievement was higher in well-established private schools than in newly created private schools (implying, the authors believe, that established schools had already snapped up the wealthier and hence higher-achieving students, leaving newer schools with the remaining poorer, lower-achieving students).

- After controlling for observable school and community characteristics, districts with a higher private enrollment share do not differ significantly from other districts in math scores, repetition rates, or student attainment (i.e., years of school completed).
- After controls, districts with higher growth in private enrollment share between 1982 and 1988 do not differ significantly in educational outcomes from districts in which private enrollment grew more modestly.
- Nationwide, "average test scores did not change," though repetition rates did fall somewhat and school attainment did rise somewhat.
- Chile dropped one place in the international ranking of countries participating in the 1970 and 1999 international tests of mathematics and science.

Contrary to the researchers' assertions, it does not necessarily follow from those findings that private voucher schools are no more effective than public schools or that the school voucher program has failed to improve overall student achievement. By looking only at the first six years of the program, the authors neglect to consider several important realities. Newly created organizations tend to have more problems than well-established ones. It is possible that, as poorly managed start-ups either went out of business or eventually improved their operations, overall private school achievement may have gone up. It is also conceivable that public schools may have been slow to react to declining enrollment in an academically effective way. Second, the introduction of a voucher program was not the only major change in government education policy during the 1980s. Total government spending also fell substantially in real terms during that decade, and that could have had a deleterious effect on achievement. Government spending began to recover only in the 1990s. Finally, it is not clear whether the cited decline in the relative international performance of Chilean students occurred between 1970 and 1982 (before the voucher program was introduced) or between 1982 and 1999 (after it was introduced).

One way to address the above concerns is to look at the performance of Chilean schools from 1988 onward. Unfortunately, it is impossible to discern reliable year-to-year test score trends before 1997 because results of the national SIMCE test were not guaranteed to be comparable from year to year prior to that date. Despite that limitation, Francisco Gallego of the Chilean Central Bank has come up with an excellent alternative statistic. Instead of charting the annual test score changes of voucher schools or public schools, Gallego decided to compare how well each type of school has performed compared with elite nonvoucher private schools—expensive private schools that have not participated in the nation's voucher program (because their tuitions exceed the voucher amount).

Gallego found that both private voucher schools and public schools steadily improved in comparison with the elite nonvoucher private schools from 1988 all the way through the most recent (year 2000) data. In 1988, fourth grade students in public schools scored only 64.7 percent as well as students in elite nonvoucher schools, but by 2000 they were scoring 81.1 percent as well as elite nonvoucher students. Private voucher schools also improved substantially relative to elite nonvoucher schools, rising from 74.0 percent to 87.4 percent of the elite nonvoucher schools' performance.

Another pattern that emerges when we look beyond the voucher program's early tumultuous years is that schools created in response to the program eventually closed the achievement gap with schools that predated it. In the words of researchers Claudio Sapelli and Bernardita Vial:

> Pre-reform schools are significantly better than post-reform schools in 1989, but the difference halves in 1993 and disappears in 1997. In 1997 both pre- and post-reform [private] schools are significantly better than municipal [i.e., public] schools.[46]

Several studies have shown that Chile's private voucher schools outperform public schools, after controlling for student and family background.[47] Some, but not all, of those studies have found that the private-sector advantage is concentrated among Catholic schools and that secular private schools perform at roughly the same level as public schools.[48] No studies have found that public schools outperform private voucher schools overall. As noted earlier, Sapelli and Vial revealed that most public schools receive substantial government funding over and above the voucher, which private schools

165

do not receive. Their study concluded that public schools that spend only modestly more than the value of the voucher perform significantly worse than both private voucher schools and high-spending public schools.[49]

The Chilean experience thus suggests that there may be an initial period following the introduction of a universal choice program during which performance may not improve because of the preponderance of new and untested schools and the shock to public schools of rapidly falling enrollments. After this period the system seems to stabilize and performance improves, especially in the private sector.

If this experience is generally representative of large-scale choice programs, then the long-established voucher program in the Netherlands should be showing strong academic achievement, and if its private schools perform better than its public schools, that should be because of their superior quality and not simply the result of a more select student body.

Of the 20 nations participating in the Third International Mathematics and Science Study (TIMSS), the Netherlands consistently scored in the top three in both subjects, at both the 8th and the 12th grade levels.[50] When fourth graders in 35 countries were tested for reading ability in 2001, students in the Netherlands placed second, behind students in Sweden (another country with a school choice program, albeit a more limited one).[51] Young adults in the Netherlands also scored well in literacy on the International Adult Literacy Survey of the mid-1990s, once again coming in second behind Sweden.[52]

From the standpoint of overall achievement, therefore, the Dutch experience is consistent with the emergent trend in Chile. But what about the relative performance of private voucher schools and public schools in the Netherlands? For historical reasons explained above, the vast majority of private schools in Holland are either Catholic or Protestant. A 2002 study by Jesse Levin reports that raw test scores for private Protestant schools are slightly, but not statistically significantly, better overall than raw test scores for public schools. Private Catholic schools, by contrast, show significantly better raw scores in most of the grades and subjects tested. To determine if this achievement difference was genuine or simply an artifact of a more elite clientele, Levin controlled for a variety of student and family background characteristics. He found that Dutch Catholic schools enroll students of *lower* overall socioeconomic status, not higher status as the cream-skimming argument would suppose. As a result, the raw score advantage of Catholic schools over public schools in Holland actually *understates* the benefit of attending a private Catholic school.

According to a research survey by Jaap Dronkers, private religious schools across Europe, most of which receive some government funding, generally perform better than public schools. He writes:

> The importance of the effectiveness differences in the cognitive domains indicates that educational systems with public and state-funded religious schools give parents a real choice between schools of different quality. Given the higher general level of achievements in both public and religious schools of European societies and the smaller differences between [the] achievement of these schools within European societies compared to the average achievement of public schools and the between-school differences in the USA, it is difficult to argue that the parental choice in these European societies has increased inequality within these societies or lowered the level of schooling.[53]

This pattern of private-sector academic superiority is not limited to religious schools or to wealthy Europe. The overwhelming majority of studies find that private schools operating in competitive markets across the developing world are more academically effective, more efficient, and more responsive to the curricular demands of parents than are state-run public schools. In a recent review of this research, I discovered 16 studies indicating superior private school academic achievement, 3 findings indicating no significant difference between the sectors, and only 1 finding showing a public school advantage.[54]

Conclusion

Because the U.S. experience can provide only limited guidance on the likely effects of introducing universal access to market education, this chapter has investigated several key criticisms of market reforms using international evidence. By comparing the actual outcomes of existing marketlike education systems with those of U.S. public schooling, it has called into question the validity of most of those criticisms.

167

The supply of private schooling certainly varies on the basis of prevailing legislative, educational, and economic contexts, but the blanket belief that markets cannot expand to serve more than a tiny fraction of students is not borne out by the international data. That is most obviously and generally true in jurisdictions that provide financial assistance to families choosing private schools, but it is also true in many nations, such as India and Pakistan, where even very poor parents choose to enroll their children in private schools in large numbers.

Markets do not, as critics rightly allege, ensure that every school can and will effectively serve every child. The same criticism applies equally well to U.S. public schools, however, despite the common but mistaken assumption that every public school accepts and serves every child. The relevant question to ask is Which system provides families with the greatest and most meaningful array of educational options? The answer to that question, based on the foreign experiences, is universal choice plans.

On the subject of social divisiveness, the lesson of the international and domestic evidence is that compulsion, not diversity, is the major cause of school-related social conflict and that it is no less likely to exist under a state-run education monopoly than under a system of government-funded school choice. Indeed, the experience of the Netherlands demonstrates that a government-funded choice program can reduce the tensions created by an official education monopoly, even if it cannot eliminate them altogether. The implication of this finding is that policymakers should be striving to come up with an education system that maximizes the ability of citizens to pursue their shared educational goals and pass on their individual traditions and beliefs without forcing them to impose their preferences on their neighbors—diversity without compulsion. Though not discussed in this chapter, I have addressed that issue at length elsewhere.[55]

Finally, the belief that universal education markets would fail to improve overall academic achievement and exacerbate the achievement gap between the haves and have-nots is not borne out by the evidence. After its first tumultuous years, the Chilean voucher program allowed students in both public schools and private voucher schools to substantially narrow the gap with their wealthier peers in nonvoucher private schools. Though before and after trend data are not available for the long-established Dutch voucher system, the Netherlands' consistent ranking among the top-achieving nations at least suggests that competition and parental choice are consistent with strong academic success. Furthermore, the fact that Dutch Catholic schools score higher than Dutch public schools, despite enrolling students of *lower* socioeconomic status, suggests that the critics have things exactly backward.

This study, by itself, is of course not definitive. There was not space to examine every relevant case, and there are other criticisms of market education not treated here. Nevertheless, it is hoped that the evidence discussed here will facilitate sound, empirically based education decisionmaking by U.S. policymakers.

Notes

1. Makani N. Themba, " 'Choice' and Other White Lies," *Rethinking Schools Online* 16, no. 1 (Fall 2001), http://www.rethinkingschools.org/archive/16_01/Lies161.shtml.

2. New Jersey Education Association, "The Truth behind Vouchers: Private Schools Do the Choosing," No Room section, August 2003, http://www.njea.org/Issues/private.asp.

3. Lana Muraskin and Stephanie Stullich, "Barriers, Benefits, and Costs of Using Private Schools to Alleviate Overcrowding in Public Schools," U.S. Department of Education, November 1998, http://www.aft.org/research/vouchers/research/usvoucher.html (Executive Summary only).

4. Richard W. Riley, "What Really Matters in American Education," White Paper prepared for a speech to the National Press Club, Washington, September 23, 1997, http://www.ed.gov/Speeches/09-1997/matters.pdf.

5. Applied Research Center, "Vouchers: A Trap, Not a Choice. California School Vouchers Will Increase Racial Inequality," Applied Research Center, October 2000, p. 19, http://www.arc.org/erase/vouchers/voucherreport.pdf.

6. Marcella R. Dianda and Ronald G. Corwin, "What a Voucher Could Buy: A Survey of California's Private Schools," Southwest Regional Laboratory, February 1993, p. 17.

7. The authors compared respondent schools with the state population of private schools on four measures: which of three affiliations they had (Catholic, other religious, nonreligious); grade level (kindergarten, elementary, K–12, high school, ungraded); which of four California regions they were in (Southern, Central, Northern, Bay Area); and total enrollment. They made no effort to determine if the respondent group differed from other private schools on the fundamental question of their propensity for expansion.

8. Emiliana Vegas, "School Choice, Student Performance, and Teacher and School Characteristics: The Chilean Case," World Bank, Development Research Group, 2001, p. 4, http://www.worldbank.org/wbi/B-SPAN/docs/school_chile_doc.pdf.

9. Organization for Economic Cooperation and Development, *Education at a Glance: OECD Indicators 2001* (Paris: OECD, 2001), table C1.4, http://www1.oecd.org/els/education/ei/eag/tables/C1.xls.

10. Geeta Gandhi Kingdon, "Private Schooling in India: Size, Nature, and Equity-Effects," *Economic and Political Weekly* 31, no. 51 (1996): 3306–14, http://www. econ.ox.ac.uk/Members/geeta.kingdon/PublishedPapers/privateschoolinginindia.pdf.

11. James Tooley and Pauline Dixon, *Private Schools for the Poor: A Case Study from India* (Reading, England: CfBT, 2003), http://www.cfbt.com/cfbt/web.nsf/ 97cae391e363b90880256b50004ff567/83d3be196fbec1b280256b610041aa24/$FILE/ Final%20Pipe.pdf.

12. Andrew J. Coulson, "Implementing Education for All: Moving from Goals to Action," paper presented at the Fondazione Liberal's Second International Education Conference, Milan, Italy, May 17, 2003, http://www.schoolchoices.org/roo/coulson_milan-(2003).pdf.

13. People for the American Way, "Vouchers vs. Public Education," undated, http://www.pfaw.org/pfaw/general/default.aspx?oid=9855.

14. Sandra Feldman, "Let's Tell the Truth," American Federation of Teachers, November 1997, http://www.aft.org/stand/previous/1997/1197.html.

15. Bob Chase, president of the National Education Association, "Toward a New Unionism: Teaching Children, Challenging Teachers," presentation in Denver, CO, April 18, 2001, http://www.nea.org/speeches/sp010418.html.

16. National Education Association, "NEA on Vouchers: Opposed," http://www. nea.org/lac/vouchers/vouchposition.html.

17. Claudio Sapelli and Bernardita Vial, "Evaluating the Chilean Education Voucher System," working paper, Instituto de Economia Pontificia Universidad Catolica de Chile, April 2002, http://www.msu.edu/~herrer20/documents/ec823/ papers/paper4.pdf.

18. All private schools in Pakistan were taken over by the state in 1972. It was not until 1979 that the creation of new private schools once again became legal. Since the relegalization of nongovernment schooling, the private education sector has grown far more rapidly than either the total student population or the public education sector (i.e., it has been increasing its share of enrollment at the expense of the public sector). While the total percentage of schools serving rural areas has always been lower in Pakistan than the percentage serving urban areas, that percentage has steadily increased since the relegalization of private schools. In other words, the private sector has been gradually expanding into lower-density rural areas as urban areas become saturated.

Private-sector enrollment is correlated with family income level in Pakistan, but that appears to be due to financial expediency rather than to admissions barriers imposed by private schools. Pakistan provides no financial assistance to families choosing private schools, and yet, as noted earlier in the text, roughly half of all families earning $1 per person per day in Lahore choose private schools. See Harold Alderman, Peter F. Orazem, and Elizabeth M. Paterno, "School Quality, School Cost, and the Public/Private School Choices of Low-Income Households in Pakistan," *Journal of Human Resources* 36, no. 2 (2001): 304–26; and Tahir Andrabi, Jishnu Das, and Asim Ijaz Khwaja, "The Rise of Private Schooling in Pakistan: Catering to the Urban Elite or Educating the Rural Poor?" working paper, Harvard University, March 21, 2002, http://ksghome.harvard.edu/~.akhwaja.academic.ksg/papers/ Pakschool%20March29.pdf.

19. Harry Anthony Patrinos, "The Netherlands as a Possible Model," Occasional Paper no. 59, National Center for the Study of Privatization in Education, Teachers College, Columbia University, November 2002, p. 2.

20. In practice, however, Dutch government officials admit that schools "rarely made a special effort (other than simply reducing class size) to meet the goal for which the extra funding was granted, namely individual attention for children from disadvantaged families." See Frans J. de Vijlder, "Dutch Education: A Closed or an Open System?" undated government report, Ministry of Education, Culture and Science, The Netherlands, p. 3, http://www1.oecd.org/els/pdfs/EDSFLLDOCA019.pdf.

21. Dinand Webbink, "School Finance in the Netherlands," University of Amsterdam, Netherlands Bureau for Economic Policy Analysis, undated, www.worldbank.lt/docs/School%20Finance%20in%20NL.ppt.

22. Sjoerd Karsten and Joost Meijer, "School-Based Management in the Netherlands: The Education Consequences of Lump-Sum Funding," *Educational Policy* 13, no. 3 (1999): 421–39. Cited in Patrinos.

23. Randall K. Filer and Daniel Münich, "Responses of Private and Public Schools to Voucher Funding: The Czech and Hungarian Experience," working paper no. 360, University of Michigan, William Davidson Institute, October 2000, p. 3, http://eres.bus.umich.edu/docs/workpap-dav/wp360.pdf.

24. "Private Schools More in Demand in Old City," *Times of India*, March 11, 2004, http://timesofindia.indiatimes.com/articleshow/553093.cms.

25. Luciana Zenti, "Objtivo: Brand-name Schooling," UNESCO, November 2000, http://www.unesco.org/courier/2000_11/uk/doss21.htm.

26. Janet R. Beales and Thomas F. Bertonneau, "Do Private Schools Serve Difficult-to-Educate Students?" research report, Mackinac Center for Public Policy, October 1997, http://www.mackinac.org/print.asp?ID = 361.

27. Jay P. Greene and Greg Forster, "Effects of Funding Incentives on Special Education Enrollment," Manhattan Institute Civic Report no. 32, December 2002. See also David F. Salisbury, "Lessons from Florida: School Choice Gives Increased Opportunities to Children with Special Needs," Cato Institute Briefing Paper no. 81, March 20, 2003.

28. The Netherlands Ministry of Education, Culture and Science, *Education, Culture and Science in the Netherlands Facts and Figures 2003* (Kelpen-Oler: Hub. Tonnaer, 2003), p. 44.

29. Lewis M. Andrews, "More Choices for Disabled Kids," *Policy Review*, April 2002, http://www.policyreview.org/APR02/andrews.html.

30. Richard W. Riley, then–secretary of education, "What Really Matters in American Education," speech to the National Press Club, Washington, September 23, 1997, http://www.ed.gov/Speeches/09-1997/matters.pdf.

31. Cited in Joanne Barkan, "Blacks, Like Jews, Finding Vouchers Divisive," *Forward*, October 20, 2000, http://www.forward.com/issues/2000/00.10.20/news3.html.

32. Justice Breyer's written dissent in *Zelman v. Simmons-Harris* (2002), argued February 20, 2002, decided June 27, 2002, http://caselaw.lp.findlaw.com/scripts/getcase.pl?court = us&vol = 000&invol = 00-1751.

33. Andrew J. Coulson, *Market Education: The Unknown History* (New Brunswick, NJ: Transaction Books, 1999), pp. 78–80.

34. Marina Brouwer, "Concern about Muslim Schools," Radio Netherlands, February 20, 2002, http://www.rnw.nl/hotspots/html/netherlands020220.html.

35. "Islamschool niet te controleren," *Het Parool* (Dutch news site), October 25, 2002, http://www.parool.nl/1035522058940.html.

36. The belief that human beings are too complex to have evolved naturally, and so must have been created by an "intelligent designer." I do not refer to this belief as a theory, because it does not share some criteria for scientific theories, namely, it is not falsifiable by any conceivable concrete evidence, and it makes no predictions about future events.

37. Coulson, *Market Education*, pp. 123–27.

38. National Education Association, "NEA on Vouchers: Opposed."

39. The literature is reviewed in Caroline M. Hoxby, "School Choice and School Competition: Evidence from the United States," *Swedish Economic Policy Review* 10, no. 11 (2003), http://post.economics.harvard.edu/faculty/hoxby/papers/hoxby_2.pdf.

40. Barbara Miner, "Vouchers and the False Promise of Academic Achievement," February 2002, http://www.rethinkingschools.org/special_reports/voucher_report/vfam.shtml.

41. Applied Research Center, "Vouchers: A Trap, Not a Choice," p. 15.

42. Harvard Graduate School of Education, "Studies Show School Choice Widens Inequality: Popular among Parents, But Little Evidence That Children Learn More," news release, July 13, 1995, http://www.gse.harvard.edu/news/features/schoolchoice07131995.html.

43. Chang-Tai Hsieh and Miguel Urquiola, "When Schools Compete, How Do They Compete? An Assessment of Chile's Nationwide School Voucher Program," Occasional Paper no. 43, National Center for the Study of Privatization in Education, Teachers College, Columbia University, January 2002.

44. Only Portugal comes close. See OECD, data tables of Annex B1 of the Programme on International Student Assessment (2001), Table 6.2, http://www.pisa.oecd.org/knowledge/annexb/t6_2.htm.

45. The discussion that follows is adapted from Andrew J. Coulson, "How Markets Affect Quality: Testing a Theory of Market Education against the International Evidence," in *Educational Freedom in Urban America*, ed. David Salisbury and Casey Lartigue (Washington: Cato Institute, 2004), pp. 265–324.

46. Sapelli and Vial, p. 6.

47. Patrick J. McEwan, "Public Subsidies for Private Schooling: A Comparative Analysis of Argentina and Chile," *Journal of Comparative Policy Analysis: Research and Practice* 4 (2002): 189–216; Vegas; Dante Contreras, "Vouchers, School Choice, and the Access to Higher Education," Discussion Paper no. 845, Yale University Economic Growth Center, June 2002; and Sapelli and Vial.

48. McEwan; and Vegas.

49. Sapelli and Vial.

50. Note that the Netherlands did not test high school seniors enrolled in apprenticeship programs, as those students were not generally studying the material tested by TIMSS. See Ina V. S. Mullis et al., *Mathematics and Science Achievement in the Final Year of Secondary School: IEA's Third International Mathematics and Science Study (TIMSS)* (Chestnut Hill, MA: TIMSS International Study Center, 1998), Figures 2.1 and 2.2.

51. Ina V. S. Mullis et al., *PIRLS 2001 International Report: IEA's Study of Reading Literacy Achievement in Primary School in 35 Countries* (Boston: International Study Center, Lynch School of Education, Boston College, 2003), pp. 26–27.

52. Defined as the percentage of 16- to 25-year-olds scoring at level 3 or above on the five-level IALS test scoring system. See Organization for Economic Co-operation and Development and Statistics Canada, *Literacy, Economy, and Society* (Paris: OECD, 1995), pp. 152–54.

53. Jaap Dronkers, "More Parental Choice in Europe? Overview of Effectiveness Differences between Religious Schools and Public Schools in several European Societies," revision of a paper originally presented at the Annual Meeting of the American Educational Research Association, April 11, 2001, Seattle WA, http://www.iue.it/Personal/Dronkers/English/AERApaper.pdf.

54. These numbers are for studies of developing countries only. The table from which they are taken also includes findings for several studies of U.S. voucher programs. See Coulson, "How Markets Affect Quality," p. 306.

55. Andrew J. Coulson, "Forging Consensus: Can the School Choice Community Come Together on an Explicit Goal and a Plan for Achieving It?" Mackinac Center for Public Policy and the LEAD Foundation, Midland, MI, 2004, http://www.mackinac.org/archives/2004/s2004-01.pdf; and Andrew J. Coulson, "Market Education and the Public Good," in *Can the Market Save Our Schools?* pp. 53–72.

10. Choice as an Education Reform Catalyst: Lessons from Chile, Milwaukee, Florida, Cleveland, Edgewood, New Zealand, and Sweden

John Merrifield

School choice policies are sweeping the globe.
Plank and Sykes[1]

The center holds.
Gauri[2]

Policymakers and intellectuals have discussed choice-based reform proposals at least since 1962 when Milton Friedman published *Capitalism and Freedom*. In a chapter on education, he advocated universal school vouchers as the best way to allocate public education funding.[3] Since then, and especially after the election of Margaret Thatcher and Ronald Reagan, a wide variety of market-oriented reforms has swept the globe, and reform of primary and secondary schooling has become a top priority in many countries.[4]

Some places managed to enact school choice programs. However, only quite limited programs emerged. One approach was just to loosen school zoning restrictions (attendance areas). When New Zealand adopted that approach, it widened the schooling options to include additional government-operated schools. Another approach, adopted in the United States, was to fund chartered public school alternatives to traditional public schools. Although chartering policies vary widely among the states, charter schools are generally more autonomous, and they enjoy some freedom from regulations that apply to the traditional public schools. Tuition vouchers have also been tried as a way to increase access to private schools, including possibly new private schools that may form to address the

175

increased interest in private schooling. Finally, some states have adopted tax credits as a way to encourage use of private schools.

Naturally, such a diverse array of possibilities, all bearing a school choice label, can create a lot of confusion. When does evidence from one program apply to another program? What kinds of differences invalidate comparisons? When is a program a meaningful experiment?[5] Unfortunately, those questions aren't asked very often. A small army of lobbyists, scholars, and journalists believes that the effects of small shifts within the system inform decisions about how to transform primary and secondary schooling. It is to be hoped that some well-placed reality checks will get the school reform debate back on the right track.

Reality Check and Roadmap

In many countries, school attendance zone boundaries decide a child's school less often than they once did. Greater financial resources now allow more families to choose privately owned schools, and other policy changes allow some families to choose from a set of government-operated schools without moving to another home. Those exceptions to school assignment by zone (expansions of parental choice opportunities collectively termed "school choice programs") are a growing global phenomenon. But since none of the programs even approaches a fundamental transformation of the prevailing system, the new programs are not worthy of the cheers and jeers that usually accompany them. For example, Chile and New Zealand eliminated school zoning, but they continued to centrally micromanage schooling practices. UCLA business management professor William Ouchi framed the issue this way: "If all schools have the same schedule, program, and staffing, what does choice mean?"[6]

The school choices of the vast majority of U.S. families are exactly the same today as they were decades ago.[7] Most families still choose a public school by picking a home, or they pay their taxes, plus tuition, to use a private school. Very few Americans have even heard of charter schools or vouchers.[8] Where charter schools or voucher programs exist, they serve small numbers of children or are restricted to children from low-income families or from the worst public schools. In New Zealand, new restrictions make it more difficult to use a school outside a family's designated attendance zone. Chile is tightening the regulatory vise that narrows the differences between the choices and tilting the playing field with new municipal-school-only subsidies.

Certainly, much more can be achieved and in many countries absolutely needs to be. Existing programs need to be seen as early mileposts, not destinations or even indefinite rest stops. Since the fog of the school choice war obscures the view from the trenches, it's time to step back from the front lines and take a fresh look at some prominent school choice programs and what has been said about them. Chile, Milwaukee, Florida, Cleveland, Edgewood, New Zealand, and Sweden were chosen for examination because of the prominent discussion of the parental choice programs recently established in those places and the mismatch between the scope of those school choice programs and the reform agendas there and elsewhere. Much of the discussion of those programs has been false, misleading, or largely irrelevant.

The following section explains why substantive reform is the relevant issue and the resulting need to determine whether school choice proposals can qualify as reform catalysts, that is, policy revisions capable of prompting a fundamental transformation of primary and secondary schooling. Next is a description of the reform avenues and the conditions that school choice programs must establish to stimulate transformation of the system. That section also discusses the key differences between varying degrees of potential rivalry and genuine competition, including an examination of which traditional economic models apply to which mix of funding and regulatory conditions. Then a section describes the key elements of school choice policies in Chile, Milwaukee, Florida, Cleveland, Edgewood, New Zealand, and Sweden. It compares the resulting conditions in those places with the conditions outlined in the previous section. The final section addresses the critical "minimum starting point" issue and describes the minimum provisions of a school choice law intended to be a catalyst for system-wide transformation.

School Choice and the Reform Imperative

Fundamental school reform is a hot topic in many countries. At opposite ends of the globe, similar issues are prompting demands for reform. Even the claims, counterclaims, and political combatants

177

are quite comparable. The similarities in the reform issues are consistent with the observation of David Plank and Gary Sykes that "there has been a dramatic decline in variation across countries in the structure and organization of national school systems."[9]

The appropriate school policy issue is which governance and funding processes most efficiently promote the intellectual development of children. It is not difficult to find solid arguments for parental choice.[10] Market forces are widely applauded for their ability to minimize cost, efficiently address diverse tastes and preferences, and maximize the rate of innovation. In *The School Choice Wars*, I argue that "competitive industries have an impressive track record and K–12 education should respond to competition at least as well as the rest of the economy. The direct evidence includes the education system of the pre-1840 United States and experience with competitive education markets in other countries."[11]

Given that evidence and the predominance of free enterprise and consumer sovereignty in developed nations, the typical primary and secondary schooling arrangements, not market-based alternatives, should seem radical. Defenders of school funding and governance arrangements that strongly favor government-owned schools should have to explain why market forces should be excluded from primary and secondary schooling. But, instead, advocates of choice have had to make the case for market accountability. And the economic case for increased choice and competition is hard for many people to understand because of past educational shortcomings.[12]

Though private schools lack many of the cost-minimizing incentives common to true market settings, comparisons of public and private schools still yield solid evidence of public school inefficiency. In the United States, Chile, and New Zealand, most private schools operate with less money per child than their public-sector counterparts yet achieve similar to slightly better test scores. That should be sufficient to demand far-reaching change in at least the public schools.

But concern about unnecessary or poorly allocated expenditures has not been the impetus for reform. Rather, the major motivation for school reform has been the unacceptably low level of academic achievement and wide disparities in achievement among students. Without the appalling statistics and shocking anecdotes of illiterate, innumerate adults oblivious to key political institutions and historical facts, calls for fundamental reform would get much less attention than they do now. Vice President Al Gore put the politically galvanizing role of crisis quite succinctly: "Scandals are front-page news, while routine failure [inefficiency] is ignored."[13]

Opting out of the assigned school is more costly in the United States than anywhere else, and the United States is a leading example of the common symptoms of huge reform opportunities. Spending is high, achievement levels are low, and harsh criticism is abundant. The existing debate, even among supporters of the present governance and funding processes, is whether U.S. public schools are "a disaster"[14] or a gold-plated disaster.[15]

A bipartisan 1983 presidential commission said the United States was a "nation at risk" and that if another country had done to us what we had done to ourselves it would have been considered an act of war.[16] In spite of that strong call for reform, the years since the 1983 *Nation at Risk* report have not produced significant, sustained academic improvement anywhere in the United States.[17] The intervening 21 years have only heightened the perception of crisis. Frightening anecdotes are commonplace, and the United States has seen periodic formal reaffirmations of the report's findings.[18] Despite decades of policy overhaul and large, real growth in spending, reform of primary and secondary schooling is still a priority of U.S. presidential candidates and state governors.

The statistics are so shocking that citing them to general audiences jeopardizes the speaker's credibility. Many people will simply refuse to believe the appalling data. For example, the 2002 and 2003 National Assessment of Educational Progress test data for fourth and eighth graders revealed that no U.S. state had even half of its students attaining proficiency in any subject at any grade level.[19] The best result was a 49 percent score earned for writing by Connecticut's 2002 fourth graders. Even so, only 49 percent of Connecticut's fourth graders can write at the official fourth grade level, but that is much better than the skill level of the vast majority of tested subjects in all of the other states. Most of the fourth and eighth grade math, reading, and writing proficiency rates are much lower than 49 percent, and they are typically lower still for later grades. Single-digit proficiency rates are quite common, even for states with high primary and secondary education spending.

The disappointing results of countless past reform efforts are strong evidence that the current funding and governance system will continue to resist repair and deteriorate further. And the general findings of Clayton Christiansen and Michael Overdorf suggest pessimism about prospects for substantial improvement in the effectiveness of the current system.[20] They found that even business organizations used to competitive markets seldom fundamentally change themselves. With very few exceptions, pressure for change causes new organizations to replace them.

Another troubling symptom of a broken, reform-resistant system is its hostility or indifference to exemplary results. The government typically fails to expand popular programs or extend them to other schools. Instead of the system expanding popular programs and seeking to further improve them—something obvious to any entrepreneur—shortages persist. That failure is obvious to parents. Where especially effective schools or outstanding programs exist, parents have "to line up days in advance seeking to have their child accepted or hope for the luck of the draw in a lottery."[21] Worse yet, administrators often see standout programs as sore thumbs and eliminate them because "they are too disruptive."[22] The people with vested interests prefer that such embarrassing examples of what is possible not arise, or quickly vanish.[23]

Getting the system out of the way is not an option for the people whose power and income depend on the existing governance and funding practices. Therefore, when confronted with the need for reform, many people within the system naturally focus on a narrow range of system-friendly policies. The recycling of system-friendly ostensible reform options even has a catchy name that captures its persistent futility: "More-of-the-Same-Harder—the MOTS-H approach."[24]

Statements like "the education standards movement is gaining momentum" are another indirect sign of serious systemic problems.[25] Such statements mean that in a system with a notoriously bad track record there is still considerable resistance to higher standards and that you have to establish semipermanent political organizations to lobby for them. A political struggle over standards also suffers severe limitations. The struggle will create a relatively stable, politically defined, academic standard for the vast majority of children, probably based on a single set of easy standardized tests. The latest American result of the ongoing standards struggle is the 2001 No Child Left Behind Act that seeks to ensure that all students meet minimum standards.[26]

A political accountability approach to defining standards implies that quality is narrowly defined and that you can't shop for the specialized standards that best suit your children. It also implies that a relatively static, narrowly defined, uniform minimum standard is acceptable. For example, in New Zealand, "the same detailed curriculum structure is imposed on all subjects, from physical education to physics. The idea that different types of learning need different types of curricula seems to have escaped the architects of the framework."[27] In contrast to the formal, top-down political accountability process, the market's bottom-up subjective accountability pushes informal, specialized standards upward continuously.[28]

Political accountability also directly drives up spending. The U.S. public school system diverts enormous resources from classrooms to political and administrative processes—more than the other members of the Organisation for Economic Co-operation and Development, who typically allow more parental choice and school-based decisionmaking than exist in the United States. According to a 1995 OECD survey, U.S. public schools employ four nonteaching staff per three classroom teachers, the highest ratio in the survey of OECD members.[29] Among OECD members, the average was two nonteaching staff per five teachers. And the high U.S. ratio of nonteaching staff to classroom teachers persists.[30]

Considerable dissatisfaction with school effectiveness exists even in some countries that fare relatively well in international comparisons, including some that recently implemented major changes and achieved some noteworthy academic gains. The debate is about whether the changes constitute reform and whether the most productive changes were made. Resistance to reform shifted policymaking from fundamental reform toward tinkering. The programs became escape hatches for the most desperate and symbols without their intended substance. It all means that a low or even mediocre rank in an international comparison of academic outcomes is probably a cause for serious concern, and because of universally strong resistance to reform (especially market accountability–based reforms), a top rank still leaves much room for improvement. As Roger Kerr, the executive director of New Zealand's Business Roundtable, wrote, "If a survey comes out saying that in certain respects we [NZ] don't compare badly to the rest of the world, my only thought is heaven help the rest of the world."[31]

At virtually opposite ends of the globe, in Chile, New Zealand, and the United States, teachers' unions and the education establishment argue for the funding and governance status quo of political account-ability, detailed rules, and uniformity. They claim that problems exist because of too little funding, inequities in the distribution of funding, and impediments to learning that result from dysfunctional home environments. They insist that parental choice will further widen already large disparities and intensify the already significant isolation of children by race and socioeconomic status. On the other side of the issue, a coalition of businesses, parents, and low–socioeco-nomic status groups argues for genuine choices to address the diver-sity of children and provide an escape hatch for children assigned to improvement-resistant schools and for increased market account-ability to drive innovation and efficiency and prompt the replace-ment of underperforming schools.

Choice as a Reform Catalyst

Paths to System Transformation

A policy change might qualify as a catalyst for reform by showcas-ing an innovation, causing educators and policymakers to "see the light." A positive demonstration followed by the appropriate policy action is what Milton Friedman meant when he said that enactment of a single, real parental choice program would quickly cause the concept to "spread like wildfire."[32] Therefore, many activists pursue a strategy of repeated, incremental enlightenment. The aim is for each modest policy adjustment to whet the appetite for further adjustments, leading ultimately to the full-blown system.

Although an incremental approach may ultimately yield all of the change that occurs—swift system transformation may be politically infeasible—it is at best a tortuously slow route to system transforma-tion. It is difficult to maintain a winning political coalition and focus on a particular final objective for the long time it can take to enact, evaluate, and debate successive pieces of legislation. System trans-formation through parental choice would require significant govern-ment retrenchment, and history does not provide much encourage-ment to those who would pursue a strategy of incremental retrenchment.

Former president Ronald Reagan once said if you can't make them see the light, make them feel the heat. So, if seeing the light doesn't motivate educators to change, we have to think of a way to make them feel the heat. "Feel the heat" means thrive through effectiveness and continuous improvement or lose the education resources to another school operator. That might mean instituting policies that demand transfer of resources to someone producing more highly valued services—a process sometimes called creative destruction. That's the normal way that most of the economy moves forward at sometimes breathtaking speed. Some producers adapt while others yield to innovative newcomers. In other words, on this route to system transformation, managers and educators more in tune with contemporary education realities and client demand would replace the less diligent and dynamic educators.

Essential Elements of a Reform Catalyst

Because of the poor track record of the political accountability approaches that prevail in most countries, this section discusses the key elements of parental choice–based, market accountability approaches to reform. The basic elements of market-based parental choice are

- opportunity to specialize;
- nondiscrimination: per child funding for all schools on the same basis;
- unbiased, low formal entry barriers, including little uncertainty about the scope of the market;
- avoid price control: no penalty for paying tuition with private funds; and
- minimal regulation of private schools.

Opportunity to Specialize. Parental choice legislation has little relevance to parents unless there are noteworthy differences between the schools.[33] The opportunity to specialize underpins the exploitation of producer comparative advantage and the ability to experiment, innovate, and adjust to changing costs.

School operators must be free to use the many important differences in educational approaches and address student diversity with specialized schooling options. If regulation or price control curbs significant specialization, a school system can offer only worse and better versions of a relatively uniform service.[34] That describes the vast majority of choices in the school systems of several countries including at least Chile, New Zealand, Sweden, and the United States. Naturally, everyone wants the best available version. The limited pressure to emulate the best version produces some benefits. But a chance to specialize would greatly increase benefits and would also avoid some of the problems inherent in widespread agreement on which school is best for most children.

A mix of oversubscribed schools and unpopular schools exists in New Zealand and Sweden and in the United States in the rare instances of genuine public school choice.[35] For example, recently when "a fairly sizeable [U.S.] school district opened enrollment at all of its public elementary schools to district parents, 85 percent of the parents applied to one school"—a school that had adopted a more effective "back-to-basics" approach to the district curriculum.[36] District-wide policy uniformity may have foreclosed even more productive avenues of specialization, including areas of specialization of greater interest to some, but not all, of the parents that preferred the popular school's back-to-basics approach to the other alternatives. Genuine opportunity to specialize allows every school to be the most popular with a subset of families large enough to generate sufficient financial support.

Because of the inevitable correlation between income and the ability to pursue the best available schooling, uniformity plus choice yields the socioeconomic sorting, or stratification, of student peer groups decried by many analysts of school choice programs.[37] Recall William Ouchi's question: "If all schools have the same schedule, program, and staffing, what does choice mean?"[38] In that case, it means that remaining differences like student body composition will dominate school choices.

A menu of specialized school choices would decrease stratification by increasing the number of dimensions in which schools differ. Several different versions of each popular topic or teaching method specialty area are much less likely to exist than several different versions of a single, centrally defined approach to schooling.

Allowing school entrepreneurs to competitively duplicate the most popular of the relatively uniform schools is helpful, but it does not eliminate the problem of having a mix of oversubscribed and unpopular schools. The longstanding presence of forced uniformity and the recent history of restriction-laden choice programs explain why a stampede from worse to better schools is already a well-known and widely alleged drawback of parental choice in general.

But if regulation does not prevent competing school operators from specializing, a stampede from worse to better schools is certain only in the early, transitional stages of a new parental choice program and unlikely thereafter.

Legislation capable of fostering a competitive, specialized education industry cannot instantly transform the menu of school choices. It will take some time for specialized offerings to develop and for parents to perceive the "best available school" as depending on the characteristics of their children. Indeed, eventually some families would shun the specialized approach of a particular school for one of their children but prefer it for another.

The widespread assumption that every school will pursue the brilliant children and shun the rest also results from the tradition of school uniformity and the resulting one-dimensional ranking of student ability. If you aim to teach nearly every child the same things in the same way, it is easy to overlook that many children are a mixture of brilliant, ordinary, and slow, depending on the subject matter and teaching method. In contrast, when you aim to fully exploit each child's academic potential rather than meet uniform objective standards, the smartest children are definitely no longer the cheapest to educate; likely the opposite.

Attempts to reconcile student diversity with school zoning have led to specialization within large schools. *The Shopping Mall High School* explains why that specialization policy is inferior to specialization by separate, autonomous, smaller schools.[39] The impersonal nature of large schools overwhelms some children. The variety of deceptively labeled choices makes it easier for children to succumb to peer pressure and other temptations to opt out of challenging courses. Large, complex schools lack the flexibility to address change, and they struggle to develop cohesive staff united behind a clearly defined, compelling mission.

Programs laden with regulations that stymie the normal inclination to specialize in areas of comparative advantage will produce much smaller benefits than programs that foster specialization. For that reason, school choice legislation must not impose uniformity on private schools or restrict the ability of school operators to focus on a specific market niche.

Nondiscrimination: Per Child Funding for All Schools on the Same Basis. Nondiscrimination in funding means universal choice on a level playing field. Unfortunately, there has been a propensity to limit parental choice eligibility to economically disadvantaged families and children enrolled in especially bad public schools. That means a slightly less tilted field for a select few. Among the key reasons for preferential treatment of some children are the political imperative to safeguard existing arrangements and the widespread fallacy that the "better" schools are necessarily good and that only disadvantaged children assigned to isolated awful schools are not well served. Also, limiting school choices to a subset of the student population—by excluding the students already enrolled in private schools or by funding public school users at a higher level than children who use vouchers to attend private schools—can save taxpayer money.

Targeting also avoids some "churn."[40] Churn is the additional cost incurred when the government pays for something most people will buy anyway. The high cost of churn includes the costs of funneling money through government channels and also the economic distortions that result from tax avoidance and tax evasion. But collecting taxes to pay the schooling costs of middle- and upper-class families also has a major advantage. It avoids a major cash flow problem that would severely reduce private spending on schooling and sharply bias many family economic and political decisions in favor of "free" public schooling. Direct private payment of tuition would concentrate the cost of schooling during the relatively few years that children are in school and that largely precede most adults' peak earning years. Using taxes to pay for schooling spreads the cost of educating children over entire lives.

So, while targeting reduces churn and might reduce government spending by funding some children below the current per pupil expenditure level, it has bigger disadvantages. As noted in *The School Choice Wars*: "Varying benefits by income makes the policy an income redistribution program, not an education program, and it raises a compelling practical issue. The political process typically ensures that 'programs for the poor (when low-income families contribute relatively little and receive relatively more per capita) become poor programs.' "[41] Means testing also has the potential to curb the social mobility that comes with the pursuit of increased earnings. Prospective loss of benefits like vouchers for children of low-income families could greatly elevate effective marginal tax rates. High marginal tax rates could stifle a considerable amount of highly beneficial movement from lower to higher income levels. For example, according to Thomas Sowell: "Only a fraction of the [American] people who are in the bottom twenty percent in income at any given time will be there for more than a few years. Most of those in the bottom twenty percent of income earners are also in the top twenty percent at some other time in their careers."[42]

The biggest disadvantage of targeting select groups of students is that it reduces the competitiveness of the education market. Since targeting means selective reduction in the financial impact of choosing a private school, fewer families will opt for a private school. That reduces the incentive to identify and correct problems in the public schools. It also reduces the incentive for potential school operators to develop new schooling choices. In other words, targeting stifles innovation and is a significant, informal market entry barrier.

Targeted school choice programs exclude the higher-income classes that usually drive innovation. Because they are willing to pay a little more, the higher-income classes are generally the early adopters of new services. Preventing their participation in school choice programs eliminates their investment in new innovations and better methods. The resulting reduction in the number of choices, the slower rate of innovation-driven improvement, and political neglect by the untargeted probably do the targeted poor children more harm than good. Harrison reaches the same conclusion: "A voucher targeted at the poor would provide benefits to the recipients—but would not introduce a competitive market. An increase in competition would improve schools and provide further benefits—to poor students and others."[43]

A second huge disadvantage of targeting is that limiting parental choice programs to a small fraction of the student population is an implied endorsement of the basic elements of the current system. It tells the largely detached, minimally informed majority of the electorate that the system does not need to be transformed.

So, to avoid discrimination and thus foster market accountability, parental choice programs should allocate 100 percent of the taxes collected to support primary and secondary schooling.[44] The same amount of taxpayer money should support a particular child, regardless of family income, at the public, private nonprofit, or private for-profit school selected by the child's parents. Avoiding targeting maximizes the competitive pressure on all schools.

Unbiased, Low Formal Entry Barriers. To maximize and accelerate the development of specialized forms of schooling, freedom to enter the arena (i.e., start a school) on formally equal terms with other school operators is one of the essential elements. Indeed, freedom to enter the market is the most essential element. Freedom to enter is more important even than a large number of schools, each with a trivial market share. Freedom to enter reinforces the ability to specialize, and it fosters rivalry sufficient to compel specialization. To maintain enrollments against existing and potential rivals, operators of existing schools will have to concentrate on their strengths and pursue continuous improvement.

Note that even in the absence of significant formal entry barriers, incumbent school operators have major informal advantages like name recognition, reputation, established adult networks, and probably less debt. Potential school operators must persuade venture capitalists or philanthropists that a new educational approach by a rookie school manager can attract enough students to cover expenses. Short of major neglect by incumbent purveyors of popular specializations, it takes a major innovation or cost advantage for a newcomer to the education market to gain some market share. The significant informal advantages of incumbency are among the critical reasons why potential competitors must be on formally equal terms with incumbents.

Freedom to enter and the pressure to innovate and create a reputation are especially relevant to profit-seeking entrepreneurs. Nonprofit school operators have different incentives, for example, to serve a particular clientele or promote a certain curriculum. Andrew Coulson notes:

> The importance of profit making can easily be grasped by looking at the different responses that non-profit and for-profit schools have to pent up consumer demand. Even the most highly regarded non-profit schools, such as Phillips Exeter and the Laboratory School at the University of Chicago, serve only about a thousand more students today than they did a century ago. They have expanded their waiting lists instead of opening new facilities [because] they lack an incentive (profits) sufficient to overcome the risks of expansion.[45]

In addition, though nonprofits cannot pursue venture capital, they may not be fully dependent on clients for their funding. They can

188

derive funding from churches or "alumni who seek to perpetuate a tradition rather than to commercialize a popular service."[46]

As long as governments don't mandate price ceilings, freedom to enter allows profit-seeking school entrepreneurs to serve as all-important barometers of changing costs, schooling preferences, and related competing investment opportunities. Absent debilitating entry barriers, entrepreneurs will innovate to create new market niches or seize market share in existing niches by cutting costs. Likewise they will exit niches where changing costs are not in synch with changes in demand.

Attracting profit-seeking entrepreneurs also requires a high degree of certainty about the scope of the market as a whole. Uncertainty about key financial support, political support for key legislation, or key programs' ability to withstand legal challenges is a major barrier to entry. Such uncertainty severely shortens the investment payback period that financial supporters will tolerate, perhaps to the point where potentially attractive long-term investments become too risky, leading to no entry or fundamentally altered entry. For example, such uncertainties may prompt entrepreneurs to forgo constructing new school buildings in favor of setting up new schools in existing rental space.

Freedom to enter ensures against "highgrading"—a fisheries term that aptly describes schools' tendency to address excess demand by keeping only the best "catches" and tossing the rest back. Allowing school operators to use tuition hikes to eliminate waiting lists is just highgrading according to ability and willingness to pay, which many people object to unless it is properly understood to be just a temporary though essential part of the market response to popularity. Higher prices are a natural response of profit-seeking entrepreneurs to increased demand. But with freedom to enter, the price increases that prevent shortages of popular products also attract copycat entrepreneurs. The resulting increased production at least partially reverses the initial price increase. The extent of reversal depends on how market growth changes production costs.

So, freedom to compete for market share leads to imitation of popular schooling practices by newcomers. That ends the opportunities to highgrade through permanently higher tuition, and it avoids the inefficiency of waiting lists or tuition levels that overstate production costs. Freedom to form new schools would also pressure schools to limit denial of enrollment requests to what a school finds necessary to pursue its specialization. Since freedom to enter the market would quickly eliminate most waiting lists, bigotry would become more costly. In the current system, the waiting lists that result from entry barriers and price control allow bigoted operators of popular schools to practice bigotry for free if they discriminate quietly enough to avoid prosecution. A waiting list means that rejection of an applicant costs oversubscribed bigots nothing. The school stays full. Waiting lists also tempt producers to save money by letting product quality deteriorate. Quality deterioration can also result from price control, and price change is an essential partner of freedom to enter in fostering innovation and curbing waiting lists.

Avoid Price Control. It is important that school management be free to vary the price of services as necessary to respond to market forces. Freedom to charge whatever they want does not mean assuring school operators enough students at whatever price they set. Nor does it mean that taxpayers should pay schools any amount they wish. It just means that there is no government-set floor or ceiling on tuition and fees. Customers' willingness to buy from a particular seller is the only constraint.

Freedom to determine price and freedom to start a school on formally equal terms are essential partners because customer willingness to buy depends on the availability of reasonable alternatives. Without the actual and potential rivalry that results from freedom to start a private school, schools could exploit the absence of alternatives by selling minimally effective schooling at a very high price. Indeed, that is the typical, current state of affairs in many reform-minded countries. Barriers to entry keep low-quality, high-cost schools in business.

Price change signals which types of education services are most sought after and provides the wherewithal and incentive to increase production of those services. Without freedom to determine price, many potentially effective forms of specialization become impossible or unattractive to educators. Some versions of schooling cost more than others, and some cost a lot to develop and launch. Later, experience and competition will bring costs down, but without the freedom to charge a relatively high price in the early stages of an innovation, many innovations would never be developed, much less get into a classroom. Regardless of the actual production expenses, the ability to charge an above-average price for schooling innovations is an important incentive to invest in the research and development necessary to bring innovations "on-line."

Unfortunately, price control is the school choice policy norm. Typically, price control results from laws that require school operators to accept government funds as full payment. In other words, the law typically bans privately funded add-on tuition or fee copayments (henceforth: "add-on bans").[47] Price control has an unbroken track record of costly failure so add-on bans are probably devastating.[48] "Probably" because we can't observe what would have happened without the bans. But we can be sure that add-on bans directly narrow the school choice menu to practices that cost less than the government funds. Add-on bans indirectly stifle competition and innovation. By discouraging private spending, add-on bans reduce total spending on formal schooling.

It is true that many people do not understand the crucial role of price change in managing scarcity and motivating innovation. But class envy could be an even larger factor. The typical rationale for add-on bans is that well-off families will use add-ons to further invest in their children, gain some sort of new advantage, and perhaps even harm less-advantaged children. But talk of subsidizing the choices of the wealthy ignores that the same kind of subsidization already exists in current systems of free government-operated schools. Wealthy people can simply decide to live in better school districts. Complaints about subsidizing the wealthy also assume that the government funds were taken from someone else. But there is no tax system in which the wealthy pay less than a per capita share of government revenue. Returning a per capita (or per student) share of the government funds collected for schooling to the middle- and upper-income households that were the major source of those funds just amounts to mandating their average minimum schooling purchase and a loan against future taxes to pay for it.[49] Upper-income taxpayers are just indirectly spending some of their own earnings while genuinely subsidizing the poor. Some drawbacks notwithstanding, forcing a minimum level of education spending has the major advantage of giving everyone a stake in the school choice program and resulting system. That is important because otherwise school choice programs are just income redistribution programs, and programs for the poor are invariably poor programs. It is very much in the interest of lower-income families that all families benefit from the tax dollars collected for the schooling of children.

Allowing add-ons will prompt some relatively wealthy families to buy even better schooling for their children, but that does not mean worse schooling for the children of lower-income families. Spending by the relatively wealthy yields innovations that ultimately benefit everyone. Additional schooling for their children is the most socially beneficial way for the wealthy to spend their earnings. Investments in human capital anywhere ultimately make the economy more productive and the political system more effective. There isn't a finite amount of opportunity to be seized by some and thus lost by others.

Focusing on the gap between more- and less-advantaged children may diminish the gains of the less advantaged. Reducing the gap by holding back the well-off does not benefit anyone. Indeed, it will lower the gains of the disadvantaged, perhaps substantially. Allowing everyone to gain from parental choice will likely narrow the gap between the most and least advantaged. After all, there is much more room for improvement in the current education system's services to the poorest families than in the schooling received by the richest families. But even if new choices for everyone were more likely to widen the gap, that's less important than maximizing the absolute gains. The key question is not the extent to which parental choice programs yield better schooling for well-off families than for less well-off families (in the unlikely event that actually happens) but whether each set of families, especially the less well-off, enjoys better schooling than they otherwise would.

Some observers may argue that add-ons will hurt less-advantaged children by allowing the wealthy to hoard the best educators. Again, that argument rests on several dubious assumptions. Certainly, the truly wealthy will always have the means to buy the best of everything. It's an outcome synonymous with higher *earnings*. Attempts to prevent that will be futile and costly to everyone. But note that "best" doesn't mean systematically and significantly better than everyone else. Most places don't have enough truly rich people to support a separate, premium set of specialized schools for just their children. Therefore, most economically advantaged children will attend the same specialized schools as their less-advantaged peers. Again, the opportunity to specialize is the key. The typical parent interested in a school with a particular teaching style or subject matter would not have premium, middle-grade, and regular versions to choose from very often.

Allowing add-ons avoids price ceilings but not a potential price floor at the per child government subsidy. To avoid price floor problems, schools must also be free to charge less than the taxpayer-funded per child payment, and parents must have an incentive to consider such schooling options. If countries like the United States that already spend a huge amount per student were to fund all children on the same basis, market entry could push some tuition quotes below the existing per child expenditure level.[50] Failure to allow the price to fall below the taxpayer-funded per child expenditure could lead to costly overinvestment in schooling and tempt some schools to offer disguised kickbacks. In addition, the availability of choiceworthy schooling for less than the per child public funding level informs adjustment of the public funding level.

With that approach to ensuring downward price flexibility, families could make intertemporal choices: less schooling now for more later. Discounts below the taxpayer-funded per child payment level in the form of credits for future schooling services (including higher education) would produce less fraudulent behavior than cash payments.[51] Cash payments could tempt some families to seek phantom schools. The resulting scandals could foster much increased, debilitating regulation. Excess supply at the taxpayer-funded per child payment level might still tempt some schools to illegally offer cash or in-kind kickbacks, but high transaction costs would cause most families to prefer credits for future schooling services or a contemporary upgrade in schooling services.

Another way to avoid a rigid price floor at the taxpayer-funded per child payment level is to specify the government payment as the lesser of a certain percentage of the tuition or a specific maximum payment. Forcing parents to share in tuition expenses has a multitude of significant political and economic advantages and disadvantages. According to Andrew Coulson's wide-ranging study of past school systems, the primary benefit of forcing parents to share in tuition expenses is increased parental involvement.[52] He found that parental responsibility for at least a share of schooling costs was a common denominator of effective school systems. Among the disadvantages is that it would create a new expense for most families.

Lower-income families would suffer disproportionately. Since they pay few taxes, they would see little, if any, benefit from lower school taxes. That might not outweigh the benefits of increased parental involvement, but it might be a moot point. The political or legal implications could prevent the program from being implemented.

Compared with the add-on or credit approach to market-based prices described above, forcing parents to share in tuition expenses reduces schools' incentive to lower tuition and increases the incentive to raise tuition to the point where the taxpayer share is the maximum payment. In other words, it may be a good idea because of increased parental involvement, but it will do little to keep the taxpayer funds from creating a price floor. For example, suppose the government's tuition-sharing policy is to pay $5,000 per child or 90 percent of tuition, whichever is less. Consider a school that charges tuition of $5,000. The government would pay $4,500 (90 percent), and parents would pay $500. Lowering the tuition to $4,500 would only lower what parents pay to $450. It saves parents only $50. Below $5,556 ($5,000 is 90 percent of $5,556) the school must forego $10 to achieve a dollar's worth of increased price competitiveness from parents' perspective. Therefore, such a policy would create a virtual price floor at $5,556. The price floor is irrelevant if that is below the tuition and fees of even the least-expensive schools, but then the affordability issue is a larger factor.

Minimal Regulation of Private Schools. To prevent fraud and promote efficient disbursement of taxes levied to support schooling, governments must establish school eligibility criteria. Recognition of private accrediting organizations is probably sufficient. The details, though beyond the scope of this chapter, are not trivial issues.

It is imperative that administrative necessities not lead to regulatory strangulation of the parental choice reform catalyst. Certainly, political and administrative strangulation in the form of detailed national curricula and even detailed physical descriptions of approved schools is a key cause of many countries' strong interest in reform. It is important that decisionmakers and activists recognize the serious consequences of going beyond the bare minimum of oversight needed to efficiently disburse funds, deter fraud, and separately manage the government-owned schools. To prescribe in detail what the vast majority of families will generally demand anyway gains little, but it eviscerates parental choice as a reform catalyst. It even sacrifices much of the value of choice as an escape hatch. An escape to a very similar school is not very helpful. Politically defined uniformity and politically correct curricula are very costly. Neglect of socially valued subject matter by some families and tolerance of some unpopular differences in what is taught are much less costly.[53]

There is little systematic evidence that private schooling promotes extremist behavior, but a few scandalous anecdotes—even hypothetical examples—are politically potent. Therefore, the formal definition of "school" should ban the advocacy of unlawful behavior. A modest minimum-size rule may also be a political necessity as a least-cost deterrent to extremist behavior that avoids violating the letter of the law but violates its spirit.

A carefully crafted minimum-size rule can achieve its aims without unpleasant regulatory side effects. To avoid banning schools that are small because they focus on a limited age cohort, the minimum-size rule should probably specify an age cohort minimum (for example, 20 children per two-year age cohort). In sparsely populated areas, significant percentages could substitute for absolute numbers per age cohort. A carefully crafted minimum-size rule, the pressure to specialize, and the inability to reject applicants on the basis of race or ethnicity would make it very difficult to recruit enough staff and students for an extremist school.[54]

Such a minimum-size rule would also keep families from earning income by educating their own children. On its face, that concern may seem inappropriate, or at least not an outcome worthy of formal opposition. Unfortunately, paying people more than actual education expenses to educate their own children can produce some significant, unintended side effects. An annual per child government payment for schooling your own children is very similar to a large increase in the per child income tax deduction. True, to legitimately earn the payments, at least one parent would have to enroll in formal schooling. But it is also true that a large family combined with payments on the order of the existing education funding per child prevailing in many countries would yield a significant annual "income." For example, the United States spends around $10,000 per child per year.[55] That times, say, five school-age children would push a family halfway to the statistically wealthy top 10 percent. Such possibilities could substantially increase the size of some families and population growth. Much smaller tax policy changes have produced significant changes in birthrates.[56] Lucrative home-schooling enterprises could also reduce labor force participation. Either or both could be unwanted side effects of school choice programs.

Helpful Elements

Among the nonessential but helpful elements is an effort to lower information costs. Markets are driven by a relatively few informed, footloose consumers. Because relatively few clients often account for the difference between profit and loss, enterprises must pay attention to their most discerning customers. But even with the growing accessibility and power of the Internet, private information sources might not adequately inform the choices of the minimum set of information conscious consumers. Those sources range from informal conversations among neighbors to accreditation and certification organizations and *Consumer Reports*–like publications. So, descriptive and basic research data, especially the types of data for which there is no immediate market, could be quite helpful.

Although permission to meet tuition costs with a combination of government and private funds (allow add-ons) is crucial, it would be helpful if the government payment per child were high enough so that competition would prompt some schools to accept the government payment as full payment. In places that constitutionally require access to a "free" education, availability of some schools that do not demand an add-on might be necessary for a school choice program to survive lawsuits from opponents of choice. But even without such legal issues, a high per child minimum would be quite helpful in addressing equity concerns and easing the transformation of the system. In the United States, existing funding levels—an average annual payment close to $10,000 per child—would eliminate income as a barrier to all but a handful of existing schools. The philanthropic dollars that already fund scholarships and full and partial vouchers could support many more children if only add-ons had to be privately funded. That would give low-income families considerable access to the few schools that would charge more than the government payment amount.

The Key Features of Seven Prominent Choice Programs

Because of the recent attention given to parental choice programs in Chile, Milwaukee, Florida, Cleveland, Edgewood, New Zealand, and Sweden, this section discusses each in terms of the key elements described above. Table 10.1, at the end of this section, summarizes key elements of each plan.

Chile

Chile has had a universal voucher system for nearly 25 years. Voucher funding means that a certain amount of government funding follows a particular child to the public or privately owned school selected by the child's parents. But tight central control survived the implementation of the voucher program. The details below demonstrate that the Chilean policy lacks most of the key elements of a school reform catalyst.

The net effect of choice within a system defined in considerable detail by the Education Ministry is that the Chilean private schools eligible for government funds do what the ministry demands of all schools a bit more efficiently than the government-owned "municipal" schools. The municipal schools generally produce slightly lower test scores, and they operate with more money per child than the voucher-funded private schools. Because funding practices favor municipal schools, new schools are not on formally equal terms with the municipal schools. Examples of preferential funding for municipal school students include the following:

- During the mid-1980s economic crisis, the ministry paid a portion of municipal deficits.[57]
- Poor students receive higher subsidies if they go to municipal schools.[58]
- Municipal schools receive extra budget (above voucher funds) from the municipalities and the ministry.[59]
- The Ministry of Education provides the physical infrastructure of municipal schools, while subsidized private ones are forced to finance all the investments by themselves.[60]
- Public schools work under a system of "soft" budget constraints and are not influenced by the competition from private voucher schools. Municipal schools with important competition from private voucher schools may actually want their students to leave, since they can preserve their jobs (no municipal schools have closed) while teaching smaller classes.[61]

The Education Ministry allows add-ons at some schools, but they are capped and progressively taxed. In other words, a school that charges, say, $100 more than the Education Ministry payment keeps less than the extra $100. The Education Ministry keeps a bigger piece of a $200 add-on, and so on. Because the Education Ministry specifies approved education practices and facilities in considerable detail, opportunities to specialize are minimal.

Beyond the documentation of ministry activity cited below, the proof that the ministry's micromanagement practices and add-on restrictions are severe is the persistence of a significant unsubsidized private school sector. If the subsidized private schools were free to produce whatever the customers of unsubsidized schools prefer to the present alternatives, a subsidized private school could offer, for a much lower price, the same services now available only at unsubsidized private schools. Unsubsidized schools would become uncompetitive and disappear. But they haven't disappeared. For nearly 10 percent of the population, the difference between what an unsubsidized school can produce and what a subsidized private school can produce is worth much more than the difference in the cost of producing it.[62]

Chile's entry barriers are formidable. The informal barrier that results from better municipal school funding is a minor factor compared with Chile's detailed regulations. They severely limit the market niches free enterprise can serve. In addition, the Education Ministry directly regulates entry. Regional offices of the Ministry of Education have to certify that there is not an excess of educational services before a private school can be formed.[63] Education services are seen as a homogenous commodity, not a mix of specialized services potentially with excess demand in some areas and excess supply in others. Taken literally, that decree means that improved service or a new market niche does not justify permission to form a new school. In addition, a school must first be recognized as a "collaborator in the educational function of the state," which means it must adhere to the ministry's curricula or propose its own, which few schools have the capacity to do.[64] According to Varun Gauri, the recognition requirement means that the Education Ministry determines if the staff, teaching materials, and building are adequate. Education Ministry inspections determine, among other things, conformity with ministerial norms. The scope of inspections has steadily expanded, especially for private schools.[65] According to Gauri: "The inspections and central government rules raise the costs of innovation for both municipal and private schools. Few are experimenting.

All schools must adhere to given curricula, organize themselves in normal cycles, and operate in a traditional building."[66] Central, standardized testing reinforces those mandates.

There is detailed central regulation of school administration, and the Education Ministry controls teacher preparation.[67] Teachers in all schools share similar backgrounds and pedagogical orientations. A Teachers Statute imposes centralized negotiation of wages so that schools lose control over their wage budgets.[68] According to Gauri, "The neoliberal reforms promoting private education have not led to educational diversity, innovation, and experimentation in Chile but have in fact brought more state control to private education, arguably even increasing homogeneity in an already uniform system."[69] Indeed, better schools have waiting lists and allegedly screen students according to parent background. Since the ministry and municipalities hinder or bar so many of the changes competition might lead to, Chile's version of parental choice has not been a reform catalyst and has little utility as a market accountability experiment.

Those compelling issues, especially Education Ministry micromanagement of Chilean schools, were largely unknown to or were ignored by the prominent school choice analysts who examined Chile's voucher system.[70] The articles authored by those analysts imply decentralized decisionmaking. Indeed, they have been willing to characterize the Chilean system as "a textbook voucher scheme," "unrestricted," and "twenty years of unrestricted school choice"— statements that are especially shocking coming from economists. No less shocking is the failure to offer ministry micromanagement as a good explanation for the lack of dramatic differences among the three voucher-funded sectors. Instead, the lack of dramatic differences was the implied result of market forces' failure to live up to the standard economic theory about the likely performance of for-profit schools.

The period during which the Chilean system was supposedly "a textbook voucher scheme" preceded the ministry decision to allow some schools to request limited, taxed add-ons (limited price decontrol). So, apparently, to those economists, price control is part of a textbook voucher scheme.[71]

Much of the evidence of Education Ministry heavy-handedness can be found in Gauri's 1998 book.[72] The alleged evidence must be refuted or taken into account. Unless Gauri overstated his findings, numerous analysts' indifference to detailed descriptions of extensive micromanagement demonstrates substantial carelessness or bias. I hope it is carelessness, but limited evidence points to bias. There aren't many studies of Chile's system, so accidentally overlooking Gauri's findings seems implausible. Gauri's micromanagement findings are in *School Choice in Chile,* a work clearly related to the subject of the careless or biased articles. None of those articles made an effort to refute Gauri's findings. One of the authors was willing to cite Gauri's findings as evidence of student screening to support the finding of "stratification" but made no mention of Gauri's description of Education Ministry micromanagement.[73] Certainly, the evolution of Chile's education system ("no dramatic differences among the three voucher-funded sectors") is consistent with relative uniformity, tight central regulation, and greater private-sector efficiency of municipal schools.

There is no basis for attaching terms like "unrestricted," "ideal," or "textbook" to Chile's system, but there is still much to be learned from it. The lessons from Chile are not lessons just for Chile. Additional evidence on the nature, extent, and effects of ministry rules could be quite helpful to policymakers around the world.

Milwaukee, Florida, and Cleveland

In terms of the key elements, the substantive differences between the three U.S. examples of publicly funded vouchers are not significant. In each instance, a small subset of low-income families gets a voucher worth much less than the per pupil expenditure in the public school system. Except for one part of the Florida program, add-ons are prohibited or capped at a very small amount.

The Milwaukee voucher ($5,882 in 2003–04) is worth slightly more than half the public school per pupil expenditure. Approximately 15,000 vouchers are available (15 percent of Milwaukee's public school enrollment) to children from low-income Milwaukee families. The 2003–04 school year saw the funding of 13,268 vouchers. In part because many Milwaukee private schools have converted to chartered schools, there hasn't been enough private school capacity to accommodate everyone eligible for a voucher. There is a waiting list for private school space.[74] Because of private school waiting lists, improvements in public or private schools do not affect enrollments or funding. Waiting lists mean that improvements anywhere change only the number hoping to leave public schools. That sharply attenuates rivalry pressures on the private and public school sectors. Nevertheless, several prominent studies imply the presence of robust competition in Milwaukee and allege that it amounts to a market education experiment.[75]

Despite the new opportunities created for some low-income Milwaukee families, the economic fundamentals are little changed. The basic economic model that applies to the Milwaukee situation now is the same as before the voucher program. There is still a very dominant "firm" (the Milwaukee Public Schools) and a "competitive" fringe. That standard economic model is about market power, not competition. Real competition is much more than the muted rivalry that exists between a dominant producer and a competitive fringe of much smaller producers. And there is much more genuine rivalry in the standard model than between private schools and the public school system. In other words, market share is even less contestable in Milwaukee than in the typical situation of a dominant firm with a competitive fringe. In the standard model, the members of the competitive fringe are businesses that can expand, and the dominant firm must finance its operations entirely from sales. Milwaukee, and most other places with a school choice program, handicap the competitive fringe with price controls and enrollment caps, and the dominant public system doesn't have to charge tuition to finance its operations.

Florida actually has three voucher programs. One is a tax credit for donating money to a private fund that provides low-income vouchers. The second program gives students publicly funded vouchers worth about half the public school per child expenditure if their assigned school gets a grade of F from the state two years out of four, an incredibly demanding standard of failure for an escape hatch that can only lead eligible escapees to really cheap private schools. In November 2003, Florida schoolchildren used 1,100 state-funded vouchers worth between $3,500 and $3,900.

A third program provides vouchers for special needs children. Because of the decision to remove the add-on ban, it's the most noteworthy element of Florida's voucher policy. Known as the McKay Scholarships Program, it began with the typical price control element; private schools that received voucher money had to accept it as full payment. Few schools participated. At the end of the first year of the McKay program, the legislature acknowledged that the program's target clientele was too diverse for the government to specify the cost of services and eliminated the add-on ban. Participation in the McKay program exploded even though many schools did not require an add-on and most add-ons were quite modest. From the fall of 2001 to February 2003, the number of participating private schools increased from 120 to 600.[76] Student enrollment reached 12,000 in the fall of 2003, more than double the first year (2001–02) enrollment of 5,019.

Cleveland's voucher is worth much less than half of the per pupil expenditure in the Cleveland public school system; in 2003–04 it was worth a maximum of 90 percent of tuition or $3,000, whichever was less. The allowed tuition payments are too small to prompt much private-sector expansion. In Cleveland, the availability of the vouchers just increased the demand for mostly church-subsidized schooling. Many churches did choose to extend church subsidies to a larger number of children (5,147 vouchers cashed in 2002–03), but ultimately many found themselves unable to continue the additional subsidies.[77]

Clearly, none of the publicly funded U.S. programs approaches the key conditions of a parental choice reform catalyst. Public school improvements are evident in Milwaukee[78] and Florida,[79] but they are quite modest in scope and size. It would take 10 to 20 years of such gains for the students in Milwaukee's public schools to reach the better, but still low, achievement levels of nearby suburban public schools.[80] Nearly 10 years into the Milwaukee voucher program, the public school system was still so bad that it barely avoided a threatened June 2000 state takeover.

Potential participation in the Milwaukee, Florida, and Cleveland programs is far from universal, and, with the exception of Florida's McKay program, price control is stringent and ubiquitous. Only the still tiny private sectors of Cleveland, Florida, and Milwaukee can pursue specialization, but price control, low funding levels, waiting lists, and participation caps reduce both the incentive and the ability to do so. Except for some periodic discussion of additional restrictions and the possibility of a higher participation cap in Milwaukee, the programs appear fairly static.

Celebration of those programs should not extend much beyond the lucky participants. As one should expect from school choices made by proactive parents, the children benefited. Given the importance mistakenly attached to comparisons of politically straitjacketed public schools and financially crippled private schools, that's quite fortunate.[81] The nature of the comparison is a powerful demonstration of the U.S. system's transformation imperative. Conclusions drawn from the studies of those programs should not go beyond the utility of parental choice as a limited escape route to elsewhere in the existing system. The modest improvements in Milwaukee and Florida did not include significant specialization. The jury is still out on those programs' potential to gradually evolve into reform catalysts or prompt wider discussion of parental choice as a reform catalyst, but the existing evidence should not bolster optimism about incremental strategies.

Edgewood

The Edgewood voucher is a privately funded, universal voucher program for the low-income residents of the Edgewood School District, one of 15 school districts in the San Antonio, Texas, metropolitan area. Because 96 percent of the district's residents meet the low-income definition, "universal" only negligibly contradicts "low income."[82] The voucher sponsors allow add-ons, but the low-income eligibility criterion limits the voucher users' willingness to pay them.

The Edgewood District spent $6,729 per public school user in 2001–02.[83] The largest voucher was $4,700. Midway through the Children's Educational Opportunity Foundation's 10-year commitment, there were 1,935 voucher users. With Edgewood's public school enrollment at 13,435 students,[84] the year five (2002–03) 14.4 percent growth over 2001–02[85] still left room for considerable growth. Language barriers, the novelty of parental choice, the district's public relations offensive, and the meager alternatives offered by the small private sector reduced interest in the voucher option. With many of those problems now resolved or diminished, program participation could still rise significantly. However, uncertainty created by the approach of the 2008 end of the program donors' 10-year funding commitment will reduce interest.

Uncertainty about longevity is probably the Edgewood program's primary shortcoming as a potential reform catalyst. The imminent 2008 expiration date probably discourages entrepreneur interest more than other lesser problems like the small, predominantly low-income market area and the district's per child funding advantage.

The effect of looming expiration on uncertainty is evident in the area's modest degree of private-sector expansion and the nature of most expansions. Because the program's funding isn't ensured for long enough to pay for major new investments, most of the new private schools formed in rented commercial space.

New Zealand

New Zealand's Education Act of 1989 implemented major decentralizing measures called for by the 1987 Picot Taskforce. The 1989 reform largely eliminated assignment by zone, and the schools became more autonomous. But again, the center held. The government maintained control of a 96.2 percent share of New Zealand's schools,[86] and the state kept or quickly reasserted control over many aspects of a school's operation.[87] Parental choice of government-owned schools suffered growing restrictions including a partial reimposition of assignment by zone. Independent private schools remained extremely rare largely because their students didn't have access to the large subsidies available to other students. Tax dollars collected to pay for schooling continued to support only the children who attend the government-owned schools and the government-controlled and government-subsidized integrated private schools.

Even more than the prominent studies of Chile's voucher program, the major studies of the New Zealand public school choice program offer examples of startling neglect of basic economic principles. The government-controlled segment (96.2 percent) of New Zealand's primary and secondary education system has no prices, profits, or instances of market entry. There have been only a few isolated school closures and little specialization. But prominent individuals ranging from former U.S. secretary of labor Robert Reich to academic economists employed by prestigious think tanks and universities see the New Zealand experience as a legitimate test of markets in action.[88] Secretary Reich and others equated the New Zealand program with a universal voucher plan, calling it an example of "unrestricted" choice, a "foray into the realm of full parental choice and competition" with "self-governing schools functioning in a competitive environment." In a recent article published in a flagship economics journal, a pair of economists noted that

- central authorities continued to retain a major role in determining teacher employment contracts, approving school charters, and maintaining educational standards; capital works continued to be the province of the Ministry of Education;

- the National Education Guidelines clearly constrained school individuality; and
- the state still controlled school capacities, curricula, and qualification systems; teacher contracts; school fees; teacher training; funding to schools; and the like; only a few of the many constraints were relaxed, and the only significant ones relaxed were on the demand side of the market.[89]

But those economists still alleged "major market-based educational reforms" in New Zealand.[90]

In reality, the New Zealand central government strictly controls the supply of schools and dictates nearly everything they do.

> For state and integrated schools, the government provides over ninety percent of the funding and the Ministry regulates the curriculum, governance arrangements, fees, student enrolment and expulsion decisions, the length of the school day and year, and approves schools' charters (and dictates a substantial portion of their content), negotiates the collective contracts with teacher unions and pays teachers through a central payroll. For state schools, the Ministry provides and allocates capital funding, owns school buildings and land, manages major maintenance, and controls school entry, exit, and expansion. It funds, provides, and regulates teacher training. The Ministry also determines the number, location, and capacity of schools for virtually every New Zealand child.[91]

Popular schools suffer crowding and have waiting lists. Space shortages persist because the government refuses to "invest in new school facilities while others remain under-utilized."[92] Space shortages at popular schools force parents to patronize unpopular schools that might otherwise be forced to close. Those shortages and excessive capacity at some schools prompted the authorities to partially reimpose school zoning. As noted previously, New Zealand's mixture of oversubscribed and underused schools demonstrates that the school choices are only among different grades of a relatively uniform schooling product. Indeed, specialization is minimal because "local goals were secondary to those imposed from the center in the form of the National Education Guidelines."[93]

Extremely rare closure of unpopular schools and the fact that enrollment is only one determinant of each school's funding indicate that school choice provides little incentive to improve schooling. Indeed, it may produce some perverse incentives. School improvements yield crowding and larger classes. Since the government almost never closes unpopular schools and salaries are centrally determined, neglecting pursuit of efficiency and innovation means classes with fewer students to teach, fewer papers to grade, and fewer parents to meet—something attractive to most teachers.[94]

Legislation "sets out in significant detail the rules governing the sector. This is true in a number of areas including hours of operation and school governance. The make-up of a school governing body is set out in much detail in the Education Act of 1989."[95] The National Curriculum has become quite detailed. Though private schools are not directly forced to offer the National Curriculum, most do. "The same detailed curriculum structure is imposed on all subjects, from physical education to physics. [There are] eight defined levels for each of a very large number of subjects. The curriculum applies to all students, irrespective of abilities or inclination. The idea that different types of learning need different types of curricula seems to have escaped the architects of the framework."[96]

Furthermore, "the industrial relations environment faced by most schools is highly centralized and complex. For the vast majority of teachers (around 90 percent), wages, terms and conditions are contained in national collective contracts (CECs) negotiated by the Ministry (via the State Sector Act)."[97] The government's highly prescriptive, homogenizing personnel policies are as follows:

> In New Zealand, state school boards appoint staff and pay the salaries of senior management (such as the principal and deputy principal) from grants they receive. The Ministry of Education sets each school's teaching staff entitlement and funds salaries that are paid to teachers through a centralized payroll system. The Ministry and teacher unions negotiate centrally the collective contracts that set pay and working conditions for most teachers. Collective contracts are negotiated for primary teachers, secondary teachers, area teachers, primary principals and support staff. The Ministry also promulgates base rates of pay for principals. Teacher central employment contracts are the only large-scale cross-employer contracts remaining in the state sector. The New

Zealand Teachers Council, which took over responsibility for registering teachers from the Teacher Registration Board in early 2002, restricts those whom boards can hire, and promises to increase regulation of teacher education, entry standards and practice.[98]

In summary, the 1989 reforms did not establish any of the key elements of a reform catalyst. Absent legislation calling for more substantial market accountability–based reforms, New Zealand will continue to offer a uniform menu of choices.

Sweden

Just over a decade ago, Sweden created a parental choice program. The Swedish reform is slightly younger than the New Zealand reform and about half the age of the Chilean reform. Much less has been written about the Swedish reform because the initial pieces of legislation merely established that approved independent schools would receive the same funding per child as the government-owned schools run by Sweden's municipalities. It took some time for a substantial number of new schools to be approved and longer still for some effects to become evident. Private-sector growth has been rapid (quadrupled since 1992), though private schools still amount to less than 5 percent of Sweden's schools.[99] But there have been no public school closures because of student losses.[100] Because rapid change is still under way, it is too early to characterize many effects of Sweden's version of parental choice. But the key program features are readily apparent. Price control in the form of add-on bans is nearly ubiquitous. However, upper secondary level schools have the right to charge modest fees, and the number of private schools is increasing especially rapidly at the upper secondary level where the ability to specialize matters the most.[101]

Bergström and Sandström discuss "strict [pre-1990] national rules and regulations,"[102] and they point out that *all* schools must still "operate in accordance with the national curriculum."[103] The central rules must be less stifling than those in Chile and New Zealand because Bergström and Sandström report that method and subject specialization dominates private-sector growth. Additional solid indicators of a lighter Swedish regulatory presence are the "better working conditions in faster-paced independent schools" where teachers noted with satisfaction that they had "more control of their own work."[104]

Holger Daun's discovery of "decreasing diversity of students within individual schools and increasing diversity between schools"[105] is consistent with the Bergström and Sandström finding that "the great majority of independent schools are specialized and/or pedagogy-based."[106] Specialized schools will attract children with similar education preferences. Daun wondered whether specialization might undermine the "fundamental tenet" of equal opportunity. A key part of the answer to that question depends on whether you define equal opportunity as learning the same things or as learning as much as possible. Shifting the definition from the former to the latter is a key reason to pursue true market-based reforms.

Since some definition of "school" must underlie government payments to private school operators, the fact that "independent schools must be approved by the National Agency for Education and meet certain criteria in order to receive funding"[107] is only noteworthy because the criteria are stringent and not entirely uniform. "More stringent conditions on the approval of new schools"[108] amount to a potentially significant entry barrier.

In the Swedish regions that have opted for the parental choice program permitted by Swedish law, the potential effects seem more substantial than in the other countries discussed. Even so, there is still little basis for substantial optimism. Key reform catalyst elements are absent or hobbled, and most of Sweden has yet to see much market entry.

Synopsis

Table 10.1 provides an overview of key elements of the parental choice programs just discussed. Since most of the key elements are completely absent or only partially present in all cases, these highly publicized parental choice programs cannot serve as reform catalysts and should not be characterized as informative market accountability experiments.

The effects of the programs listed in Table 10.1 support Milton Friedman's hypothesis that parental choice will not be a reform catalyst unless it is universal (or nearly so) and promises potentially significant consequences for everyone in the education system. Anything that permanently limits eligibility for parental choice or attenuates effects prevents the program from becoming a catalyst for system-wide transformation. Also, limiting programs to a subgroup of

Table 10.1
OVERVIEW OF KEY ELEMENTS

Location	Freedom to Specialize	Key Elements Present?			
		Nondiscrimination*	Low Formal Entry Barriers**	Avoid Price Control	Little Private School Reg.
Chile	Virtually no	No	No	Some schools and taxed	No
Milwaukee, Florida, Cleveland, USA	Private only	No	Yes	No except FL special needs	Yes
Edgewood, Texas, USA	Private only	Close	Uncertainty issues	Yes	Yes
New Zealand	Virtually no	No	No	No	No
Sweden	Limited	Yes	Modest	Some schools and capped	No

* Nondiscrimination means that government payments don't depend on school ownership; government funds support every child on the same basis.
**Discrimination against private school users can be—and often is—a formidable barrier even in the absence of formal entry restrictions.

students disguises the scope of the problems by implying that the problems are isolated and can be fixed in other ways.

The tendency to state the core problem in terms of the worst schools or inequity in the distribution of resources marginalizes parental choice as a policy tool. Both perspectives imply that the better schools are an appropriate standard and that the key elements of the current system are not the problem. The policy issues become the reform of isolated, individual schools, not system transformation. The implementation challenges are seen as adjustment of individual schools' personnel and funding. From that perspective, many policy activists see parental choice only as an obligatory escape hatch— something appropriate so that victims of a low-performing school can have access to another part of the existing system. Some activists note that escape hatch programs give problem schools a needed extra jolt of unfavorable publicity and "competition."[109] But since the aim is to resuscitate problem schools (rather than maximize the academic progress of children), school choice offers an escape hatch only on terms favorable to the problem schools. It stifles entry and rules out exit.

Certainly, a combination of factors can lead program authors and program evaluators to lose sight of the low-performing, inefficient system, core problem. Economic illiteracy, faith in incrementalism, imagined or exaggerated tradeoffs, and paranoia that already well-off people might also benefit from reform combine to prevent school choice from becoming a reform catalyst. Studies of escape hatch versions of choice mistakenly labeled "experiments" have yielded lackluster data that are widely imagined to be general evidence. The studies have generally shown that the escapees and the children that remain in their assigned schools benefited from the escape hatch programs, but the modest gains convinced many policymakers that they could or should (depending on their political position) seek reform by other means.

It may be politically attractive to start out with a limited program, but advocates and policymakers who are so inclined should keep in mind that, once in place, limited programs are difficult to expand and initial restrictions are typically quite resistant to change. Indeed, the Center for Education Reform noted that "it's often harder to improve a law than to do it right the first time."[110]

The Minimum Starting Point

Activists who believe that parental choice programs are the key to needed system transformation have to figure out the minimum starting point for a program that is likely to become a reform catalyst. That is, advocates must design policies that will eventually yield a program with little regulation, noteworthy specialization, entry on formally equal terms with existing schools, and no price control. The relatively static critical features of the existing choice programs (especially narrow targeting, participation caps, add-on bans, and detailed regulation) belie confidence in incremental development of parental choice as a reform catalyst.

Perhaps modest escape hatch–style programs and public school choice are necessary precursors to programs with far fewer restrictions. Modest programs may inform some people who are not in the loop, deflate the anxieties of a political swing group, whet some appetites, and clear the legal underbrush enough to improve the feasibility of larger, unrestricted parental choice programs. Unfortunately, there are some reasons to believe that just the opposite is true; that is, modest programs can work to typecast parental choice as an escape hatch only for children in the worse circumstances. In addition, the lackluster results of modest programs can decrease the political feasibility of large, unrestricted programs. Those are issues that serious advocates of reform can ill afford to ignore.

Advocates of choice need to identify and implement the critical market elements necessary to push the system the rest of the way toward system transformation. The minimum starting point may be well short of outright privatization of government-run schools, but the starting point is well beyond any of the school choice programs in place now and probably involves shifting the allocation of funds from politicians to parents.

There is a good theoretical case for and some evidence to support allowing parental choice alone to allocate public funding to particular schools. Such a proposal would allow activists and policymakers to temporarily set aside controversial issues like funding levels, revenue sources, regulations, compulsory education, and whether the government should own and run schools at all. Using parental choice alone as the funding mechanism also limits the intellectual argument solely to the issue of political accountability versus market accountability.

Shifting the allocation of government funds from politicians to parents would create a dynamic from which the total separation of school and state could eventually follow. Since there is always plenty of political competition for public funds, add-ons could become a growing share of tuition spending. Charity funding of add-ons for the poor would make it politically feasible for the authorities to allow the government share of school funding to shrink at least in real terms and perhaps in absolute terms. The add-on share of tuition could gradually rise to 100 percent, perhaps aided by nonrefundable tuition tax credit programs like the one described by Andrew Coulson.[111] Separation of school and state could become a reality without ever having to call for a vote on it. It is probably the only politically feasible way to achieve complete separation. If tax credits and charities don't adequately support children of low socioeconomic status, then something short of complete separation (a Friedman-style voucher program, for example) is probably a better idea. We already know from the high adult illiteracy rates and especially dismal performance of children of low socioeconomic status in the current system that we cannot afford a vast uneducated underclass. It endangers our political freedom and economic prosperity.

The minimum starting point could be a real experiment in market-driven primary and secondary schooling. A real experiment would be an area that had all of the key elements of a reform catalyst. The areas remaining under the current system would serve as the benchmark against which we could gauge the effects of market-based reforms. The problem with this potential starting point is the long time frame needed for such an experiment. It could take 20 years to establish that competition and free enterprise work for primary and secondary schooling just like they work for the rest of the economy.

Summary and Conclusion

Though much has been written about the modest parental choice programs that are becoming commonplace around the globe, there is typically little widespread awareness of them. Indeed, the low level of awareness is perhaps the most compelling demonstration of the limited nature of the changes. The parental choice programs have generally amounted to slightly increased mobility within a system of little-changed, largely uniform schooling alternatives.

Studies of the effects of those limited parental choice programs have shed light on some important issues. Unfortunately, many of the analysts allege that those programs are generally insightful experiments. They are not. The potential evidence is as limited as the policy changes. The limited, restriction-laden parental choice programs are not insightful experiments in market accountability–driven primary and secondary schooling. And the programs are too limited to gradually initiate the system transformation urgently needed by many countries. Since false, misleading, and irrelevant statements about the effects of limited parental choice programs are quite common—perhaps the norm—we should be grateful that not many people are aware of them.

Mark Harrison's review of existing programs demonstrates that escape hatch programs are at least helpful in the short run and yield some modest system-wide benefits in some cases.[112] The participants benefit; advocates of choice are energized with a genuine, major sense of accomplishment; modest rivalry pressures on and media attention to low-performing schools prompt some improvements; and publicity generally increases the comfort level with a concept that might otherwise be seen as novel and suspect. Choice programs are harmful in the long run only if a perception that they are insightful experiments or reform catalysts aborts policy changes that would provide greater benefits to a larger number of children.

Before the limited programs and the numerous studies that are excessively exuberant or inappropriately alarmist become more widely known, the record must be corrected. The perception that we have considerable direct, positive, but unspectacular evidence of the effects of market accountability in primary and secondary education could spread.[113] That would be catastrophic. Programs that could actually harness and test market forces would probably become increasingly politically infeasible.

Advocates of choice must decide how to accept escape hatch programs without undermining the pursuit of market accountability–driven system transformation. The incrementalism philosophy of many advocates of choice argues that escape hatch programs are a steppingstone on the path to system transformation. The improbability of that is arguably one of the genuine lessons of the parental choice programs of Chile, New Zealand, Sweden, and the United States. For that reason, advocates of choice need to engage in more research and discussion of the minimum starting point. Advocates of choice have to determine how much needs to be accomplished in the initial parental choice legislation so that a diverse menu of competing, rapidly improving school choices will establish itself in an acceptably short time frame.

One of the reasons that the starting point is so important is that many analysts will read the evidence presented above (especially on the micromanagement of private schools by the Chilean and New Zealand central governments) as further proof that regulatory control and derailing of school reform will follow government funding of children enrolled in private schools. They may be right. But an alternate explanation is that a reform is inadequate, perhaps even counterproductive, if it leaves the beneficiaries of the status quo in positions of power from which they can at least try to stifle competition and specialization or use regulatory micromanagement to extend government control to private schools.

Notes

1. David N. Plank and Gary Sykes, preface to *Choosing Choice: School Choice in International Perspective*, ed. David N. Plank and Gary Sykes (New York: Teachers College Press, 2003), p. vii.

2. Varun Gauri, *School Choice in Chile* (Pittsburgh: University of Pittsburgh Press, 1998), p. 26.

3. Milton Friedman, *Capitalism and Freedom* (Chicago: University of Chicago Press, 1962), chap. 6.

4. Daniel Yergin and Joseph Stanislaw, *The Commanding Heights: The Battle for the World Economy* (New York: Simon and Schuster, 1998).

5. "Tentative procedure" is one of the Webster Dictionary definitions of "experiment."

6. William G. Ouchi, "Making Schools Work," *Education Week*, September 3, 2003, pp. 56, 44.

7. Home schooling has gotten easier in most states.

8. Education Policy Institute, "New Poll Finds Public in Dark about Charters and Vouchers," *EPI-Update*, November 19, 1999; and Terry Moe, *Schools, Vouchers, and the American Public* (Washington: Brookings Institution, 2001).

9. Plank and Sykes, p. xii.

10. Mark Harrison, *Education Matters: Government, Markets, and New Zealand Schools* (Wellington, NZ: Education Forum, 2004), p. 2; Herbert J. Walberg and Joseph L. Bast, *Education and Capitalism* (Stanford, CA: Hoover Institution Press, 2003), p. 3; Friedman, *Capitalism and Freedom*; and John Merrifield, *The School Choice Wars* (Lanham, MD: Scarecrow Education Press, 2001).

11. Ibid., chap. 4. See also Samuel Blumenfeld, *Is Public Education Necessary?* (Boise, ID: Paradigm, 1981); and Andrew Coulson, *Market Education* (New Brunswick, NJ: Transaction, 1999).

214

12. Myron Lieberman. *Public Education: An Autopsy* (Cambridge, MA: Harvard University Press, 1993), p. 160.

13. Seymour Sarason, *Revisiting the Culture of the School and the Problem of Change* (New York: Teachers College Press, 1996), p. 346. Inefficiency includes failure to relentlessly pursue improvement.

14. Gray Davis, governor of California, quoted in David Broder, "Reforming Education a Tough Assignment," *San Antonio Express-News*, March 2, 1999, p. 7B.

15. See the findings of the U.S. Congress cited in David Kirkpatrick, *School Choice: The Idea That Will Not Die* (Mesa, AZ: Bluebird, 1997).

16. National Commission on Excellence in Education, *A Nation at Risk: The Imperative for Educational Reform* (Washington: U.S. Department of Education, 1983).

17. No doubt there are minor and therefore largely secret exceptions. Some especially troubled systems have improved to where they approach or attain the dismal national norms of *A Nation at Risk*.

18. It appeared most recently in the February 15, 2001, report of the United States Commission on National Security. See *21st Century: Road Map for National Security: Imperative for Change—Phase III Report*. See also Marjorie Coeyman, "Twenty Years after 'A Nation at Risk,' " *Christian Science Monitor*, April 22, 2003; Laurence Steinberg, "Failure Outside the Classroom," *Wall Street Journal*, July 1, 1996; Paul Gray, "Debating Standards," *Time*, April 8, 1996, p. 40; William J. Bennett et al., "A Nation Still at Risk," *Policy Review* 90 (July–August, 1998); George Clowes, "After 15 Years, Nation Is Still at Risk," *Intellectual Ammunition* 7, no. 4 (September–October 1998): 5; and David Kirkpatrick, "A Nation Still at Risk," *School Reform News*, April 2003.

19. NAEP data from 2002 and 2003. See "Quality Counts," *Education Week*, January 8, 2004, p. 100.

20. Clayton M. Christensen and Michael Overdorf, "Meeting the Challenge of Disruptive Change," *Harvard Business Review*, March–April 2000, pp. 66–76.

21. David W. Kirkpatrick, "What Will It Take?" *School Report*, November 6, 2003.

22. Ibid.

23. "Creative insubordination," "mavericks who buck the system," and "low flyers who get the job done quietly" describe many noted, effective public school principals. Samuel Casey Carter, *No Excuses* (Washington: Heritage Foundation, 2000), p. 9.

24. Wayne B. Jennings, "Let's Ride the Wave of Change," *Enterprising Educators* 6, no. 2 (Spring 1998): 1.

25. Hugh B. Price, "Establish an Academic Bill of Rights," *Education Week*, March 17, 1999, pp. 54–55.

26. Margaret DeLacy, "The 'No Child' Law's Biggest Victims?" *Education Week*, June 23, 2004, p. 40.

27. Martin Hames, *The Crisis in New Zealand Schools* (Palmerston North, NZ: Dunmore, 2002), p. 77.

28. John Pisciotta, "School Accountability: Top-Down or Bottom-Up?" *Veritas*, October 2001, pp. 19–25, http://www.texaspolicy.com/pdf/2001-veritas-2-3-school.pdf.

29. OECD, *Education at a Glance: OECD Indicators* (Paris: OECD, 1995), pp. 176–77.

30. New Zealand did not report data on nonteaching staff.

31. Hames, p. 21.

32. Milton Friedman, "Public Schools: Make Them Private," *Washington Post*, Weekly Edition, February 19, 1995.

33. Differences in what is taught include extracurricular programs, and differences in how it is taught include cost, staff qualifications, use of technology, approach to discipline, and opportunities for parental involvement.

34. Plank and Sykes, p. x, call it "standardized public educational provision." Byron Brown, "Why Governments Run Schools," *Economics of Education Review* 11, no. 4 (1992): 287–300, calls it "comprehensive uniformity."

35. Edward B. Fiske and Helen F. Ladd, *When Schools Compete: A Cautionary Tale* (Washington: Brookings Institution Press, 2000).

36. Kirkpatrick, "What Will It Take?"

37. See, for example, Dennis Epple and Richard Romano, "Neighborhood Schools, Choice, and the Distribution of Education Benefits"; and David Figlio and Marianne Page, "Can School Choice and School Accountability Successfully Coexist?" both in *The Economics of School Choice*, ed. Caroline Hoxby (Chicago: University of Chicago Press, 2003).

38. Ouchi, pp. 56, 44.

39. A. G. Powell, E. Farrar, and D. K. Cohen, *The Shopping Mall High School: Winners and Losers in the Educational Marketplace* (Boston: Houghton Mifflin, 1985).

40. Harrison.

41. Merrifield, *The School Choice Wars*, pp. 50–51. The insightful phrase in quotes surfaces frequently. Milton Friedman said he heard it in a 1972 debate on Social Security from Wilbur Cohen, secretary of health, education, and welfare during the Johnson administration. It still appears frequently. For example, see Paul Romer, "Redistributional Consequences of Educational Reform," in *Education in the 21st Century*, ed. Edward P. Lazear (Stanford, CA: Hoover Institution Press, 2002), p. 65.

42. Thomas Sowell, "The Big Lie of 'Working Poor' Returns," *San Antonio Express-News*, March 2, 2004.

43. Harrison, p. 324.

44. Some taxpayer funds will have to pay for enrollment monitoring, disbursement of funds to schools, and prevention and detection of fraud.

45. Andrew Coulson, "Forging Consensus," *Mackinac Center Report*, April 2004, p. 13, http://www.mackinac.org/archives/2004/s2004-01.pdf.

46. Ibid., p. 14.

47. Terms like "private copayments," "private topping off," and "topping up" are synonymous with add-ons. Each term refers to parents making up the difference between a student's taxpayer-funded support and the higher cost of tuition at the school preferred by the parents. For example, suppose the government funds $5,000 per child vouchers. A family that prefers a school that charges tuition of $7,000/child pays the tuition with the voucher and $2,000 of its own money.

48. See Robert L. Schuettinger and Eamonn F. Butler, *Forty Centuries of Wage and Price Controls* (Thornwood, NY: Caroline House, 1979).

49. "Average" minimum because, to avoid price floors as well as ceilings, families should be given credits to spend on future education services whenever current schooling costs less than the annual per child public funding available for the current year. See below for the price floor discussion.

50. The estimated average annual total expenditure per child in the United States was $9,354 in 2001–02. See National Center for Education Statistics, http://nces.ed.gov/programs/digest/d02/tables/dt166.asp.

51. Walberg and Bast, pp. 301–02, advocate allowing credits for education savings accounts that can be used to pay college expenses.

52. Coulson, *Market Education.*

53. Stephen Arons, *Short Route to Chaos: Conscience, Community, and the Re-Constitution of American Schooling* (Amherst: University of Massachusetts Press, 1997).

54. Lieberman, pp. 290–92.

55. An estimated $9,354 total expenditure per student in 2001–02, a figure that does not include state administrative spending. The table at http://nces.ed.gov/programs/digest/d02/tables/dt166.asp does not mention the federal administrative spending that I suspect is also not reflected in the $9,354.

56. Leslie A. Whittington, James Alm, and H. Elizabeth Peters, "Fertility and the Personal Exemption: Implicit Pronatalist Policy in the United States," *American Economic Review* 80, no. 3 (1990): 545–56.

57. Patricia Matte and Antonio Sancho, "Primary and Secondary School Education," in *Private Solutions to Social Problems*, ed. Cristián Larroulet (Santiago, Chile: Libertad y Desarrollo, 1991), p. 8.

58. Claudio Sapelli and Bernardita Vial, "Evaluating the Chilean Education Voucher System," *Cuadernos de Economia* 39, no. 118 (December 2002): 423–54.

59. Ibid.

60. Washington, DC Nucleus, "School Vouchers: An Alternative for Venezuela," *Electronic Bilingual Review* 10 (December, 1996).

61. Sapelli and Vial.

62. For example, suppose the per child government payment is $2,000 and the private school can earn a maximum additional $600 by charging a taxed $1,000 add-on. Then suppose an unsubsidized private school charges $5,000. A family will pay it only if the extra $2,400 ($5,000 − [$2,000 + $600]) worth of schooling services is worth at least the extra $4,000 ($5,000 − $1,000) out-of-pocket cost of the unsubsidized school.

63. Decree Law 3476, article 3, letter h. See Matte and Sancho, p. 8.

64. Gauri, p. 26.

65. Ibid., p. 27.

66. Ibid., p. 28.

67. Ibid.

68. Sapelli and Vial.

69. Gauri, p. 28.

70. I'd prefer to focus my criticisms on issues and ideas and avoid making it personal. Like Henry Hazlitt's classic *Economics in One Lesson* (New York: Three Rivers Press, 1979: p 11), my aim "is not to expose the special errors of particular writers, but economic errors in their most frequent, widespread, or influential form." Still, to maintain the credibility of my observations, I feel compelled, with reluctance, to cite the published source of the materials. The peer-reviewed nature of the publications means that the reviewers and editors of the publications are accomplices, either unwittingly through carelessness or because past flawed analyses created imagined stylized facts. Perhaps the editors shared the authors' bias and chose to publish the articles in spite of reviewer criticism. For example, the unpublished version of the paper that characterized the micromanaged Chilean voucher system as "a textbook voucher scheme" listed Milton Friedman as a reviewer. No doubt, Friedman was at least partially responsible for the "textbook" comment's absence from the published draft. But the authors and editors must have ignored Friedman's objections to many other claims nearly as shocking and clearly false as the textbook claim (for example: price control doesn't matter and "twenty years of unrestricted school choice").

Because I want to stay focused on what was said rather than who said it, I made you read this far to get the sources. The "textbook" remark appears on page one of Hsieh and Urquiola, January 2002 draft. The published version lacking the "textbook" remark, but containing the "twenty years" comment and failing to note price control, is Chang-Tai Hsieh and Miguel Urquiola, "When Schools Compete, How Do They Compete? An Assessment of Chile's Nationwide School Voucher Program," NBER Working Paper 10008, 2003, http://papers.nber.org/papers/w10008.pdf. Henry Levin, director of the National Center for the Study of Privatization in Education at Columbia University Teachers' College cites the Chilean experience as useful evidence for evaluating the likely performance of for-profit schools. Levin does not mention Education Ministry micromanagement of schooling, even though it is a very good explanation for his concluding observation that "there are no dramatic differences among [Chile's] three voucher-funded sectors." Henry M. Levin, "Bear Market," *Education Next*, Spring 2001, pp. 6–15. The following publications also ignored Ministry of Education micromanagement: Martin Carnoy and Patrick McEwan, "Does Privatization Improve Education? The Case of Chile's National Voucher Plan," in *Choosing Choice*, pp. 24–44; Martin Carnoy, "School Choice? Or is it Privatization," *Educational Researcher* 29, no. 7 (October, 2000): 15–20; and Helen F. Ladd, "School Vouchers: A Critical View," *Journal of Economic Perspectives* 16, no. 4 (Fall 2002): pp. 3–24.

71. Hsieh and Urquiola.

72. Gauri.

73. Hsieh and Urquiola. p. 34.

74. Marya DeGrow, "Milwaukee Voucher Program Continues to Expand," *School Reform News*, May 2003, p. 6.

75. Caroline M. Hoxby, "Rising Tide,"*Education Next* (Winter 2001), http://educationnext.org/20014/68.html; and John Witte, *The Market Approach to Education: An Analysis of America's First Voucher Program* (Princeton, NJ: Princeton University Press, 2000).

76. February 6, 2003, e-mail from Bill Greiner, Florida Department of Education.

77. Mary Ann Zehr, "Cleveland Voucher Aid No Panacea for Hard-Pressed Catholic Schools," *Education Week*, June 18, 2003, p. 9.

78. Hoxby, "Rising Tide"; and William G. Howell and Paul E. Peterson, *The Education Gap: Vouchers and Urban Schools* (Washington: Brookings Institution, 2002).

79. Alan Murray, "Florida's Experience May Aid Argument for School Vouchers," *Wall Street Journal*, November 4, 2003.

80. Hoxby, "Rising Tide."

81. Howell and Peterson, *The Education Gap*.

82. John Merrifield, "The Edgewood Voucher Program: Some Preliminary Findings," *Cato Journal* 23, no. 3 (Winter, 2004).

83. Texas Education Agency, "Snapshot" Reports. See http://deleon.tea.state.tx.us/.

84. http://deleon.tea.state.tx.us/SDL/.

85. Personal communication with the CEO Horizon office, February 11, 2003.

86. July 2003 numbers in Harrison, p. 4. Nominally private, but state-controlled, integrated schools are 10.5 percent, while 85.7 percent are literally government owned. Only 3.8 percent of New Zealand schools are independent, private schools.

87. Ibid., p. 235.

88. Carnoy, pp. 15–20; Ladd, "School Vouchers"; and Fiske and Ladd.

89. Alan Woodfield and Philip Gunby, "The Marketization of New Zealand Schools: Assessing Fiske and Ladd," *Journal of Economic Literature* 61 (September 2003): 863–84.

90. Woodfield and Gunby, p. 863.

91. Harrison, p. 4.

92. Fiske and Ladd, p. 298. This book also asserted that the New Zealand program represented "market competition" (p. 292) with "self-governing schools functioning in a competitive environment" (p. 297). Clearly, the authors were aware of significant central control but did not think it inconsistent with "market competition" and "self-governing schools functioning in a competitive environment."

93. Ibid., p. 298.

94. Class-size regulation precludes large reductions in class size, but small reductions can occur.

95. Norman LaRocque, *The Regulatory Framework for the New Zealand School Sector: A Description* (Wellington: New Zealand Business Roundtable, February 2001), p. 5.

96. Hames, p. 77.

97. LaRocque, p. x.

98. Harrison, p. 198.

99. Fredrik Bergström and F. Mikael Sandström, *School Choice Works! The Case of Sweden* (Indianapolis: Friedman Foundation, 2002).

100. Holger Daun, "Market Forces and Decentralization in Sweden: Impetus for School Development or Threat to Comprehensiveness and Equity?" in *Choosing Choice*, pp. 92–111.

101. E. G. West Centre, "Customer Choice Systems in Nacka, Sweden," Newcastle, UK, 2003, www.ncl.ac.uk/egwest/nacka.html.

102. Bergström and Sandström, p. 4.

103. Ibid., p. 5.

104. Ibid., p. 16.

105. Daun, p. 92.

106. Bergström and Sandström, p. 8.

107. Ibid., p. 1.

108. Ibid., p. 6.

109. Murray.

110. Center for Education Reform, May 2000 Report, http://www.edreform.com/.

111. Andrew Coulson, "Toward Market Education: Are Vouchers or Tax Credits the Better Path?" Cato Institute Policy Analysis no. 392, February 23, 2001, www.cato.org/pubs/pas/pa392.pdf.

112. Harrison.

113. Choosers and children left behind typically enjoy some academic gains, but their skills remain far from what they should be and core problems remain.

Contributors

Lewis M. Andrews is executive director of the Yankee Institute for Public Policy, a Connecticut research and educational institute.

Andrew Coulson is senior fellow in education policy at Michigan's Mackinac Center for Public Policy and serves on the Advisory Council of the E. G. West Centre for Market Solutions in Education at the University of Newcastle, UK.

Charles L. Glenn is professor and chairman of educational administration and policy studies at Boston University.

Claudia R. Hepburn is the managing director of the Fraser Institute, Ontario Office, and the institute's director of education policy.

Norman LaRocque is policy adviser with the New Zealand Business Roundtable and the Education Forum, based in Wellington, New Zealand.

John Merrifield is professor of economics at the University of Texas, San Antonio.

David Salisbury is director of the Center for Educational Freedom at the Cato Institute in Washington, D.C.

F. Mikael Sandström works as a political adviser for the Moderate Party of the Swedish parliament.

Claudio Sapelli is a professor in the Department of Economics at the Catholic University of Chile.

James Tooley is director of the E. G. West Centre for Market Solutions in Education at the University of Newcastle, UK. He was, until 2002, director of education at the Institute of Economic Affairs and is professor of education policy at the University of Newcastle Upon Tyne, England.

Ludger Woessmann is the head of the Human Capital and Structural Exchange Department at the Ifo Institute for Economic Research in Munich, Germany, and works at the Center for Economic Studies.

Index

Cato Institute

Founded in 1977, the Cato Institute is a public policy research foundation dedicated to broadening the parameters of policy debate to allow consideration of more options that are consistent with the traditional American principles of limited government, individual liberty, and peace. To that end, the Institute strives to achieve greater involvement of the intelligent, concerned lay public in questions of policy and the proper role of government.

The Institute is named for *Cato's Letters*, libertarian pamphlets that were widely read in the American Colonies in the early 18th century and played a major role in laying the philosophical foundation for the American Revolution.

Despite the achievement of the nation's Founders, today virtually no aspect of life is free from government encroachment. A pervasive intolerance for individual rights is shown by government's arbitrary intrusions into private economic transactions and its disregard for civil liberties.

To counter that trend, the Cato Institute undertakes an extensive publications program that addresses the complete spectrum of policy issues. Books, monographs, and shorter studies are commissioned to examine the federal budget, Social Security, regulation, military spending, international trade, and myriad other issues. Major policy conferences are held throughout the year, from which papers are published thrice yearly in the *Cato Journal*. The Institute also publishes the quarterly magazine *Regulation*.

In order to maintain its independence, the Cato Institute accepts no government funding. Contributions are received from foundations, corporations, and individuals, and other revenue is generated from the sale of publications. The Institute is a nonprofit, tax-exempt, educational foundation under Section 501(c)3 of the Internal Revenue Code.

CATO INSTITUTE
1000 Massachusetts Ave., N.W.
Washington, D.C. 20001
www.cato.org